IN HIS IMAGE

IN HIS IMAGE

Dr. Paul Brand

and

Philip Yancey

HODDER AND STOUGHTON
LONDON SYDNEY AUCKLAND TORONTO

British Library Cataloguing in Publication Data

Brand, Paul
   In his image.—(Hodder Christian
   paperbacks)
   1. Jesus Christ—Mystical body
   I. Title   II. Yancey, Philip
   262'.77   BV600.5

ISBN 0-340-36327-4

Copyright © 1982 by Dr Paul Brand and Philip Yancey. First printed in Great Britain 1984. All rights reserved. No part of this publication may be reproduced or transmitted in any form or by any means, electronic or mechanical, including photocopy, recording, or any information storage or retrieval system, without permission in writing from the publisher. Printed in Great Britain for Hodder and Stoughton Limited, Mill Road, Dunton Green, Sevenoaks, Kent by Cox & Wyman Limited, Reading. Photoset by Rowland Phototypesetting Limited, Bury St Edmunds, Suffolk. Hodder and Stoughton Editorial Office: 47 Bedford Square, London WC1B 3DP

Contents

SPIRIT

PAIN

Acknowledgments

G. K. Chesterton once dedicated a book to his secretary, 'without whose help this book would have been published upside down.' Our publisher probably would have found a way to print right side up regardless of the condition of our submitted manuscript, but we do know the finished product would have suffered were it not for the contributions of certain people. Doctors Christopher Fung and Kenneth Phillips checked over medical details, and John Skillen, Tim Stafford, and Harold Fickett each made enormously helpful editorial suggestions. Typist Harriet Long imposed order on hopelessly scrawled-up drafts of the book. And our editor at Zondervan, Judith Markham, did her usual fine job of guiding the whole merry process. We are grateful to all.

Preface

Unless all existence is a medium of revelation, no particular revelation is possible.

William Temple

When *Fearfully and Wonderfully Made* first went to press in 1980, Dr Brand and I, as well as our publisher, awaited results with some trepidation. It was a difficult book to describe and present. Very few books of analogies exist, and we could not predict how the public would respond.

While writing that book I had the sense of working on three different books at once. I wanted to capture the essence of Dr Brand's life and to tell biographically some of his remarkable experiences in England and India. In addition, I also hoped to convey an appreciation for the human body by rendering medical facts in an appealing style. And, of course, the real core of the book lay in a third kind of approach: a spiritual application, drawn from analogy, that sometimes expressed wonder, sometimes praise, and sometimes prophetic challenge.

In every chapter, on almost every page, I strained to keep these three disparate kinds of material in balance. I often felt as if each of the three books was growing disproportionately, and I struggled to shape one book out of the three. I persevered because I recognised that Dr Brand offers a unique blend of gifts. Even after forty years of medical practice, he retains a boyish enthusiasm for the grandeur of the human body. In two decades of missionary service in India he has gained fresh and profound insights into Christian truth. And, along the way, he has experienced adventures and personal encounters with patients that are as dramatic and poignant as any I have come across.

This book, *In His Image*, continues the approach begun

in *Fearfully and Wonderfully Made*. It is not a sequel in the strictest sense because we had both volumes in mind from the beginning. Whereas *Fearfully and Wonderfully Made* placed emphasis on individual cells and the varying roles within the Body, this book will focus more on the connections, the forces uniting and guiding that Body, and the involvement of God Himself.

We begin each major section with a survey of how the human body functions. Since Sophocles first declared the human body the most wondrous of the world's wonders, several thousand years of scientific discovery have only served to underscore his words. The body is far more wondrous than Sophocles could have imagined.

We believe studying the human body, a worthy endeavour in itself, yields an unexpected bonus. It sheds light on a metaphor used over thirty times in the New Testament: the Body of Christ. Christians are compared to individual members in a universal Body in which Jesus Christ serves as Head. We do not, of course, imply that God created the cells in human bodies in order to make a spiritual point, or that the biological facts precisely mirror spiritual truth. But a likeness does exist between the human body and spiritual Body, a likeness that derives from common authorship.

A great artist may use a variety of media for expression, but common themes of style, content, and approach will run through all the works. It should not surprise us, then, that the Supreme Artist has left His signature in many different forms. If you train a telescope on the galaxies and stars and planets of the universe, and then look through a powerful microscope at tiny molecules and atoms and electrons, and you will notice an unmistakable similarity in structure and pattern. The same Creator designed both levels of reality. So, too, the same Creator designed the human body and then inspired New Testament authors to look there for a model of spiritual truth.

The word *symbol* comes from two Greek words meaning 'to throw across.' In this book, we attempt to provide a bridge from a visible, natural world to an invisible, spiritual world. If we go too far and stretch the symbol beyond what it can bear, forgive us. We do not intend a new theology; rather, we hope to illumine one already revealed, by the analogy of the human body.

Up until the late eighteenth century, science was seen as a direct search for God. When Copernicus, Kepler, Galileo, and Newton made their discoveries, they believed their results taught humanity about God as well. The created world, they felt, revealed His nature. Not many people approach science that way any more. We hope this book stands as an exception. William Blake said it well: 'If the doors of perception were cleansed, everything will appear to man as it is, infinite.'

Philip Yancey

My partnership with Philip Yancey has resulted in two books that are quite different from what I could have written on my own. The original concepts and most of the stories came out of my own experience as a surgeon and biologist. They began to take shape initially in India as I tried to help my medical students integrate and enrich their Christian faith with their new knowledge in medicine. Those thoughts, delivered first as chapel messages at the Christian Medical College in Vellore, lay in a drawer for years. Finally I felt the time had come to share the ideas with a larger audience, and at that point Philip and I were brought together.

I had hoped that Philip would use his writing skills to shape my material into something more readable than what I could write myself. This he has done. But he has done much more. Long before we first met, Philip had been thinking and writing about pain and suffering and its impact on people and their faith. Now, armed with my notes and tapes of our conversations, he began further research into the writings of others and into the anatomy of the body and function of its cells. When he began to write, it was as an expert in many aspects of biology and theology.

Very quickly the material became not 'my' book, but our book. He refined and polished some of my rough-hewn concepts and challenged others. When early drafts began to come across my desk, I found I had to stop and think about ideas in biology and interpretations of Christian theology that had not come from me at all. The material began to fit together as an obvious enhancement of what I had first expressed. Some of the ideas were quite new to me and led us into further discussion and then into further rewriting. Both of us have grown because of this dynamic creative experience.

Philip insisted that for the sake of coherence the books must be written in the first person 'I' rather than the 'we' of joint authorship. Because of this, all the thoughts are told from my perspective as physician in the partnership. However, it has bothered me that most readers of *Fearfully and Wonderfully Made* who have written to me seem to have assumed that all ideas were mine and that Philip simply recorded them in a readable style. Nothing is further from the truth. Some of the writing is mine, pure and un-varnished. Some is his editing and rewriting of what I have written. But some is entirely the result of Philip's own reading and thought. There are even a few places where I have reversed roles and revised the wording of his own writing.

In this Preface, Philip has already written of the difficulty of containing three different kinds of books in a balanced tension. The process also included blending together two different authors. We still use the format of 'I' as if it were all mine, but in fact it is a true co-authorship. More, both of us have increasingly felt that we two were not alone. This book is written to the glory of God, and the Holy Spirit, the Go-Between God, has joined the process. May the same Holy Spirit be your Counsellor as you read, so that the words may come alive and speak to you, not as my voice or Philip's, but as a voice from fellow-members of the Body of Christ, under the direction of the Head.

Paul Brand

Numberless are the world's wonders, but none – none more wondrous than the body of man.

Sophocles

Man cannot afford to be a naturalist, to look at Nature directly, but only with the side of his eye. He must look through and beyond her.

Henry David Thoreau

IMAGE

1 Likeness

What a piece of work is a man! how noble in reason! how infinite in faculties! in form and moving how express and admirable! in action how like an angel, in apprehension how like a god!

William Shakespeare

Man is not a balloon going up into the sky, nor a mole burrowing merely in the earth; but rather a thing like a tree, whose roots are fed from the earth, while its highest branches seem to rise almost to the stars.

G. K. Chesterton

What indeed is Earth but a Nest, from whose rim we are all falling?

Emily Dickinson

Curtains screened my group of ten interns and medical students from the rest of the forty-bed ward. Externally, the Christian Medical College Hospital in Vellore resembled a modern Western facility, but inside it was all Indian. Activity throbbed just beyond our curtain: patients' families bringing in home-cooked food and nurses chasing away the scavengers that followed, crows, and an occasional monkey.

Those of us inside the curtains, however, were giving full attention to our young colleague as he made his diagnosis. He was half-kneeling, in the posture I had taught him, with his warm hand slipped under the sheet and resting on the patient's bare abdomen. While his fingers probed gently for telltale signs of distress, he continued a line of questioning that showed he was weighing the possibility of appendicitis against an ovarian infection.

Suddenly something caught my eye – a slight twitch of movement on the intern's face. Was it the eyebrow arching upward? A vague memory stirred in my mind, but one I could not fully recall. His questions were leading into a delicate area, especially for demure Hindu society. Had the woman ever been exposed to a venereal infection? The intern's facial muscles contracted into an expression combining sympathy, inquisitiveness, and disarming warmth as he looked straight in the patient's face and asked the questions. His very countenance coaxed the woman to relax, put aside the awkwardness, and tell us the truth.

At that moment my memory snapped into place. Of course! The left eyebrow cocked up with the right one trailing down, the wry, enticing smile, the head tilted to one side, the twinkling eyes – these were unmistakably the features of my old chief surgeon in London, Professor Robin Pilcher. I sucked in my breath sharply and exclaimed. The students looked up, startled by my reaction. I could not help it; it seemed as if the intern had studied Professor Pilcher's face for an acting audition and was now drawing from his repertoire to impress me.

Answering their questioning looks, I explained myself. 'That is the face of my old chief! What a coincidence – you have *exactly* the same expression, yet you've never been to England and Pilcher certainly has never visited India.'

At first the students stared at me in confused silence. Finally two or three of them grinned. 'We don't know any Professor Pilcher,' one said. 'But Dr Brand, that was *your* expression he was wearing.'

Later that evening, alone in my office, I thought back to my days under Pilcher. I had thought I was learning from him techniques of surgery and diagnostic procedures. But he had also imprinted his instincts, his expression, his very smile so that they, too, would be passed down from generation to generation in an unbroken human chain. It was a kindly smile, perfect for cutting through the fog of embarrassment to encourage a patient's honesty. What textbook or computer programme could have charted out the facial expression needed at that exact moment within the curtain?

Now I, Pilcher's student, had become a link in the chain, a carrier of his wisdom to students some nine thousand miles away. The Indian doctor, young and brown-skinned, speaking in Tamil, shared few obvious resemblances with either Pilcher or me. Yet somehow he had conveyed the likeness of my old chief so accurately that it had transported me back to university days with a start. The thought gave me a crystalline insight into the concept of 'image'.

The word *image* is familiar to us today, but the meaning of the word has leaked away so that now it connotes virtually the opposite of its former meaning of 'likeness'. Today, a politician hires an image-maker, a job applicant dresses for image, a corporation seeks the right image. In all these usages, image has come to mean the illusion of what something is presented to be, rather than the essence of what it really is.*

---

* An example of the change in meaning: advertising agencies huddle daily and debate how to reposition the 'image' of their clients' products. Twenty years ago a cigarette brand with the rather dandified name of Marlborough was experiencing a decline in sales; men avoided it because

In this book entitled *In His Image* I want to reinforce the original meaning of image as an exact likeness, not a deceptive illusion. We must return to the concept of likeness to understand the 'image of God' we are intended to carry. Glimpses into that former meaning still endure. For instance, when I gaze at a nerve cell through a scanning electron microscope, I study the neuron's image. I am looking not at the neuron itself – its small size precludes that – but at a reassembled image that faithfully reproduces it for my eye. In this case the image enhances, rather than distorts, the essence of the cell.

Similarly, photographers use the word *image* to describe their finished product. The image of a sequoia redwood grove flattened onto a small black-and-white rectangle surely does not express the totality of the original, but when developed by a master like Ansel Adams it may convey the original essence with great force.

Or, think of a ten-pound bundle of protoplasm squirming fitfully in a blanket. The baby's father weighs fifteen times as much and has a vastly larger range of ability and personality. Yet the mother announces proudly that the baby is the 'spitting image' of his father. A visitor peers closely. Yes, a resemblance does exist, evident now in a dimple, slightly flared nostrils, a peculiar earlobe. Before long, mannerisms of speech and posture and a thousand other mimetic traits will bring the father unmistakably to mind.

These usages of image, applied to the microscope and photograph and offspring, carry a meaning similar to the 'image' of Professor Pilcher that I unwittingly passed along to scores of Indian students. All are true images, a likeness of one subject expressed visibly through another. And all shed light on the grand and mysterious phrase from the

---

of its primly feminine image. A massive advertising campaign reshaped that cigarette's image, changing the brand's spelling and creating 'The Marlboro Man'. Now the cigarette conjures up the image of a rugged cowboy, alone on the range, lighting up a Marlboro during a welcome pause from his demanding chores. The essential reality did not change: same old cigarette. Only the illusion – the image – of the cigarette changed. As a result, Marlboro became America's best-selling brand.

Bible: the image of God. That phrase appears in the very first chapter of Genesis, and its author seems to stutter with excitement, twice affirming a concept just mentioned in the preceding verse: 'So God created man in his own image, in the image of God he created him' (1:27). The image of God – the first man on earth received it, and in some refracted way each one of us possesses this quality 'wondrous strange'.

How can visible human beings express the image of God? We certainly cannot look like Him, sharing characteristic features of eyebrow or earlobe, for God is invisible spirit. Philosophers and theologians have long speculated on all that could be contained within the mystery of that single phrase. Predictably, they tend to project onto their definitions the principal concerns of their own era. The Enlightenment age assures us the image of God is the ability to reason, the Pietists identify it as the spiritual faculty, the Victorians claim it as the capacity to make moral judgments, and the Renaissance thinkers locate the image of God in artistic creativity. As for our own psychology-dominated age? What else could that image be, we are now advised, than our capacity for relationships with other people and with God.

Because even professional theologians have failed to reach a consensus over the centuries, I will not attempt a comprehensive definition saying the image of God is *this* and not *that*. But since it stands for all that is unique about humanity among God's creations, the phrase deserves a few moments' reflection.

In the Genesis narrative, the concept 'image of God' appears at the consummation of all creation. At each stage of progress, Genesis note punctiliously, God looks back on His creation and pronounces it 'good'. But creation still lacks a creature to contain God's own image. Only after all that preparation does God announce the culmination of life on earth: 'Let us make man in our image, in our likeness, and let them rule over the fish of the sea and the birds of the air, over the livestock, over all the earth, and over all the creatures that move along the ground' (1:26).

Among all God's creatures, only humanity receives the image of God, and that quality separates us from all else. We possess what no other animal does; we are linked in our essence to God. (Later, as God discusses with Noah the extent of human dominion over the animals, this quality of the image of God looms up again, as a decisive and awesome demarcation between man and other creatures. Killing an animal means one thing; killing a fellow human is an entirely different matter, 'for in the image of God has God made man' 9:6.)

One of the supreme artists of history rendered the Creation sequence on the vaulted stone ceiling of the Sistine Chapel in Rome. Michelangelo chose as the centrepiece of his great work the precise moment when God awakened man into His image.

I have visited the Sistine Chapel, in its contemporary ambience far different from what Michelangelo probably had in mind as a setting for his art. Tourists are admitted in groups running to several hundred, many of them clasping white plastic headphones to their ears like painful growths. They are listening to a recording that guides them through the chapel. Instead of looking up when they walk into that splendid room, they look down, following the trail of red tape that marks off an area where the recording is being transmitted.

Nothing can quite prepare the visitors for what they see when, on cue, they raise their heads. Magnificent works of art cover every inch of the large room: the division of light and darkness, the creation of the sun and planets, the days of Noah, the last judgment. And in the focal centre, the calm eye in the swirl of frescoes, Michelangelo has painted the creation of man.

Adam's muscular body reclines on the ground in the classical pose of the ancients' river gods. Slumbrous, he is lifting up his hand, stretching it out toward heaven from where God Himself reaches down. The hands of God and Adam do not actually touch. A gap separates their fingers, like a synapse across which the energy of God is flowing.

In some respects, Michelangelo captured man's creation as no artist ever has. The very word Adam in Hebrew refers to ground or dust, and Adam is set on the physical earth. Yet Michelangelo also expressed Adam's dual nature by portraying the instant when God reached across the void to convey spiritual life. The second account of man's creation, in Genesis 2, adds more detail: 'And the Lord God formed man from the dust of the ground and breathed into his nostrils the breath of life, and man became a living being' (2:7).

When I heard that verse as a child, I imagined Adam lying on the ground, perfectly formed but not yet alive, with God leaning over him and performing a sort of mouth-to-mouth resuscitation. Now I picture that scene differently. I assume that Adam was already biologically alive – the other animals needed no special puff of oxygen, nitrogen, and carbon dioxide to start them breathing, so why should man? The breath of God now symbolises for me a spiritual reality. I see Adam as alive, but possessing only an animal vitality. Then God breathes into him a new spirit, and infills him with His own image. Adam becomes a living soul, not just a living body. God's image is not an arrangement of skin cells or a physical shape, but rather an inbreathed spirit.

This single act of special creation, God breathing into man 'the breath of life', distinguished humanity from all other creatures. We share with the animals a biological shell composed, in our case, of bone, organs, muscle, fat, and skin. In truth, we fall short in direct comparison to the strictly biological features of some animals. Who would compete in beauty with a splashy macaw or even a lowly luna moth? A horse easily outruns us, a hawk sees far better, a dog detects odours and sounds imperceptible to us. The total sum of our sheer physical qualities is no more godlike than a cat's.

And yet, *we* are made in the image of God. For us, the shell of skin and muscle and bones serves as a vessel, a repository for His image. We can comprehend and even convey something of the Creator. Our cellular constructions of proteins arranged by DNA can become temples of the Holy Spirit. We are not 'mere mortals'. We are, all of us, immortals.

I began with the image of Professor Robin Pilcher, my old surgical chief from London. As a young student I absorbed something from his image that I carried nine thousand miles to India and in turn transferred to scores of Indians. Today, those former students work in hospitals all over the world. An exact copy of Pilcher's expression may appear at critical moments in Borneo, in the Philippines, in Africa. Pilcher died years ago, but that one small aspect of him – a small pattern of facial muscles appropriate for a particular medical situation – remains alive and visible on my face and the faces of my students.

What God has in mind for us is similar, but far greater. He is asking us to be the chief bearers of His likeness in the world. As spirit, He remains invisible on this planet. He relies on us to give flesh to that spirit, to bear the image of God.

2 Mirrors

> Materialists mistake that which limits life for life itself.
>
> *Leo Tolstoy*

> Know thyself, since thou art my image. So shalt thou know me, whose image thou art and so shalt thou find me in thyself.
>
> *William of St Thierry*

In forty years of surgery I have encountered my share of human drama, but nothing has surpassed my early experiences as a surgical student during the German bombings of London in World War II. Daily, squadrons of ugly, fat *Luftwaffe* bombers filled the sky, their engines growling like unbroken thunder, their bomb bays belching out cargoes of destruction.

Several scenes scarred my memory so that forty years later they still come to me vividly. I remember one direct hit on a Turkish bathhouse in the Imperial Hotel. The raid had come without much warning, and the baths were still full when the bomb exploded. When I arrived at the site I found a scene straight out of Dante. Partitions in the baths had all been glass, and now shattered glass literally paved the streets. Enormously fat men, stark naked, were climbing out of the glowing rubble and stumbling onto the glass-strewn street. Blood from dozens of small cuts flecked their bodies; on some, blood spurted from huge gashes. In the background, air raid sirens howled a belated, plangent wail. Everything was glistening: the blood, the naked, pinguid flesh, the eerily shining streets. Ambulance workers did their best to calm the injured, carefully picking shards of glass from skin and binding up the worst wounds, while we interns rushed to our hospital to prepare for treatment.

Another night, I was watching from my hospital roof when a bomb fell into the infant ward at the nearby Royal Free Hospital, causing the upper floors to collapse into smouldering ruins. I ran to the scene. There, volunteers dug for the newborns, most of them less than a week old, and found both survivors and casualties covered with blood, grime, and glass. Rescuers set up a human chain, like a fire brigade, to pass the bundled infants out from the hospital rubble to waiting ambulances. The babies' thin cries seemed a pathetically inadequate response to the horror of that scene. To the side, mothers in bathrobes watched with fear and despair flickering across their faces. Had their babies survived? All the infants looked alike in the smoke and darkness.

To this day, when I hear the undulating pitch of a siren that approximates the air-raid warning in London, adrenaline floods my body, resurrecting the fear and tension.

During one period, the *Luftwaffe* attacked our city on fifty-seven consecutive nights, with the raids lasting as long as eight hours without pause. Fifteen hundred planes came each night, in waves of 250. In those dark days, we could not help believing that everything we cherished – our freedom, our nation, our families, our civilisation – would be buried in the wasteland created by those hated bombers. Only one thing gave us hope: the courage of Royal Air Force pilots who rose in the skies each day to battle the Germans.

We could watch the aerial confrontations from the ground. RAF Hurricanes and Spitfires, tiny and manoeuverable, looked like mosquitoes pestering the huge German bombers. Although their cause seemed futile, and more than half of their own fighters were soon shot down, the RAF pilots never gave up. Each day they sent a few more of the dreaded bombers cartwheeling in flames toward the earth, and all of us spectators cheered loudly. Eventually, Germany could not sustain further losses from the increasingly accurate fighter pilots and Hitler called off the raids. London slept again.

I cannot possibly exaggerate the adoration that Londoners gave to those brave RAF pilots. Winston Churchill, if anything, understated our gratitude when he said, 'Never in the history of human conflict has so much been owed by so many to so few.' I doubt whether a more adulated group of young men has ever lived. They were the cream of England, the brightest, healthiest, most confident and dedicated, and often the handsomest men in the entire country. When they walked the streets in their decorated uniforms, the population treated them as gods. All eyes turned their way. Young boys ran up to touch them and to stare at close range. All other girls envied the ones who were fortunate enough to walk beside a man in Air Force blue.

I came to know some of these young men, though in far

less idyllic circumstances. The Hurricane, agile and effective as it was, had one fatal design flaw. The single propeller engine was mounted in front, a scant foot or so from the cockpit, and fuel lines snaked alongside the cockpit toward the engine. In a direct hit, the cockpit would erupt in an inferno of flames. The pilot could eject, but in the one or two seconds it took him to find the lever, heat would melt off every feature of his face: his nose, his eyelids, his lips, often his cheeks. I met the RAF heroes swathed in bandages as they began the torturous series of surgeries required to refashion their faces. I helped treat the damaged hands and feet of the downed airmen, even as a team of plastic surgeons went to work on their burned faces.

Sir Archibald McIndoe and his plastic surgeons performed miracles of reconstruction, inventing many new procedures along the way. For facial work they usually used skin grafts from the abdomen and chest. In the days before microvascular surgery, full thicknesses of skin and fat could not simply be sliced away from one part of the body and stitched onto another. Swatches of skin had to be coaxed away, with one end remaining attached to the old blood supply while the other was connected to the graft site until new vessels grew to nourish it. Often surgeons used a two-stage process, temporarily attaching one end of the patient's abdominal skin flap to an arm until a blood supply developed on the arm. They then cut the flap of skin from the abdomen so that it dangled only from the arm, and sewed the loose end to the forehead or cheek or nose. Eventually a blood supply would develop on the facial graft site and the skin could be cut free from its temporary host, the arm.

As a result of these complex techniques, bizarre sights flourished in the wards: arms growing out of heads, a long tube of skin extending from a nasal cavity like an elephant trunk, eyelids made of skin flaps so thick they could not open. An airman commonly endured twenty to forty such surgical procedures before being ready for dismissal.

Throughout the tedious progression of surgeries, morale remained surprisingly high among the pilots, who were fully aware of their patriotic contribution. Wonderful nurses did their best to create an atmosphere of cheerfulness and warmth. The pilots discounted the pain and teased each other about their elephant-man features. They were ideal patients.

But gradually, as the last few weeks of recuperation drew to a close, a change would set in. We noticed that many of the pilots kept asking for minor alterations: a nose flap tucked in just a bit, a mouth turned up some at the corner, a slight thinning down of the right eyelid. Soon the realisation dawned on all of us, including the patients, that they were simply stalling. They could not face the world outside.

Despite the miracles wrought by McIndoe with his marvellous techniques, each face had changed irreparably. No surgeon could possibly restore the protean range of expression of a handsome young face. Although technically a good piece of work, the new face was essentially a scar. You cannot appreciate the flexible, nearly diaphanous delicacy of the eyelid until you try to fashion one out of coarser skin from the abdomen. That bulgy, stiff tissue will protect the eye adequately, but without beauty.

I especially remember an RAF pilot named Peter Foster, who described to me his mounting anxiety as the release day approached. Your fears and concerns, he said, come to a focus in the mirror. For some months you use the mirror daily, as an objective measuring device, to scrutinise the progress your surgeons have made. You study scar tissue, the odd wrinkling of the skin, the thickness of lips and shape of the nose. From this survey, you ask for certain adjustments to improve appearance, and the doctors tell you whether your request is reasonable.

But nearer the day of release, your view of the mirror changes. Now, as you gaze at the reflection of a new face, not the one you were born with but an inferior imitation, you try to see yourself as strangers will see you. In the hospital you have been an object of pride, supported by the camaraderie of your friends and the ministrations of the staff. On the outside, you will be a freak. Fear creeps in.

Will any girl dare to marry that face? Will anyone give it a job?

At that critical moment, concluded Foster, as each airman contemplated the new image of himself as viewed by the rest of the world, one factor alone mattered: the response of family and intimate friends. The surgeons' relative success in remaking the face counted for little. The future hinged on the reactions of family members to the news that the surgeons had done all they could and the face before them would never improve. Did the airman sense loving acceptance or recoiling hesitance?

These distinctly different reactions cleaved the airmen into two groups in as dramatic a demarcation as I have ever seen. Psychologists followed their progress. In one group were some whose girl friends and wives could not accept the new faces. These women, who once had idolised their heroic lovers, quietly stole away or filed for divorce. Airmen who encountered this reaction changed in personality. They stayed indoors, refusing to venture outside except at night, and looked for some kind of work to do at home. In contrast, those whose wives and girl friends stuck by them went on to tremendous success – they were, after all, the elite of England. Many became executives and professionals, leaders of their communities.

Peter Foster gratefully admitted belonging to the fortunate group. His own girl friend assured him that nothing had changed but a few millimetres' thickness of skin. She loved *him*, not his facial membrane, she said. The two got married just before Peter left the hospital.

Naturally, Peter encountered painful rejection from some. Many adults quickly looked away when he approached. Children, cruel in their honesty, made faces, laughed, and mocked him.

Peter wanted to cry out, 'Inside I am the same person you knew before! Don't you recognise me?' Instead, he learned to turn toward his wife. '*She* became my mirror. She gave me a new image of myself,' he said with appreciation. 'Even now, regardless of how I feel, when I look at her she gives me a warm, loving smile. That tells me I am OK.'

Years after I worked with the airmen, I read a profoundly disturbing article entitled 'The Quasimodo Complex' in the *British Journal of Plastic Surgery*. In it, two physicians reported on their study of 11,000 prison inmates who had committed murder, prostitution, rape, or other serious crimes. They carefully documented a trend that I will summarise with one overall comparison. In the normal adult population, 20.2 percent of all people may be said to have surgically correctable facial deformities (protruding ears, misshapen noses, receding chins, acne scars, birthmarks, eye deformities). But research revealed that among the 11,000 offenders fully *60 percent* showed such characteristics.

The authors, who named the phenomenon after Quasimodo, Victor Hugo's 'hunchback of Notre Dame', ended the article with some disquieting questions. Had these criminals encountered hostility and rejection from classmates in grammar school and high school because of their deformities? Could the cruel japery of other children have pushed them toward the state of emotional imbalance that ultimately led to criminal acts?

The authors went on to propose a programme of corrective plastic surgery for prison inmate volunteers.* If the surface appearance had made society reject these people and possibly push them toward crime, they reasoned, perhaps changing that surface appearance would help rehabilitate them by changing their self-image. Whether a murderer on death row or a crack pilot in the RAF, a person forms a self-image based largely on what kind of image other people mirror back.

The report on the Quasimodo complex reduces to statistics a truth that haunts every burn victim, handicapped person, and leprosy patient. We humans give inordinate regard to the physical body, or shell, that we live in. It takes a rare person indeed, someone like Peter Foster's wife, to

---

* Due partly to the authors' (F. W. Masters and D. C. Greaves) findings, many US states have instituted comprehensive programmes of free plastic surgery for prisoners with deformities.

look through that shell and acknowledge the inherent human worth, the image of God inside.

As I have pondered the Quasimodo complex I realise that in subtle and not-so-subtle ways I too have judged and labelled people by their external appearances. I think back to an old family tradition I used to practise with my children. Each year during summer holidays I devised a serial adventure story that featured every member of the family by name and character. Continuing the story each night at bedtime, I tried to weave in some helpful aspects: the children heard of themselves showing unexpected displays of courage and unselfishness that perhaps they would later try to exercise in real life.

Yet the stories contained villains also. I heightened tension and excitement from day to day by having these villains lure the children into impossible situations from which they would somehow have to extricate themselves. Now, as I recall these stories, I remember with a wince that my chief villains, who reappeared in the stories annually, bore the names Scarface and Hunchback. One had an ugly scar across his face; the other was short with a hump on his back. In the running plots, the two would attempt to disguise these features, but sooner or later one of the children would see through the disguises and unmask the villains.

Why, I now wonder, did I give the bad men of my stories those names and characteristics? Undoubtedly I followed the universal stereotype of equating ugly with bad and beautiful with good. Did I inadvertently encourage my own children to equate ugliness with evil, possibly as a result making it harder for them to love those bearing deformities or scars?

Medieval princes used to collect midgets, monsters, and hunchbacks for their own entertainment. Our sophistication does not allow that sort of practice, but do we slip into subtle kinds of rejection just as powerful? After reading about the Quasimodo complex and recognising overtones of labelling and judgment in my own story-telling, I started noticing more carefully the cultural influences that determine our standards for human worth and acceptance. In America the national ideal is a tall, handsome, and confident male or a slender-yet-shapely, smiling female. Advertisements for body-building programmes, diet plans, facial treatments, and clothes for 'the right image' underscore our cultural commitment to physical beauty. If we judged the American population by the images that appear in magazines and on television, we would conclude we live in a society of gods and goddesses.

I have seen the long-term impact of our devotion to physical perfection on my leprosy patients, who will never achieve the image of an Olympic athlete or a Miss America. And I have watched more subtle forces at work in my own children as they have attended state schools. Somehow our cultural ideals have placed us in such bondage that we find no room for a child who is clumsy, shy, or unattractive. Those children meet constant, unrelieved rejection. The 'mirrors' around them determine their self-images, and they do not measure up. How many Salks or Pasteurs have been lost because of this deadly process of rejection by peers? We too have much to learn about mirroring.

I have spent my life in medicine trying to improve the 'shells' of my patients. I strive to restore their damaged hands, feet, and faces to the body's original design specifications. I have felt deep satisfaction in seeing those patients relearn how to walk and use their fingers and then return to their communities and families with an opportunity to live a normal life.

Yet increasingly I have come to realise that the physical shell I devote so much energy to is not the whole person. My patients are not mere collections of tendons, muscles, hair follicles, nerve cells, and skin cells. Each of them, regardless of deformed appearance and physical damage, contains an immortal spirit and is a vessel of the image of God. Their physical cells will one day rejoin the basic elements of earth, the 'humus' that constitutes the material part of humanity. But their souls will live on, and my effect on those souls may have far more significance than my attempts to improve their physical bodies.

Although I live in a society that honours strength, wealth, and beauty, God has placed me among leprosy patients who are often weak, poor, and unattractive. In that environment, I have learned all of us are, like Peter Foster's wife, mirrors. Each of us has the potential to help summon up in the people we meet the image of God, the spark of Godlikeness in the human spirit. Or, instead, we can ignore or squelch that image and judge only on the basis of external appearance. I pray that when I see a person I will see the image of God inside, and ultimate worth, not just the cultural 'image' that we all strive to attain.*

Mother Teresa says that when she looks into the face of a dying beggar in Calcutta, she prays to see the face of Jesus so that she might serve the beggar as she would serve Christ. In an often quoted passage, C. S. Lewis expressed a related thought: 'It is a serious thing to live in a society of possible gods and goddesses, to remember that the dullest and most uninteresting person you talk to may one day be a creature which, if you saw it now, you would be strongly tempted to worship, or else a horror and a corruption such as you now meet, if at all, only in a nightmare. All day long we are, in some degree, helping each other to one of these destinations.'

---

* The author of *Proverbs* points to the inherent worth in every person in this intriguing statement: 'He who oppresses the poor shows contempt for their Maker, but whoever is kind to the needy honours God' (14:31).

3 Restoration

Adam himself lies now scattered on the whole surface of the earth. Formerly concentrated in one place, he has fallen; having been broken to pieces, as it were, he has filled the universe with his debris. However, God's mercy has gathered together from everywhere his fragments and by fusing them in the fire of his charity, has reconstituted their broken unity.

St Augustine
City of God

The Christian ideal changed and re-versed everything so that, as the gospel puts it, 'That which was exalted among men has become an abomination in the sight of God.' The ideal is no longer the greatness of Pharaoh or of a Roman emperor, not the beauty of a Greek nor the wealth of Phoenicia, but humility, purity, compassion, love. The hero is no longer Dives, but Lazarus the beggar; not Mary Magdalene in the day of her beauty, but the day of her repentance; not those who acquire wealth, but those who have abandoned it; not those who dwell in palaces, but those who dwell in catacombs and huts; not those who rule over others, but those who acknowledge no authority but God's.

Leo Tolstoy
What Is Art

I am standing in the sublime Sistine Chapel. Most tourists have left, twilight approaches, and the light has ripened to a golden hue. My neck aches slightly from supporting my head at odd angles, and I wonder fleetingly how Michelangelo felt after a day of working on these ceiling murals.

My eyes keep drifting back to the pivotal scene which shows God imparting life to man. The image of God stands for all that gives worth and dignity to individual men and women, and nothing could better display that indwelling power than the paintings that surround me. And yet even as I stare at the creation scene something troubles me. Michelangelo succeeded wonderfully at depicting human duality and the drama of creation. But he clearly failed, as all artists must, at portraying God Himself. Michelangelo's God is no spirit, but a God made in the image of man.

Six centuries before Christ, the Greek philosopher Xenophanes observed that 'If oxen and horses and lions had hands or could draw with hands and create works of art like those made by men, horses would draw pictures of gods like horses, and oxen of gods like oxen. . . . Ethiopians have gods with snub noses and black hair; Thracians have gods with grey eyes and red hair.' Michelangelo's God has the shape and texture of humanity – even a sloping Roman nose just like Adam's. The artist portrayed the likeness between God and man literally and physically, not spiritually. In fact, if you took Adam's face in the painting, aged it around the eyes, and crowned it with flowing white locks and a beard, you would have Michelangelo's depiction of God the Father.

How can an artist possibly represent a God who is spirit? And if we cannot see Him, how can we contemplate His image? Our vocabulary, superb and precise when describing the material world, falls silent before the inner processes of spirit. The very word 'spirit' in many languages means nothing more than breath or wind. But the entire Old Testament insists upon the central truth that God is spirit and that no physical image can capture His essence.

The second of the Ten Commandments forbids drawing

a picture or making a sculptured image intended to represent God. Whenever the Jews tried, God viewed it as profanation. After living in a country where graven images and idols abound, I can well understand the prohibition.

Hinduism has over a thousand different images, and I could hardly walk a block in an Indian town without seeing an idol or representation. As I watched the effects of those images on the average Indian, I observed two common results. For most, the images trivialise the gods. The gods lose any aura of sacredness and mystery and become rather like mascots or good luck charms. A taxi driver mounts a goddess statue on his taxicab and offers flowers and incense as a prayer for safety. For other Indians, the gods may become grotesque symbols that evoke an attitude of fear and bondage. Calcutta's violent goddess Kali, for example, has a fiery tongue and wears a garland of bloody heads around her waist. Hindus may worship a snake, a rat, a phallic symbol, even a goddess of smallpox; such images crowd the ornate temples.

Wisely, the Bible warns us against reducing the image of God to the level of physical matter; such an image too easily limits our concept of His real nature. We may begin to think of Him as a bearded old man in the sky, like the figure in Michelangelo's painting. Being a spirit, present everywhere, God can have no confining shape. 'To whom, then, will you compare God?' asks Isaiah. 'What image will you compare him to?' (40:18).*

We have, therefore, a God who cannot be captured in a visible image. But what does God look like? How can I find him? Where is His image? Somehow the essence of God entered the bodies of the first created humans, and *they* bore His image on this planet. For a time the two natures, the physical nature of organs and blood and bone and a

---

* See Isaiah 44:9–19 for a speech from God that gives a forceful and yet witty summary of the foolishness of making idols.

spiritual nature allowing direct communion with God, fit together in harmony. Sadly, that condition failed to last.

An event recorded in Genesis 3 disrupted the harmony between the two natures. Adam's and Eve's rebellion forever marred the image of God they carried, and at that moment a huge gulf fissured open, destroying the unity between God and mankind. Now when we gaze on human beings we find lurking among them the likes of Genghis Khan, Josef Stalin, and Adolf Hitler. And, yes, dramatic evidence of the broken image spills out of every one of us. Individual human beings can no longer express adequately a likeness to God; history proves darkly our unlikeness to Him.

It is not enough for us to mirror forth the residue of spirit and worth inside each person. We need something greater, far greater, to know what God is like. We need a new image, a new demonstration of God's likeness on our planet.

Christians believe we got such an image in the person of Jesus Christ, the Second Adam, whose comimg proved so revolutionary that it became the exact centre of a new religion. God the spirit agreed to become a man and incarnate His spirit. Inside a body of skin and bone and blood, the divine lived in matter as a microcosm, like the sun in a drop of water. In G. K. Chesterton's succinct phrase, 'God who had been only a circumference was seen as a centre'.

In three places the New Testament applies the word image to Jesus Christ (Col 1:15; 2 Cor. 4:4; Heb. 1:3). He is, says the Hebrews passage, the 'radiance of God's glory and the exact representation of his being'. Christ came to earth to offer us an image in the purest sense of the word: a precise reflection of what the Father is like, in bodily form. 'In the Father,' says Michael Ramsey, 'there is no unChrist-likeness at all.'

Doctors warn against glancing into the sky to look at the brilliance of the sun, even for an instant. Doing so would overwhelm light-receptor cells so that even with our eyes closed the image of that star would still appear, seared into our retinas like a brand of fire. It is the same with Jesus Christ: in a form we can visualise He sears our perception with the image of God.

Here is a strange truth, though: the image Jesus revealed surprised nearly everyone. Most of us have heard and seen the Jesus story portrayed so often that we have firm, preconceived notions of what Jesus was like. We will never be able to recapture the shock, the cataclysmic shock of the incognito form God took upon Himself. For His entrance He bypassed Rome, of course, and even Jerusalem, selecting instead a tiny, backwater town. He missed the people's expectations of divinity so widely that some asked, incredulous, 'Isn't this the carpenter's son?' The inevitable ethnic slur followed, 'Nazareth! Can anything good come from there?' Even His brothers did not believe Him; at least once they judged Him insane. John the Baptist, who had foretold Christ and baptised Him, wavered in faith toward the end. Jesus' closest follower cursed Him.

Jesus claimed to be a king greater than David, but little about Him suited the image of royalty. He carried no weapons, waved no banners, and the one time He permitted a procession He rode on a donkey, with His feet dragging the ground. Clearly, Jesus did not measure up to the image expected of a king or a God.

We instinctively think of Jesus as a perfect physical specimen, and in art He is portrayed as tall, with flowing hair and fine features modelled after the accepted ideals of the artist's culture. But on what basis? From the evidence of Scripture, nothing about Jesus made Him very special as a physical specimen either.

Once in my childhood my gentle Aunt Eunice came home from a Bible study in an absolute rage. Someone had read a description of Jesus, written by Josephus or another historian, that characterised Him as a hunchback. Aunt Eunice trembled with shame and anger, and her face flushed scarlet. It was blasphemy, she declared. 'Utter blasphemy! That is a horrid caricature, not a description of my Lord!' As an impressionable child, I could not help nodding in sympathetic indignation.

Although the notion shocked me greatly at that time, now it would not shock me at all to discover that Jesus was not a handsome, shining ideal in His personal looks and physique. Although the Bible does not include a description of Jesus' face and body, there is a description of sorts, in a prophecy of the suffering Servant in Isaiah:

'. . . there were many who were
            appalled at him –
    his appearance was so disfigured
            beyond that of any man
    and his form marred beyond
            human likeness . . .
He had no beauty or majesty to
            attract us to him,
    nothing in his appearance that we
            should desire him.
He was despised and rejected by men,
    a man of sorrows, and familiar with
            suffering.
Like one from whom men hide their
            faces
    he was despised, and we esteemed
            him not' (52:14; 53:2–3).

Socially, in His own teaching about Himself, Jesus identified with the hungry, the sick, the estranged, the naked, and the imprisoned so totally that, He said, whatever we do for one of the least of those people, we do for Him (Matt. 25:40). We meet the Son of God not in the corridors of power and wealth, but in the byways of human suffering and need. Christ chose to identify most intimately with those who appeared ugly and useless in the world's eyes.

It is this fact of Jesus' personal identification with the lowly, more than any other, that has taught me the stark distinctions in uses of the word *image*. In the image of the world – the image we exploit today in status games, beauty contests, advertising campaigns – God on earth made no special mark. Yet even one from insignificant Nazareth, a carpenter's son, a bruised body twitching on a cross – even He could express the image, the exact likeness of God.

I cannot tell you what impact that single truth can have when it fully dawns on a person who will never measure up – a leprosy victim in India, for example, unspeakably poor and physically deformed. For such a person Jesus becomes the only hope for restoration.

Jesus, the exact likeness of God in flesh, expressed the image of God in human form. But from the very beginning He warned that His physical presence was temporary. He had in mind a further goal: to restore the broken image of God in humanity.

God's activity on earth did not end with Jesus, and His image on earth did not vanish when Jesus departed. New Testament authors extend the term to a new Body God is creating composed of 'members' – men and women joining together to do the work of God. In referring to this Body, these writers pointedly use the same word that first described the spark of the divine in man and later described Christ. We are called, said Paul, to be 'the likeness [image] of his Son, that he might be the firstborn among many brothers' (Rom. 8:29).

This book, *In His Image*, is not primarily a treatise on the nature of individual men and women. We will not explore the psychological and mental attributes in each one of us that might reflect the image of God. Instead, we will centre on a community, that group of God's people who are called, more than two dozen times in the New Testament, Christ's Body. All of us joined to Him are an extension of the Incarnation. God reproduces and lives out His image in millions of ordinary people like us. It is a supreme mystery.

We are called to bear that image as a Body because any one of us taken individually would present an incomplete image, one partly false and always distorted, like a single glass chip hacked from a mirror. But collectively, in all our diversity, we can come together as a community of believers to restore the image of God in the world.

For a pattern to follow, we need only look back at Jesus, that divine image seared into our consciousness. The surprising qualities He showed – humility, servanthood, love – become the model for His Body also. No longer must we struggle to build up our own images, to prove ourselves. Rather, we can focus our lives on showing forth His image. And what counts for great success in popular culture – strength, intelligence, wealth, beauty, power – means little to that image.*

I had never grasped the revolutionary pattern Jesus laid down until I began working among leprosy patients in India. Again and again I saw these people, so cruelly ostracised from society, somehow radiate the love and goodness of God far better than wealthy, handsome and comfortable Christians I had known. Just as God Himself had taken on a lowly image, so it seemed His most faithful followers commonly revealed that same homeliness. They had a more natural right to anger and bitterness, yet the level of dedication and spiritual maturity among patients who came to know Christ shamed us doctors and missionaries. I wrestled with the paradox that those who seemingly had least reason to be grateful to God showed His love best.

The trend appeared with such force and consistency that it drove me to examine biblical passages that I had never taken seriously and that, I confess, had caused me embarrassment. Describing the church in Corinth, Paul said, 'Not many of you were wise by human standards; not many were influential; not many were of noble birth. But God chose the foolish things of the world to shame the wise; God chose

---

* 'Let not the wise man boast of his wisdom
  or the strong man boast of his strength
  or the rich man boast of his riches,
but let him who boasts boast about this;
  that he understands and knows me,
that I am the Lord, who exercises kindness,
  justice and righteousness on earth,
  For in these I delight' (Jer. 9:23–24).

the weak things of the world to shame the strong. He chose the lowly things of this world and the despised things – and the things that are not – to nullify the things that are, so that no one may boast before him' (I Cor. 1:26–29). Statements from Jesus also came to mind: the Sermon on the Mount, in which He enigmatically blesses the poor, the mourning, the persecuted; His comments on how difficult it is for the rich to enter the kingdom of heaven; His condemnation of pride and self-sufficiency.

Inevitably, as I read these passages now, my thoughts keep circling back to that single word we have been discussing: image. I strive with all my energy to improve the damaged self-images of the patients I treat. But when I approach Scripture, I encounter a new kind of image, one for which the same rules do not apply. If anything, the opposite principles hold true, a sort of 'reverse Quasimodo complex'.

Human self-image thrives on physical attractiveness, athletic ability, a worthwhile occupation; I worked to give those gifts to injured fliers in Britain and leprosy patients in India and now America. But, paradoxically, any of those desirable qualities may raise a barrier against the image of God, for virtually any quality that a person can rely on makes it more difficult for that person to rely on the spirit of God. The beautiful, the strong, the politically powerful, and the rich do not easily represent God's image. Rather, His spirit shines most brightly through the frailty of the weak, the impotence of the poor, the deformity of the hunchback. Even as bodies are broken, His image can grow brighter.

Initially, I found this insight into the nature of Christ's Body jarring, perhaps because it brought a gnawing awareness that I had often sought to surround myself with the successful, the intelligent, and the beautiful. Too often I had judged by the image of people rather than the image of God. But as I have reflected on my life and the people who have most powerfully presented God's image to me, my mind keeps fixing on three people especially. And none of them met human standards of success.

As a child, I often attended large churches and retreat centres where I listened to some of the most famous Christian speakers in England, many of whom demonstrated great eloquence and erudition. But another kind of speaker holds a special place in my memory: Willie Long, a man I encountered in a Primitive Methodist church at a seaside resort. Willie would mount the pulpit in his blue fisherman's jersey, with the fish scales still clinging to its sides contributing a salty aroma to the church hall. Yet this uneducated man with a thick Norfolk accent, unconventional grammar, and simple faith probably did more to nudge my own faith in those formative years than the entire company of famous men. When he stood to speak of Christ, he spoke of a personal friend, and the love of God radiated from him, through his tears. Willie Long, of little consequence in the image of men, showed me the image of God.

Later, in India, I observed with awe the spiritual rapport that bonded patients to the surgeon Mary Verghese. Mary was unique: a paraplegic surgeon.

One of my most promising students, Mary had suffered a terrible road accident that left her paralysed from the waist down. For months she lay in her hospital bed, resisting rehabilitation. She was staking her hopes on divine healing, she said, and rehabilitation exercises for paraplegia would merely waste her time. One day soon God would restore the full use of her legs.

Ultimately, however, Mary gained the courage to relinquish that demand for miraculous healing in exchange for the sense of the power of the Spirit revealed best in her weakness. Against all odds, she completed her surgery requirements and became a powerful spiritual force in the Christian Medical College hospital.

In addition to the paraplegia, Mary had also suffered severe facial injuries. After a series of operations to rebuild the bony infrastructure of Mary's cheeks, the plastic surgeon had no choice but to leave a large, ungainly scar right across her face. As a result, she had an odd, asymmetrical smile. By standards of physical perfection, she did not rate high. Yet she had a profound impact on the patients at Vellore.

Dejected leprosy patients would loiter aimlessly in the hallways of their wards (at that time their movements in the main hospital were restricted). Suddenly they would hear a small squeak that signified the approach of Mary's wheelchair. At once the row of faces lit up in bright smiles as though someone had just pronounced them all cured. Mary had a power to renew their faith and hope. Thus, when I think of Mary Verghese, I see not her face, but its reflection in the smiling faces of so many others; not her image, but the image of God poured through her broken human body.

One last figure towers above all others who have influenced my life: my mother, known as Granny Brand. I say it kindly and in love, but in old age my mother had little of physical beauty left in her. She had been a classic beauty as a young woman – I have photographs to prove it – but not in old age. The rugged conditions in India, combined with crippling falls and her battles with typhoid, dysentery, and malaria had made her a thin, hunched-over old woman. Years of exposure to wind and sun had toughened her facial skin into leather and furrowed it with wrinkles as deep and extensive as any I have seen on a human face. She knew better than anyone that her physical appearance had long since failed her – for this reason she adamantly refused to keep a mirror in her house.

At the age of seventy-five, while working in the mountains of South India, my mother fell and broke her hip. She lay all night on the floor in pain until a workman found her the next morning. Four men carried her on a string-and-wood cot down the mountain path to the plains and put her in a jeep for an agonising 150-mile ride over rutted roads. (She had made this trip before, after a head-first fall off a horse on a rocky mountain path, and already had experienced some paralysis below her knees.)

I soon scheduled a visit to my mother's mud-walled home in the mountains in order to persuade her to retire. By then she could walk only with the aid of two bamboo canes taller than she was, planting the canes and lifting her legs high with each painful step to keep her paralysed feet from dragging on the ground. Yet she continued to travel on horseback and camp in the outlying villages in order to preach the gospel and treat sicknesses and pull the decayed teeth of the villagers.

I came with compelling arguments for her retirement. It was not safe for her to go on living alone in such a remote place with good help a day's journey away. With her faulty sense of balance and paralysed legs, she presented a constant medical hazard. Already she had endured fractures of vertebrae and ribs, pressure on her spinal nerve roots, a brain concussion, a fractured femur, and severe infection of her hand. 'Even the best of people do sometimes retire when they reach their seventies,' I said with a smile. 'Why not come to Vellore and live near us?'

Granny threw off my arguments like so much nonsense and shot back a reprimand. Who would continue the work? There was no one else in the entire mountain range to preach, to bind up wounds, and to pull teeth. 'In any case,' she concluded, 'what is the use of preserving my old body if it is not going to be used where God needs me?'

And so she stayed. Eighteen years later, at the age of ninety-three, she reluctantly gave up sitting on her pony because she was falling all too frequently. Devoted Indian villagers began bearing her on a hammock from town to town. After two more years of mission work, she finally died aged ninety-five. She was buried, at her request, in a simple, well-used sheet laid in the ground – no coffin. She abhorred the notion of wasting precious wood on coffins. Also, she liked the symbolism of returning her physical body to its original humus even as her spirit was set free.

One of my last and strongest visual memories of my mother is set in a village in the mountains she loved, perhaps the last time I saw her in her own environment. She is sitting on a low stone wall that circles the village, with people pressing in from all sides. They are listening to all she has to say about Jesus. Heads are nodding in encouragement, and deep, searching questions come from the crowd. Granny's own rheumy eyes are shining, and standing beside her I can see what she must be seeing through failing eyes: intent faces gazing with absolute trust and affection on one they have grown to love.

I know that even with my relative youth and strength and all my specialised knowledge about health and agricultural techniques, I could never command that kind of devotion and love from these people. They are looking at a wrinkled old face, but somehow her shrunken tissues have become transparent and she is all lambent spirit. To them, she is beautiful.

Granny Brand had no need for a mirror made of glass and polished chromium; she had the incandescent faces of thousands of Indian villagers. Her worn-out physical image did nothing but enhance the image of God beaming through her like a beacon.

Willie Long, Mary Verghese, Granny Brand – these are three in whom I have seen the image of God most clearly. I do not say that a Miss Universe or a handsome Olympian can never show forth the love and power of God, but I do believe that such a person is, in some ways, at a disadvantage. Talent, a pleasing physical appearance, and the adulation of crowds tend to shove aside the qualities of humility and selflessness and love that Christ demands of those who would bear His image.

The message is clear: 'God has combined the members of the body and *has given greater honour to the parts that lacked it*, so that there should be no division in the body, but that its parts should have equal concern for each other' (1 Cor. 12:24–25). In our own physical bodies, Paul points out, those parts that seem to be weakest prove indispensable and the unpresentable parts call for special modesty. In Christ's Body, too, the analogy holds. When we join his Body, it is the image of God Himself we must find, not our own. We find it not by proving ourselves, but by releasing that desperate dependence on our own self-images in favour of taking on His glorious image.

I, Paul Brand, approaching my seventieth year with

more wrinkles and less hair than I would prefer, can let go the anxiety about my health and appearance and abilities that are slipping away. The painful and competitive dependence on my own self-image yields to a freeing, joyful dependence on God's own image.

Admittedly, I lose some autonomy and a chance to nurture my ego. But belonging to Christ's Body offers its reward too. From God's viewpoint we members are in fact swallowed up, surrounded by Christ's Body, 'in Christ', as Paul keeps repeating. New Testament authors stretch for metaphors to express the reality. We live or 'abide' in him, they say (1 John 2:6). We are 'the aroma of Christ' to God (2 Cor. 2:15). We 'shine like stars in the universe' (Phil. 2:15) and are 'holy and blameless in his sight' (Eph. 1:4). Those are just a sampling; the message resounds throughout the Epistles. We are God's delight, His pride, His experiment on earth meant to display His wisdom even to the 'rulers and authorities in the heavenly realms' (Eph. 3:10). A restoration of His image on earth is underway, through us.

For membership in His Body, God has drawn from all races and groups, since in Him there is neither Greek nor Jew, slave nor free. A simple fisherman, a scar-faced pilot, a paraplegic, a crone can take their rightful places there with joy. It is His glory we take on, not our own. The cost may increase for those with wealth, physical attraction, and security. But for all of us, the reward is the same: a chance to be judged not for what we are but for what Christ is. When God looks upon us He sees his beloved Son.

'But we all, with unveiled faces beholding as in a mirror the glory of the Lord, are being transformed into the same image from glory to glory, just as from the Lord, the Spirit' (2 Cor. 3:18 NASB).

BLOOD

4 Power

A fly is a nobler creature than the sun, because a fly hath life, and the sun hath not.

St Augustine

My entire career in medicine traces back to one dreary night at Connaught Hospital in East London. Before that night I had stubbornly resisted all pressures to enter medical school. For some time my family had tried to influence me toward medicine, even to the extent of an uncle offering to pay all school expenses. And just before I left high school my mother's return from India gave us an opportunity for a serious talk about my future.

We sat together before a hissing gas fire in her bedroom. After a separation of six years, I was struck by her changed appearance. Twenty years in rural India had worn away the soft facade of British gentility and etched an unmistakable resolve in the lines of her face. Grief covered her face like a mask – my father had died of blackwater fever that same year. She had come home a desperately broken person, seeking a place of refuge.

It seemed strange for me to be abruptly planning my future with someone I had not seen in six years. 'You know how much your father loved the medical work in the mountains,' she began gently. 'He always wished he had become a doctor with a proper degree instead of having to rely on a short training course at Livingston College. If he had . . . who knows, he might still be with us. He would have known how to treat the fever.'

Her eyes filled up and she paused a few minutes, swallowing repeatedly. She went on to tell me of new laws in India that would prohibit all but qualified doctors from practising medicine. Then she looked directly into my eyes and said gravely, 'Paul, your father always dreamed that you could take up where he left off and return as a real doctor –'

'No, mother!' I stopped her in mid-sentence. 'I don't want to be a doctor. I don't like medical work. I'd rather be a builder. I could build houses and schools and even hospitals. Anyhow, I don't want to be a doctor.'

Although she did not argue, I could sense a barrier had arisen between us. I mumbled some excuse and left, with a gnawing awareness that I was disappointing her as well as my father and my generous uncle by not studying medicine.

I could not tell my mother, and probably did not even admit to myself at the time, the real reason: a visceral reaction against blood and pus. Memories had sickened me ever since childhood.

As small children in India my sister and I had shared in everything my parents did. Sometimes a patient came for treatment of a tumid abcess, and when Dad dressed the wound we held the bandages. If we were on camp, my father would cart his steriliser out to a shady tree, boil the instruments, and prepare to lance the abcess. He had no anaesthetics, so the patient would cling fiercely to a relative during the incision and drainage. My sister turned her head the instant she saw the flash of the knife. I laughed at her and boasted that boys were not afraid.

But I was afraid, and also repulsed by the sight of the blood and the pus. I hated those scenes and the sticky cleanup that followed. Vivid memories, years later, were still keeping me from becoming a doctor. I could not brave a whole lifetime of dealing with blood and pus and sickness.

Five years after my awkward conversation with Mother, I found myself unavoidably working at Connaught, a small hospital in London's East End. I had kept my promise of learning the building trade, having apprenticed as a carpenter, a mason, a painter, and a bricklayer. I loved it. Evening classes in civil engineering had also exposed me to the theories behind construction. I chafed to return to India to practise my trade. The mission advised enrolling in the same Livingston College course in hygiene and tropical medicine that my father had taken. I was assigned to a local hospital to do dressings in the wards and to learn basic principles of diagnosis and treatment.

It was during one evening of my stint at Connaught that my whole view of medicine – and of blood – permanently shifted. That night hospital orderlies wheeled a beautiful young accident victim into my ward. Loss of blood had given her skin an unearthly paleness, and her brownish hair seemed jet-black in contrast. Oxygen starvation had shut down her brain into a state of unconscious.

The hospital staff lurched into their controlled-panic response to a trauma patient. A nurse dashed down a corridor for a bottle of blood while a doctor fumbled with the transfusion apparatus. Another doctor, glancing at my white coat, thrust a blood pressure cuff at me. Fortunately, I had already learned to read pulse and blood pressure. I could not detect the faintest flicker of a pulse on the woman's cold, damp wrist.

In the glare of hospital lights she looked like a waxwork Madonna or an alabaster saint from a cathedral. Even her lips were pallid, and as the doctor searched her chest with his stethoscope I noticed whitened nipples on her small breasts. Only a few freckles stood out against the pallor. She did not seem to be breathing. I felt sure she was dead.

The nurse arrived with a bottle of blood and buckled it into a metal stand as the doctor punctured the woman's vein with a large needle. They fastened the bottle high and used an extra-long tube so that the increase in pressure would push the blood into her body faster. The staff told me to keep watch over the emptying bottle while they scurried off for more blood.

Nothing in my memory can compare to the excitement of what happened next. Certainly the details of that scene come to me even now with a start. As the others all left, I nervously held the woman's wrist. Suddenly I could feel the faintest press of a pulse. Or was it my own finger's pulse? I searched again – it was there, a tremor barely perceptible, but regular. The next bottle of blood arrived and was quickly connected. A spot of pink appeared like a drop of watercolour on her cheek. It began to spread into a beautiful flush. Her lips darkened pink, then red, and her body quivered with a kind of sighing breath.

Then her eyelids fluttered lightly and parted. She squinted at first, and her pupils constricted, reacting to the bright lights of the room. At last she looked directly at me. To my enormous surprise, she spoke, asking for water.

That young woman entered my life for only an hour or so, but the experience left me utterly changed. I had seen a miracle: a corpse resurrected, the creation of Eve when breath entered into and animated her body. If medicine, if blood could do this. . . .

I picked up the empty glass bottle, streaks of blood still smearing its side, and read the label. Who had given these pints of life? I wanted some mental picture of the donor who had made the miracle possible. In our registry I discovered the donor lived in Seven Kings, Essex, a town where I had worked for a building construction firm. With eyes closed I envisioned one of the burly workmen from that blue-collar neighbourhood. At that moment he could have been out climbing ladders, or laying bricks, exuding strength and vigour, oblivious to the frail young woman revived by his own blood cells miles away.

By the time I finished my year at Livingston College I was incurably in love with medicine. A short time later, feeling some shame at my vacillation, but compelled by an inner sense, I turned back and accepted my uncle's offer of support for medical school. The memory of shed blood had kept me out of medicine; the power of shared blood ultimately brought me to it.

For most of us, the organ of blood, if one can think of this fluid mass as an organ, comes to consciousness mainly when we begin to lose it. Then, the sight of it in tinted urine, a nosebleed, or a weeping wound provokes alarm. We miss the dramatic sense of blood's power that I saw demonstrated in the Connaught patient – the power that sustains our lives at every moment.

'What does my blood *do* all day?' a five-year-old child asked, peering dubiously at his scraped knee. Whereas the ancients would have responded with elegant references to ethers and humours borne in that 'pure clear lovely and amiable juice', perhaps a technological metaphor would serve best today. Imagine an enormous tube snaking southward from Canada through the Amazon delta, plunging into oceans only to surface at every inhabited island, shooting out eastward through every jungle, plain, and desert in Africa, forking near Egypt to join all of Europe and Russia as well as the entire Middle East and Asia – a pipeline so global and pervasive that it links every person worldwide. Inside that tube an endless plenitude of treasures floats along on rafts: mangoes, coconuts, asparagus, and produce from every continent; watches, calculators, and cameras; gems and minerals; forty-nine brands of cereals; all styles and sizes of clothing; the contents of entire shopping centres. Four billion people have access: at a moment of need or want, they simply reach into the tube and seize whatever product suits them. Somewhere far down the pipeline a replacement is manufactured and inserted.

Such a pipeline exists inside each one of us, servicing not four billion but one hundred trillion cells in the human body. An endless supply of oxygen, amino acids, nitrogen, sodium, potassium, calcium, magnesium, sugars, lipids, cholesterols, and hormones surges past our cells, carried on blood cell rafts or suspended in the fluid. Each cell has special withdrawal privileges to gather the resources needed to fuel a tiny engine for its complex chemical reactions.

In addition, that same pipeline ferries away refuse, exhaust gases, and worn-out chemicals. In the interest of economical transport, the body dissolves its vital substances into a liquid (much as coal is shipped more efficiently through a slurry pipeline than by truck or train). Five or six quarts of this all-purpose fluid suffice for the body's hundred trillion cells.

When blood spills, it appears as a uniform, syrupy substance ranging in colour from bright red to dark purple. The late Loren Eiseley, a naturalist and anthropologist, more accurately recognised it as a teeming population. Near the end of his life, he tripped while walking to his office one afternoon. He fell face downward, and blood spilled from a gash on his forehead. Somewhat dazed, Eiseley sat up and stared at the blot on the pavement. Later, he wrote:

Confusedly, painfully, I murmured, 'Oh, don't go. I'm sorry.' The words were spoken to no one, but to a part of myself. I was quite sane, only it was an oddly detached sanity, for I was addressing blood cells, phagocytes, platelets – all the crawling, living independent wonders that had been part of me and now, through my folly and lack of care, were dying like beached fish on the hot pavement. I was made up of millions of these tiny creatures, their toil, their sacrifices, as they hurried to seal and repair the rent fabric of this vast being whom they had unknowingly, but in love, compounded. I was their galaxy, their creation. For the first time, I loved them consciously. It seemed to me then, and does now in retrospect, that I had caused to the universe I inhabited as many deaths as the explosion of a supernova in the cosmos.

A simple experiment confirms the composite nature of blood. Pour a quantity of red blood into any clear glass and simply wait. Horizontal bands of colour will appear as various cells settle by weight, until the final multi-layered result resembles an exotic cocktail. The deepest reds, comprising clumps of red cells, sink to the bottom; plasma, a thin yellow fluid, fills the top part of the flask; platelets and white cells congregate in a pale grey band in between.

What the telescope does to nearby galaxies, the microscope does to a drop of blood: it unveils the staggering reality. A speck of blood the size of this letter 'o' contains 5,000,000 red cells, 300,000 platelets and 7,000 white cells. The fluid is actually an ocean stocked with living matter. Red cells alone, if removed from a single person and laid side by side, would carpet an area of 3,500 square yards.

Red cells and white cells make appearances in other portions of this book and are examined in detail elsewhere. But the body's survival depends just as surely on the cells with a delicate flower-like shape, the platelets. Their function remained hidden until recently. Now scientists recognise that platelets, which circulate only six to twelve days in the blood, play a crucial role in the life-saving process of clotting; they serve as mobile first-aid boxes by detecting leaks, plugging them, and tidying up the debris.

When a blood vessel is cut, the fluid that sustains life begins to leak away. In response, tiny platelets melt, like snowflakes, spinning out a gossamer web of fibrinogen. Red blood cells collect in this web, like cars crashing into each other when the road is blocked. Soon the tenuous wall of red cells thickens enough to stanch the flow of blood.

Platelets have a very small margin of error. Any clot that extends beyond the vessel wall and threatens to obstruct the vessel itself will stop the flow of blood through the vessel and perhaps lead to a stroke or coronary thrombosis and possibly death. On the other hand, people whose blood has no ability to clot live short lives: even a tooth extraction may prove fatal. The body cannily gauges when a clot is large enough to stop the loss of blood but not so large as to impede the flow within the vessel itself.*

A view through a microscope clarifies the various components of blood but gives no picture of the daily frenzy encountered by each cell. Red cells, for example, never sit motionless. From their first entrance into the bloodstream they are pushed and shoved through rush hour traffic. Beginning the cycle at the heart, they take a short

---

* India has a very feared species of snake, the 'eleven-step adder', so named because its toxic bite is said to allow the victim time for just eleven more steps. Like all vipers, it kills with a clotting toxin. If its fang penetrates a major vein, say, in the leg, all the blood in the channel between the heart and leg clots at once. If the toxin merely reaches a minor vessel, an amazing thing happens. The poison draws platelets to the tissue like a magnet. Elsewhere in the body platelets simply vanish so that the blood cannot clot anywhere. Then, the smallest scratch will kill the victim or he may bleed internally in brain or intestine. Bleeding cannot be stopped. Thus a viper's toxin can kill in two opposite ways: a devastating clot or an equally devastating inability to clot. The Haffkeine Institute in Bombay milks these adders and uses infinitesimal amounts of the dried toxin to treat excess bleeding in patients.

jaunt to the lungs to pick up a heavy load of oxygen. Immediately they return to the heart, which propels them violently over the Niagara Falls of the aortic arch. From there, highways crowded with billions of red cells branch out to the brain, the limbs, and vital internal organs.

Sixty thousand miles of blood vessels link every living cell; even the blood vessels themselves are fed by blood vessels. Highways narrow down to one-lane roads, then bike paths, then footpaths, until finally the red cell must bow sideways and edge through a capillary one-tenth the diameter of a human hair. In such narrow confines the cells are stripped of food and oxygen and loaded down with carbon dioxide and urea. If shrunken down to their size, we would see red cells as bloated bags of jelly and iron drifting along in a river until they reach the smallest capillary, where gases fizz and wheeze in and out of surface membranes. From there red cells rush to the kidneys for a thorough scrubbing, then back to the lungs for a refill. And the journey begins anew.

A person can live a day or two without water and several weeks without food, but only a few minutes without oxygen, the main fuel for our hundred trillion cells. Heavy exercise may increase the demand for oxygen from the normal four gallons up to seventy-five gallons an hour, prompting the heart to double or even triple its rate to speed red cells to the heaving lungs. If the lungs alone cannot overcome the oxygen shortage, the red cells call up reinforcements. Instead of five million red cells in a speck of blood, seven or eight million will gradually appear. After a few months in the rarified atmosphere of Colorado's mountains, for example, up to ten million red cells will fill each drop of blood, compensating for the thinner air.

The pellmell journey, even to the extremity of the big toe, lasts a mere twenty seconds. An average red cell endures the cycle of loading, unloading, and jostling through the body for a half million round trips over four months. In one final journey, to the spleen, the battered cell is stripped bare by scavenger cells and recycled into new cells. Three hundred billion such red cells die and are replaced every day, leaving behind various parts to reincarnate in a hair follicle or a taste bud.*

The components of this circulatory system cooperate to accomplish a simple goal: nourishing and cleansing each living cell. If any part of the network breaks down – the heart takes an unscheduled rest, a clot overgrows and blocks an artery, a defect diminishes the red cells' oxygen capacity – life ebbs away. The brain, master of the body, can survive intact only five minutes without replenishment.

Blood once repulsed me. I saw it as the most distasteful part of medical treatment. Now, however, I share the grateful sentiments of Loren Eiseley. I feel like assembling all my blood cells and singing them a hymn of praise. The drama of resurrection enacted before me in Connaught Hospital takes place without fanfare in each heartbeat of a healthy human being. Every cell in every body lives at the mercy of blood.

---

* The body provides the energy for the red cells' travels by employing the heart, an organ that deserves a book exclusively devoted to it. Primitive artificial hearts are now available, but I would like to see a government design specification sheet for a truly adequate replacement.
  BIDS ACCEPTED FOR:
  – Fluid pump with 75-year life expectancy (2,500,000,000 cycles).
  – No maintenance or lubrication required.
  – Output: must vary between .025 horsepower at rest and short bursts of 1 horse power determined by such factors as stress and exercise.
  – Weight: not to exceed 10.5 ounces (300 grams).
  – Capacity: 2,000 gallons per day.
  – Valves: each to operate 4,000–5,000 times per hour.

5 Life

The line between the living and the dead is a sharp line. When the dead atoms of Carbon, Hydrogen, Oxygen, Nitrogen, are seized upon by Life, the organism at first is very lowly. It possesses few functions. It has little beauty. Growth is the work of time. But Life is not. That comes in a moment. At one moment it was dead; the next it lived. This is conversion, the 'passing', as the Bible calls it, 'from Death unto Life'. Those who have stood by another's side at the solemn hour of this dread possession have been conscious sometimes of an experience which words are not allowed to utter – a something like the sudden snapping of a chain, the waking from a dream.

Henry Drummond
Natural Law in the
Spiritual World

Blood spatters the pages of mythology and history. Drinking it gave strength and new life to the ghosts of the dead in *The Odyssey*, to the Roman epileptics who dashed onto the floor of the Colosseum to lap up the blood of dying gladiators, to Kenya's Masai tribesmen who still celebrate feast days by quaffing blood freshly drawn from a cow or goat.

In human relations, blood had a mysterious, almost sacred aura. An oath held more power than a person's word, but blood made a contract nearly inviolable. The ancients, unashamed to act out their symbols, sometimes sealed contracts by slashing themselves and commingling their blood.

We moderns have inherited quaint tokens of the intrinsic mystery of blood: a wedding ring placed on the 'leech finger' that was once believed to contain a vein leading directly to the heart; a child's game of 'blood brothers' by which two participants solemnly and unhygienically pledge their undying loyalty. We echo misconceptions, too, when we use such terms as 'pure blood', 'mixed blood', 'blood relations', or 'hot-blooded' and 'cold-blooded', harking back to the days when the liquid was presumed to carry heredity and temperament.

Even now, after it has been centrifuged in laboratories and demythologised, blood still retains mystic power, if only in the queasy sensation it evokes when we see it shed. There is something horribly unnatural, even nauseating, about watching the fluid of life pour uncontrollably from a living body. Little wonder religions throughout history have honoured blood as a sacral substance. A ravaging plague, a minor drought, or, perhaps, a desire to triumph over enemies or decoy the gods' anger – anything of major import can prompt a bloody sacrifice in a primitive religion.

Although worshippers may feel uncomfortable with the fact, Christianity too is inescapably blood-based. Old Testament writers graphically describe blood sacrifices, and their New Testament counterparts overlay those symbolic rituals with theological interpretations. In their writings, they choose the word 'blood' three times as often as the 'cross' of Christ, five times as frequently as 'death'. And daily, weekly, monthly (or whenever, depending on denomination) we are called upon to commemorate Christ's death with a ceremony centred in His blood.

As a surgeon, I come into contact with blood almost daily. I read it as a measure of my patients' health. I suction it away from areas where I am cutting. I order neatly labelled pints of it from a refrigerator when a patient needs an extra supply. I know well the warm, slightly acrid substance pumping around inside each of my patients – blotches of it soil every lab coat I own.

But as a Christian, I confess I used to recoil instinctively from the blood symbol that suffuses our religion. Unlike our forefathers, we have not grown up in a cultural environment stocked with mystagogic religions and animal sacrifices. For most of us, blood is not an everyday metaphor, and over time blood-linked concepts may lose their meanings or, worse, unnecessarily repel people from the faith. A challenge arises. Can we discover insights into the biblical symbolism of blood that fit more naturally within our culture while preserving the essence of the metaphor?

Blood works as a religious symbol because of what it is, and the more we know about the properties of actual blood, the better we will grasp its metaphoric connotations. I have already described how the innate power of blood so impressed me that I changed careers. Because I am a surgeon and not a theologian, I will restrict the next few chapters to the specific functions of blood I have encountered in medicine. I will keep before me the actual warm and sticky fluid I wash off my gloves each day.

To people who practise medicine, blood represents life; that quality overarches all other aspects. Every time I pick up a scalpel I have an almost reverent sense of the vital nature of blood.

When performing surgery, I must continually control bleeding, for each quiver of the scalpel leaves a thin wake of blood. Most often it comes from a few of the millions of tiny capillaries, and I disregard them, knowing they will seal up of their own accord. Every minute or two a spurt of bright blood tells me an artery has been cut, and I must either clamp it or sear it with a cautery. The slow ooze of darker blood indicates a punctured vein, and I pay even closer attention. A cut vein is dangerous: with far less muscle in its wall than an artery, it cannot easily close itself off. To avoid these problems, I strive to locate each significant vessel before I make a cut. Then I can clamp it twice and slice between the clamps without the loss of a drop of blood. After years of surgical practise, all this routine proceeds without producing stress or emotion.

Despite all precautions, a different level of bleeding may occur – one that no surgeon ever gets used to. Sometimes, through an error of judgment or loss of manual dexterity, a really large vessel is cut or tears open and the wound gushes with blood. It wells up in a cavity like the abdomen or the chest and totally obscures the rip in the vessel from which it comes. The surgeon, fumbling in the sump of blood up to his wrists, shouts for suction and gauze sponges – inevitably, this is when the suction nozzle gets blocked or the lights go out. No surgeon goes through a career without such incidents.

I shall never forget the horror-struck face of one of my London students during one such experience. He was performing a routine procedure on a woman in our out-patient clinic, excising a tiny lymphatic node from her neck for biopsy. It was a minor procedure, performed with local anesthetic. I was working in an adjacent room. Suddenly, a nurse appeared in my doorway, her hands and uniform splashed with fresh blood. 'Come quick!' she cried, and I dashed next door to find the intern, white as a corpse, working frantically on a woman from whose neck blood was gushing. It was hard to tell who was more terrified: my intern or the patient.

Fortunately, a wonderful teacher in England had drilled into me the appropriate reflexes. I ran to the woman's side and, quickly removing all instruments from the wound, grasped her neck and simply applied firm pressure on the wound with my thumb. As my thumb filled in the broken part of the blood vessel wall, bleeding stopped, and I stayed in that position until the woman calmed down enough for me to extend the anesthesia and repair the vessel. I learned that the intern had dissected the nodal area and had conscientiously tried to clip it free from all its roots. But in doing so he had inadvertently snipped off a small section of the jugular vein!

A crisis with blood – and it *will* occur sometime – tells a student whether or not to continue in the profession. If a young surgeon panics, he or she should move over to a branch of medicine less likely to produce fearsome situations.

My London teacher, who had the grand name Sir Launcelot Barrington-Ward, had fiercely tried to prepare his students for just such an emergency. Sir Launcelot, surgeon to England's royal family, taught me paediatric surgery. As his assistant, I would hear him ask each fresh student, 'In case of massive bleeding, what is your most useful instrument?' At first the newcomer would propose exotic surgical tools, and the old teacher would frown and shake his head. There was only one acceptable answer: 'Your thumb, sir.' Why? The thumb is readily available – every doctor has one – and offers a perfect blend of strong pressure and gentle compliancy.

Then Sir Launcelot would ask, 'What is your greatest enemy when there is bleeding?' and we would say, 'Time, sir.' And he would ask, 'What is your greatest friend?' and we would say again, 'Time.'

Sir Launcelot impressed on us the fact that as long as blood is being lost, time is the enemy. Second by second, life will leak away as the patient grows weaker and approaches the point of no return. The temptation is to panic, to grab at vessels and clamp them off with forceps here and there, often causing more damage.

But once I have my thumb on the bleeding point, time becomes my friend. There is no hurry; I can stop and plan what to do next. The body busies itself helping: clots form to repair the breach. I can take time to clean up and arrange a transfusion, or to send for a special instrument, or to call for an extra assistant, or to enlarge the incision to get a better view. (Once, I held a clump of blood vessels in my fist for twenty-five minutes while removing a diseased spleen, operating with one hand while I held off the flow of blood with the other.) All this can happen if my thumb is pressing firmly on the area of bleeding. Finally, when all is ready, I slowly remove my thumb while my other hand and my assistants are poised to take action – and I find that no action is needed. The bleeding has stopped.

At those moments, in the rush of adrenaline brought on by the crisis, I often have a sense of spiritual exaltation. I feel at one with the millions of living cells in that wound fighting for survival. I realise that, incredibly, the common thumb is the only thing between my patient and death.

After many such experiences in the electric atmosphere of the operating room, every surgeon learns to identify blood with life. The two are inseparable: you lose one, you lose both.

Why, then, does blood as a Christian symbol seem to contradict what I learn at such moments?

I admit at the outset that I sometimes find the associations of the blood symbol in Christendom distasteful. I switch on my radio on a Sunday morning while driving from my hospital in Carville to New Orleans. A heavy-breathing pastor is conducting a communion service in a church in the bayous. He gives a maudlin commentary on the final agony of Jesus on the cross. He vividly describes the scene of a cross being strapped to a back bloodied by whips. The congregation murmurs as he evidently holds up a four-inch thorn and illustrates how barbarously the soldiers jammed a crown of them onto Jesus' head. Every occasion for the word blood (which his drawl stretches into two syllables) – the nailing, the thud of the cross in the ground, the spear in the side – seems to give this preacher a fresh burst of energy.

The theme of *death* and unrelieved gloom hangs darkly over the entire hour. I drive along in bright Louisiana sunshine, glancing at the stately egrets, white as clouds, bobbing for food in the canals lining the highway. The preacher asks his parishioners to think of all their recent sins, one by one, and to contemplate the horrible guilt that led to such a bloody death on their behalf.

A ceremony follows, the sacrament itself. My mind, jarred from the solemn service on the radio, returns to the literal substance of blood – not the watery purple substance in the communion glasses but, the rich scarlet soup of proteins and cells that keeps my patients alive. Again I wonder; has something been lost over the centuries, something foundational? Has the intent and meaning of the symbol evaporated? The Louisiana pastor concentrates exclusively on blood that was *shed* – but does not the sacrament centre also on blood that is *shared*?

William Harvey, the seventeenth-century British scientist who revolutionised our understanding of circulation and blood, stated the medical fact: 'Blood is the cause not only of life in general but also of longer or shorter life, of sleep and watching, of genius, aptitude and strength. It is the first to live and the last to die.' Medically, blood signifies life and not death. It feeds and sustains every cell in the body with its precious nutrients. When it seeps away, life falters. Has our modern interpretation of the symbol, as exemplified by the radio preacher's fixation on death, strayed so far from the original meaning?

We must find the decisive clue of meaning not from medicine but from Jesus and from the authors of the Bible who introduced that symbol. To them, shed blood could stand for death ('[Abel's] blood cries out to me from the ground' Gen. 4:10). And yet, deep in every Jewish person's consciousness lay a fundamental association of blood with life. God Himself had given it that meaning. As a new era of world history began, in a covenant with Noah, God commanded, 'But you must not eat meat that has its lifeblood still in it' (Gen. 9:4). Later, in the formal legal code given to Moses and the Israelites, God reiterated His command as 'a lasting ordinance for the generations to come.' He explained the reason, 'For the life of a creature is in the blood' (Lev. 3:17; 7:26–27; 17:11, 14; Deut. 12:23).

Old Testament Jews, inured to violent death and capital punishment, were not squeamish about blood. Israel had no aseptic slaughter-houses for sheep and cattle, so each Jew must have viewed the bloody deaths of many animals. But still, every good Jewish housewife checked her meat to see that no blood remained. The rule was absolute: do not eat the blood, for it contains life. Kosher cuisine developed, using elaborate techniques to assure that no blood contaminated the meat.

So ingrained was this prohibition against ingesting blood that thousands of years later, when the apostles distilled what indispensable customs must be honoured by the new Gentile Christians, two rules about blood made the list of only four taboos (Acts 15:29). Though flexible on such long-held practices as circumcision, the apostles forbade drinking blood and eating meat improperly butchered (in strangled animals the blood would not have drained out).*

In view of this background of rigid Jewish assumptions about blood, consider the shocking, almost revolting message Jesus brought to that culture:

> I tell you the truth, unless you eat the flesh of the Son of Man and drink his blood, you have no life in you. Whoever eats my flesh and drinks my blood has eternal life, and I will raise him up at the dark day. For my flesh is real food and my blood is real drink. Whoever eats my flesh and drinks my blood remains in me, and I in him. Just as the living Father sent me and I live because of the Father, so the one who feeds on me will live because of me. (John 6:53–57)

A call for gross immorality would hardly have jolted Jesus' followers more severely. His words, coming at the

---

* Curiously, even the most literalistic Christians today ignore this direct command to the New Testament church.

peak of His popularity just after the feeding of the five thousand, signalled a drastic turning point in His public acceptance. The Jews became so confused and outraged that a crowd of thousands, who had pursued Jesus around a lake in order to crown Him king forcibly, silently melted away. Many of His closest disciples deserted Him; His own brothers judged Him insane; plots to kill him suddenly sprang up. This time, Jesus had simply gone too far.

At least those first hearers caught the dramatic sweep of what Jesus had done. He had siphoned from the word *blood* four thousand years of deeply felt associations. No Jew ingested blood – only savages and the uncircumcised did that. Blood was always poured out before God as an offering, for life belonged to Him. Yet to those very people Jesus said, 'Drink my blood.' Is it any wonder the Jews bristled and the disciples slunk away?

A question looms. Knowing – as he must have known – the offence His words would cause, why did Jesus say them? Why not draw a more reasonable parallel to Jewish sacrifice? If He had said, 'Eat my flesh and pour out my blood,' or 'Eat my flesh and sprinkle my blood,' His hearers would not have been offended. But they would not have grasped Jesus' intent. Instead, He told them, 'Drink it.'

Jesus spoke as He did not to offend, but to effect a radical transformation in the symbol. God had said to Noah, if you drink the blood of a lamb, the life of the lamb enters you – don't do it. Jesus said, in effect, if you drink my blood, my life will enter you – do it! Thus, I believe Jesus intended our ceremony to include not only remembrance of His past death but also realisation of His present life. We cannot live without the nourishment His life provides.

The ceremony we call Eucharist (or Lord's Supper or Holy Communion) formally traces back to Jesus' last night with the disciples before His crucifixion. There, amid a stuffy roomful of His frightened disciples, Jesus first said the words that have been repeated millions of times: 'This is my blood of the new covenant, which is poured out for many for the forgiveness of sins' (Matt. 26:28). Jesus commanded his disciples to drink the wine, representing His blood. The offering was not merely poured out, but rather taken in, ingested. He repeated those shocking words, 'Drink from it, all of you' (v. 27).

That same evening Jesus used another metaphor, perhaps to shed light on the meaning of shared blood. 'I am the vine; you are the branches,' he declared. 'If a man remains in me and I in him, he will bear much fruit; apart from me you can do nothing' (John 15:5 – note parallel wording to John 6:56). Surrounded by the vineyard-covered hillsides that ringed Jerusalem, the disciples could more easily comprehend this metaphor. A grape branch disconnected from the nutrients of the vine becomes withered, dry, and dead, useless for anything except kindling. Only when connected to the vine can it grow, prosper, and bear fruit.

Even in the doom-shrouded atmosphere of that last night, at the meal from which the sacrament derives, the image of life welled up. For the disciples, the wine was to symbolise His blood that could vitalise them much as the sap does the grapevine.*

If I read these accounts correctly, they correspond to my medical experience exactly. It is not true that blood represents life to the surgeon but death to the Christian. Rather, we come to the table also to partake of His life. 'For my flesh is real food and my blood is real drink. Whoever eats my flesh and drinks my blood remains in me, and I in him' – at last those words make sense. Christ came not just to give us an example of a way of life but to give us life itself. Spiritual life is not ethereal and outside us,

---

* The earliest Christians seemed to get the meaning: their Eucharist feasts invariably celebrated the risen Christ, memorialising not so much the Last Supper as the Easter meals when Jesus shared fish and broke bread with the disciples. Works of art lining the one hundred miles of dark corridors in the Roman Catacombs vividly illustrate that point. Among twenty thousand frescoes amateurishly painted on those stone walls, not a single death theme or cross appears. Whenever the Eucharist is portrayed, fish, a symbol of life, is always present on the table.

something that we must work hard to obtain; it is in us, pervading us, as blood is in every living being.

Theologian Oscar Cullmann, in *Early Christian Worship*, presents a fresh interpretation of an event that has often puzzled Bible scholars: Jesus' first miracle, when He turned water into wine at a wedding banquet in Cana. Cullmann says this miracle or 'sign', like all others in John's gospel, points to a deeper spiritual teaching. Relying on key phrases such as 'My time has not yet come' (John 2:4), he concludes that the Cana story points to the new covenant to come with Christ. As the bread in John 6 connects to the bread of the Last Supper, the wine here may point to the wine of the Last Supper.

I will leave to Bible scholars the judgment on Cullmann's interpretation. If true, the setting could hardly be more appropriate to introduce this great symbol: a wedding feast, filled with joyous music, the laughter of guests, the clink of pottery, the sounds of excitement as two families are joined together. Sharing the wine that stands for Christ's blood fits in much better with that tone than with the dreary sounds I heard on my radio in Louisiana. Eucharist, celebrated in memory of the death of Jesus, is also a toast, if you will, to the Life that conquered even death and that is now offered freely to each of us.

6 Cleansing

Do you want to punish him fearfully, terribly, with the most awful punishment that could be imagined, and at the same time to save him and regenerate his soul? If so, overwhelm him with your mercy! You will see, you will hear how he will tremble and be horror-struck. 'How can I endure this mercy? How can I endure so much love? Am I worthy of it?' That is what he will exclaim.

Fyodor Dostoevsky
The Brothers Karamazov

I turn up the collar of my wool topcoat and lower my head against the moisture-laden wind. Snow is gradually transforming the tired modern city of London into a Dickensian Christmas card. On a deserted street I stop under an ancient streetlamp and look up. Snow flakes arc from the light like an endless shower of electrical sparks, then float down to cover potholes, gutter, cars, and sidewalk with a coat of softly glowing white.

From somewhere I hear music, the muffled tones of brass and what seems like human voices. On a night like this? I walk toward the sound, the music growing louder with each step, until I round a corner and see its source: a Salvation Army band. A man and a woman are playing a trombone and trumpet, and I wince as I imagine metal pressed against lips in the numbing wind. Three others, evidently new recruits, are lustily singing a hymn based on a poem by William Cowper.

Only two other people are listening: a drunkard who is propping himself against the stone porch of a Georgian-style townhouse and a businessman on the corner who keeps glancing at his pocket watch.

The words of Cowper's hymn are familiar to me:

There is a fountain filled with blood
Drawn from Emmanuel's veins;
And sinners, plunged beneath that flood,
Lose all their guilty stains. . . .

An unavoidable smile crosses my face as I hear those words. I have just come from hospital rounds where real blood was being drawn from some veins, transfused into others, and diligently scrubbed off surgical smocks and nurses' uniforms. With my church background, I understand the origin and meaning of the Christian symbol. But these two bystanders, listening half-heartedly – what images fill their minds as they hear that hymn? Would not such a phrase as 'washed in the blood of the Lamb?' seem to the modern Englishman as bizarre as a report of animal sacrifice in Papua, New Guinea?

In addition to our culture's resistance to the intrusion of blood in religion, an even greater barrier blocks Cowper's blood symbol from modern hearers. Consider the phrase 'washed in the blood': nothing in modern culture corresponds to the idea of blood as a cleansing agent. We use water, with soap or detergent, to clean. Blood, in contrast, soils or stains. It is something we try to scrub *off*, not scrub with. What possible meaning could the hymn writer, and Bible writers before him, have intended?

Blood's quality of cleansing appears throughout the Bible, from the earliest books to the latest. In Leviticus 14, for example, a priest sprinkles cleansing blood on a person with an infectious skin disease and on the mildewed walls of a house. New Testament authors often refer to Jesus' blood 'cleansing' us (e.g. 1 John 1:7), and Revelation describes a multitude who 'have washed their robes and made them white in the blood of the Lamb' (Rev. 7:14).

Does this frequent reference to blood indicate primitive Christianity's remoteness from modern culture? To the contrary, modern medical science has shown that the symbol of cleansing conforms closely to the function of the actual substance. Presumably biblical writers did not know the physiology behind their metaphor, but the Creator chose a theological symbol with an exact analogue in the medical world. All that we have learned about physiology in recent years confirms the accuracy of the still-jarring linking of blood and cleansing. The theological image immortalised by William Cowper's hymn makes for good biology as well.

If you truly wish to grasp the function of blood as a cleansing agent, I suggest a simple experiment. Find a blood pressure test kit and wrap the cuff around your upper arm. Have a friend pump it up to about 200 mm. of mercury, a sufficient pressure to stop the flow of blood in your arm. Initially your arm will feel an uncomfortable tightness beneath the cuff. Now comes the revealing part of the experiment: Perform any easy task with your cuffed arm. Merely flex your fingers and make a fist about ten times in succession, or cut paper with scissors, or drive a nail into wood with a hammer.

The first few movements seem quite normal at first as the muscles obediently contract and relax. Then you feel a slight weakness. Almost without warning, after perhaps ten movements, a hot flash of pain strikes. Your muscles cramp violently. If you force yourself to continue the simple task, you will likely cry out in absolute agony. Finally, you cannot force yourself to continue; the pain overwhelms you.

When you release the tourniquet and air escapes from the cuff with a hiss, blood rushes into your aching arm and a wonderfully soothing sense of relief floods your muscles. The pain is worth enduring just to experience that acute relief. Your muscles move freely, soreness vanishes. Physiologically, you have just experienced the cleansing power of blood.

The pain came because you forced your muscles to keep working while the blood supply to your arm was shut off. As muscles converted oxygen into energy, they produced certain waste products (metabolites) that normally would have been flushed away instantly in the bloodstream. Because of the constricted bloodflow, however, these metabolites accumulated in your cells. They were not *cleansed* by the swirling stream of blood, and therefore in a few minutes you felt the agony of retained toxins.

The body performs its janitorial duties with such impressive speed and efficiency that I cannot resist at least a summary of them. Hold the theological metaphor of cleansing in abeyance while I indulge in a quick scan of the body's cleansing processes.

No cell lies more than a hair's breadth from a blood capillary, lest poisonous by-products pile up and cause the same ill-effects demonstrated in the tourniquet experiment. Through a basic chemical process of gas diffusion and transfer, individual red blood cells drifting along inside narrow capillaries simultaneously release their cargoes of fresh oxygen and absorb waste products (carbon dioxide, urea, and uric acid etc.) from these cells. The red cells then deliver the hazardous waste chemicals to organs that can dump them outside the body.

In the lungs, carbon dioxide collects in small pockets to be exhaled with every breath. The body monitors the expiration cycle and makes instantaneous adjustments. If too much carbon dioxide accumulates, as when I burn more energy by climbing a flight of stairs, an involuntary switch increases my breathing to speed up the process. (Conversely, no one can commit suicide by not breathing – the involuntary trigger 'forces' you to breathe).

Complex chemical wastes are left to a more discriminating organ, the kidney. I must restrain myself from writing long, rhapsodic chapters about the kidneys. Some observers judge them second in complexity only to the brain. The body obviously values them greatly, for one-fourth of the blood from each heartbeat courses down the renal artery to the twin kidneys. That artery divides and subdivides into a tracery of tubules so intricate as to bedazzle the finest Venetian glassblower.

Filtering is what the kidney is all about, but in very little space and time. The kidney manages speed by coiling the tubules into a million crystal loops, where chemicals can be picked over one by one. Since red cells are too bulky for those tiny passageways, the kidney extracts the sugars, salts, and water from the blood and deals with them separately. This segregation process roughly compares to a master mechanic who has a garage too small to fit a whole car inside. To repair a car engine, he hoists it out of the car, carries it to the garage, disassembles and scours each individual valve, piston, and ring, then reassembles the hundreds of parts minus the grime and corrosion.

After the kidney has removed the red cell's entire payload to extract some thirty chemicals, its enzymes promptly reinsert 99 percent of the volume into the bloodstream. The 1 percent remaining, mostly urea, is hustled away to the bladder to await expulsion, along with whatever excess water the kidney deems expendable. One second later, the thunder of the heart resounds throughout the body and fresh blood surges in to fill the tubules.

An elite coterie of people view the kidney with an attitude approaching reverence. These are the few without kidneys or with useless kidneys. Thirty years ago all of those people would have died. Now they have time to contemplate the wonders of the kidney – too much time. Three times a week for five hours they lie or sit motionless while a tube drains all their blood through a noisy, clanging machine the size of a large suitcase. The function of this technological monster, a kidney dialysis machine, crudely approximates the intricate work of the soft, bean-shaped human kidney. Our natural one, however, weighs only one pound, works around the clock, and normally repairs itself. Just to be sure, our body provides a spare – one kidney would do the job just fine.

Other organs enter into the scavenging process also. A durable red cell can only sustain the rough sequence of freight-loading and unloading for a half million circuits or so until, battered and leaky as a worn-out river barge, it nudges its way to the liver and spleen for one last unloading. This time, the red cell itself is picked clean, broken down into amino acids and bile pigments for recycling. The tiny heart of iron, 'magnet' for the crucial haemoglobin molecule, is escorted back to the bone marrow for reincarnation in another red cell. A new cycle of fuelling and cleansing begins.

This seeming digression into the process of cleansing actually leads back to the meaning of the metaphor. Medically, blood sustains life by carrying away the chemical by-products that would interfere with it – in short, by cleansing. As I reflect on the Body of Christ, the blood metaphor offers a fresh and enlightening perspective on a perpetual problem in that Body: sin.

To some, the word *sin* has become dusty, timeworn, and freighted with unfortunate connotations. And the metaphors commonly used to describe God's relationship with sinful creatures have faded too. God is the judge, we the accused – although biblically accurate, that metaphor loses force as the modern legal system grows less trustworthy and more capricious. Metaphors age over time; as culture and language change, sometimes they crack and the concept inside them leaks away.

In blood, however, we have the perfect analogue to reveal the nature of sin and forgiveness with startling clarity. Medical knowledge has only enhanced our understanding. Just as blood cleanses the body of harmful metabolites, forgiveness through Christ's blood cleanses away the waste products, sins, that impede true health.

Too often we tend to view sin as a private list of grievances that happen to irk God the Father, and in the Old Testament He seems easily irritated. But even a casual reading of the Old Testament shows that sin is a blockage, a paralysing toxin that restricts our realisation of our full humanity. God gave laws for our sakes, not His own. In the midst of a withering attack on Israel recorded in Jeremiah, God makes this poignant observation: 'They pour out drink offerings to other gods to provoke me to anger. But am I the one they are provoking? . . . Are they not rather harming themselves, to their own shame?' (7:19).

Pride, egotism, lust, and covetousness are simply poisons that interfere with our relationship to God and to other people. Sin results in separation: separation from God, other people, and our true selves. The more we cling to our private desires, our thirsts for success, our own satisfactions at the expense of others, the farther we will drift from God and others.

The Old Testament Israelites had a stark pictorial representation of this state of separation between God and humanity. God's presence rested in a most Holy Place, approachable only once a year (the Day of Atonement) by one man, the high priest, who had purified himself through an elaborate ritual. Jesus Christ made that ceremony obsolete by a historical once-for-all sacrifice. 'This is the blood of the covenant, which is poured out for many *for the forgiveness of sins* (Matt. 26:28), He said as He instituted the Last Supper.*

The Lord's Supper, or Mass, as celebrated today contrasts sharply with that Old Testament ceremony on the Day of Atonement. No longer must we approach God through a ritually purified high priest, no longer await the Day of Atonement to enter the most Holy Place. On the day Christ died, the thick temple veil of separation split from top to bottom. Now all of us can enter into direct communion with God: 'We have confidence to enter the Most Holy Place by the blood of Jesus, by a new and living way opened for us through the curtain, that is, his body' (Heb. 10:19–20).

The Lord's Supper dramatises that the effect of Christ's sacrifice is continuous and ongoing. Wine is taken personally, symbolising that the same living blood that bathes every cell with the nutrients of life also carries away all the accumulated waste and refuse. By His blood we are forgiven, made clean.

The word *repentance* describes the process each cell undergoes in that cleansing action. C. S. Lewis reminds us that repentance 'is not something God demands of you before He will take you back and which He could let you off if He chose; it is simply a description of what going back is like.' The past hanging thickly over us needs to be remembered

---

* The author of Hebrews explains the theological shift that has taken place: 'When Christ came as high priest of the good things that are already here, he went through the greater and more perfect tabernacle that is not man-made, that is to say, not a part of this creation. He did not enter by means of the blood of goats and calves; but he entered the Most Holy Place once for all by his own blood, having obtained eternal redemption. The blood of goats and bulls and the ashes of a heifer sprinkled on those who are ceremonially unclean sanctify them so that they are outwardly clean. How much more, then, will the blood of Christ, who through the eternal Spirit offered himself unblemished to God, cleanse our consciences from acts that lead to death, so that we may serve the living God!' (Heb. 9:11–14).

in order to be forgotten. In the terms of our analogy, in repentance each cell willingly avails itself of the cleansing action of blood. Repentance is for our sakes, not to punish us, but to free us from the harmful effects of accumulated sins. 'This is His body, broken *for you*' . . . *for your* gossiping, *your* lust, *your* pride, *your* insensitivity . . . broken to remove all those and replace them with His perfect obedience.

Why do any of us go to church and sit on rather uncomfortable furniture, in stiff clothes, lined up in rows as in a high school classroom, singing songs unlike any we have heard all week? Is it not because in each of us a spark of hope has been lit – a hope to be known, to be forgiven, to be healed, to be loved? Something like this yearning lies at the heart of the ceremony of the Lord's Supper.

Symbols are weaker than the reality behind them. But Christ has given us the wine and the bread as proof that we are forgiven, healed, and loved. The symbol works its way inside us, becoming material as well as spiritual nourishment, carrying its message to individual cells throughout each body.

In the Eucharist, we are reminded of the overarching forgiveness accomplished in Christ's sacrifice that made obsolete the whole Jewish sacrificial system. And we also experience the particular, cell-by-cell cleansing of toxins that have accumulated and will not easily release their grip. 'For if, when we were God's enemies, we were reconciled to him through the death of his son, how much more, having been reconciled, shall we be saved through his life!' (Rom. 5:10). If sin is the great separator, Christ is the great reconciler. He dissolves the membrane of separation that grows up every day between ourselves and others, ourselves and God. 'Now in Christ Jesus,' said Paul elsewhere, 'you who once were far away have been brought near through the blood of Christ. For he himself is our peace' (Eph. 2:13–14).

Near the end of his life, François Mauriac, the French Catholic novelist who received the Nobel Prize for Literature, reflected on his own love-hate history with the church.

He detailed the ways in which the church had not kept its promise: the petty rifts and compromises that have always characterised it. The church, he concluded, has strayed far from the precepts and example of its Founder. And yet, added Mauriac, despite all its failings the church has at least remembered two words of Christ: 'Your sins are forgiven you', and 'This is my body broken for you'. The Lord's Supper brings together those two words in a quiet ceremony of healing by cleansing individual cells in His Body of all impurities.

7 Overcoming

Hark, hark, the wise eternal Word
Like a weak infant cries.
In form of servant is the Lord,
And God in cradle lies.

T. Pestel

If our God were a pagan god or the god
of intellectuals – and for me it comes to
much the same – He might fly to His
remotest heaven and our grief would
force him down to earth again. But you
know that our God came to be among
us. Shake your fist at Him, spit in His
face, scourge Him, and finally crucify
Him: what does it matter? . . . It's
already been done to him.

George Bernanos
Diary of a Country Priest

Each day we live at the mercy of organisms one-trillionth our size. Medical author Ronald J. Glasser concludes rather humbly, 'No matter how we may wish to view ourselves, despite all our fantasies of grandeur and dominion, all our fragile human successes, the real struggle . . . has always been against bacteria and viruses, against adversaries never more than seven microns wide.'

Wars, fires, and earthquakes get far more press coverage today than this war of microbes, but it was not always so. The great plague of the fourteenth century, for example, killed one-third of all people in Europe. Over a million pilgrims visited Rome the Easter of 1348; ninety percent went home infected, spreading its horror and death around the world. Ships drifted crewless at sea. Vast estates went untended. Traffic disappeared from highways.

Early in our own century the 'war to end all wars' cost the greatest toll in the history of human conflict: eight-and-a-half million lives. But during the year of armistice an influenza epidemic broke out that would eventually triple the carnage – twenty-five million deaths worldwide.

Battle imagery is particularly appropriate to describe what happens inside our bodies, for with an array of menacing weapons and defenders, our bodies, quite simply, declare war on invaders. At the first sign of invasion, a chemical Paul Revere alarm sounds, and numerous body systems hasten into action. Capillaries dilate, like inflatable tunnels, to allow a swarm of armed defenders into the combat zone. White blood cells of five distinct types form the initial assault forces. Transparent, bristling with weapons and possessing a Houdini-like ability to slip between other cells, the white cells are the body's chief fighters.

Flattened on a microscope slide, white cells resemble fried eggs sprinkled with pepper, each dot marking a deadly chemical weapon. As the white cells circulate in the body they assume roughly spherical shapes and resemble pale glass eyes aimlessly adrift in the blood vessels. When an invasion hits, they abruptly come alive.

Some white cells, armed with crude chemicals, serve as shock troops and attempt to overwhelm the invaders through sheer numbers. Others with massively shielded cell walls roll in with heavier ammunition, like battle tanks. Attack strategy differs also. Some white cells free-float in the bloodstream, sniping at strays. Some stalk the vital organs, alert for any invader that may slip through initial defences. Others try to corral invaders into a fortress-like lymph gland for execution. And still others, the sanitary corps, linger until the battlefield is strewn with bits of cells and leaking protoplasm, then move in to clean up after the melee.

During healthy periods, twenty-five billion white cells circulate freely throughout the blood and twenty-five billion more loiter on blood vessel walls. When an infection occurs, billions of reserves leap from the marshes of bone marrow, some in inchoate form like beardless young recruits pressed into service. The body can quickly mobilise ten times the normal number of white cells; in fact, doctors use a census of them as a diagnostic blood test to judge the severity of infection.

We need vast numbers of white cells for one reason: some lymphocytes are 'specific' defenders, programmed against only one type of disease. In truth the battle within resembles not so much a one-on-one infantry assault as a furious mating dance in which white cells crowd against the bacteria or viruses seeking the right 'fit' before calling up reserves. The average white cell lives merely ten hours. But a select few live for sixty or seventy years and preserve the chemical memory of dangerous invaders, all the while checking in at their assigned lymph gland every few minutes. These master cells safeguard the chemical secrets that remind the body how to respond to any invader previously encountered.

A white cell must somehow home in on the actual invaders who are camouflaged by the chemical smoke-screen of battle and the rubble of leaking cells, clotting agents, and broken membranes. Antibodies (a misleading name, since no substance in the body is so pro-body) guide the white cell through the fray to its intended target. Only 1/1000 the size of bacteria, antibodies cling to the enemy like moss to a tree, softening them up for the approaching white cells and neutralising their destructive spike shapes. A single antibody protects against only one disease; for example, measles antibody has no effect against infantile paralysis.

Because of the staggering range of invaders confronting a person in a lifetime, the body must stockpile an enormous arsenal of weapons. Immunologists share a little joke which they cite when asked how the body can possibly prepare every type of antibody required in our parlous world: 'GOD', they reply. In this case GOD is an acronym for Generator of Diversity, expressing the body's astounding ability to manufacture whatever defence is needed. Dr Ronald Glasser calls the process ' a mixture of mystery and chemistry . . . a combination of physics and grace down at the molecular level.'

If I cut my hand, roaming antibodies tag the known invaders, or antigens, almost immediately. In the event a new one is spotted, a circulating lymphocyte cell touches it, memorises its shape, and rushes to the nearest lymph node. There, that lymphocyte transmogrifies into a veritable chemical factory and conveys the newly acquired information to thousands of other lymphocytes that in turn produce billions of antibodies. Once the lymph produces an antibody, it permanently stores the formula so that a subsequent invasion will incite a fast-motion repeat of the process.*

---

* The body faces its most hazardous moments when a baby emerges from a sterile uterus into a deadly world, having had no exposure to germs. For that event, too, the body provides a life-preserving system. Just before the birth, the mother's placenta floods the foetus's bloodstream with gamma globulin containing agents to fight scarlet fever, whooping cough, typhus, typhoid, pneumonia, diphtheria, tetanus, chicken pox, mumps, measles, polio – any disease, in fact, that the mother has already encountered. Even more immunities flow from the mother's milk until the infant begins to manufacture its own antibodies.

Occasionally, a new antigen comes along with a shape utterly different from any previously known. The lymph cells fumble around for the precise combination, trying and abandoning formula after formula. Meanwhile the mystery invader, oblivious to the stunned and feckless white cells, wreaks havoc. The great plague of the fourteenth century was caused by such a newcomer. European blood had no previous experience with such a disease, which had migrated from Asia.

Still today, diseases like measles and influenza, minor annoyances in developed countries, can sweep through remote cultures with devastating impact. Gradually, however, bodies accumulate a culturally shared knowledge of such diseases, lessening the impact of successive outbreaks.

Timing presents by far the biggest challenge to the body's protective system. Because bodily defences are strictly that, defences, and always counterattack, never attack, we must live in the perilous time gap between infection and adequate response. Antibiotic drugs merely buy precious hours for the body's own mobilisation. (Antibiotics indiscriminately slaughter millions of invaders, but some survivors will always slip through the chemical barrier. And if just one bacterium survives, a million offspring can generate in just eight hours. To win, the body must kill 100 percent of invading microbes, a task as difficult as killing all mosquitoes in a given city. No antibiotic can accomplish that task, as shown by the fact that antibiotics prove ineffective for people with immuno-deficiency diseases like AIDS.)

For centuries humanity lived at the mercy of this deadly time gap, which sometimes resulted in the annihilation of entire populations. But one technique ingeniously solved the time problem and has done more to conquer disease than any other medical procedure. Called 'immunisation', it derives from brilliant pioneering work by Jenner, Pasteur and others. Diseases that once held nations hostage and struck terror into every village and hamlet are now virtually unknown in developed countries. Yellow fever, diphtheria, smallpox, rabies, cholera, typhus, typhoid, polio, measles – each of these has killed and maimed more people than a world war; now immunisation gives us the tools to defeat them all.

Normally, the body loses crucial hours while breaking the code of a new invader and manufacturing appropriate antibodies to combat it. With immunisation, a prior injection exposes the body to polio or smallpox virus in a safe form: either a weakened or 'tired' virus or a 'killed' virus with its outer shell intact to stimulate antibody production. Immunisation gives the body an advantage: with antibodies targeted against polio or smallpox now strategically deployed, the time gap shrinks. When invaded, the body can flood the scene with a prepared assortment of antibodies and quickly overwhelm the intruders.

The story of smallpox vaccination, one of the proudest chapters in medical history, wonderfully typifies the success of the vaccination procedure. Smallpox ravaged the world and was often more feared than the Black Death, bubonic plague. Wrote Thomas Babington Macaulay in his *History of England*, 'The havoc of the plague had been far more rapid; but plague had visited our shores only once or twice within living memory; and the smallpox was always present, filling the churchyard with corpses, tormenting with constant fears all whom it had not yet stricken, leaving on those whose lives it spared the hideous traces of its power, turning the babe into a changeling at which the mother shuddered, and making the eyes and cheeks of a betrothed maiden objects of horror to the lover.'

The disease ravaged Europe for centuries. When introduced to an unexposed population, smallpox showed even more ferocity. One of Cortes's warriors, wounded and left behind after a skirmish, infected the Aztec Indians with smallpox. In two years, four million died, far more than were destroyed by all Cortes's soldiers. In Missouri, the Mandan Indian tribe, with no natural immunities, was reduced from thirty thousand to thirty people. Incredulous traders and scouts of the time filed reports of whole villages huddled in their tents, all dead. Vast prairies displayed no rising smoke, no signs of life, only corpses.

One man, Edward Jenner, the pastor's son, changed all that. Just as Pasteur was forever haunted by the memory of a rabid wolf, Jenner carried with him dreadful memories of the summer of 1757. That year, at the age of eight, he was chosen for a procedure called 'buying the pox,' a crude attempt to ward off an epidemic. For six weeks the town doctor bled the boy repeatedly and virtually starved him. Then, at the village apothecary the physician scratched his arm with a knife and placed over the fresh cut the dried scab of a smallpox victim. For the sake of observation Jenner was kept in a stable, surrounded by other boys in various stages of 'cure'. After a month he recovered, forever immune to smallpox, but the terror of that summer never left him.

Jenner's doctor was utilising what had been known about smallpox for centuries: once infected with a mild case, a person became immune to the disease. Unfortunately, the unsterile procedures and the virulence of the microbe made the practice only marginally safer than an epidemic.

A stray bit of peasant wisdom started Jenner down the path to scientific immortality. After years of studying the disease in the British Isles, Jenner came across a milkmaid who calmly told him she had no fear of smallpox because she had once had cowpox. The idea ignited Jenner. Could the mild disease of cowpox somehow make a person immune to smallpox? He collected data, performed experiments (some flawed), coined the term 'vaccination', perfected his procedures, and presented his findings to the Royal Society in London. Rather predictably, the stuffy medical establishment scoffed at the young researcher's conclusions and refused to publish his paper.

Debate over Jenner's procedure raged for over a

century. Some countries banned it, while others made it compulsory.*

In the year 1802, smallpox broke out among the Indians and Spanish settlers of Bogotá, Colombia. Aware that the disease could easily decimate an unprotected population, the ruling council of Bogotá petitioned Spain's King Carlos IV for help. Their letter described a city paralysed by the fear of a disease which was spreading epidemically through its neighbourhoods.

King Carlos (though remembered by historians as an incompetent ruler) had an active interest in the new technique of vaccination. His three children had received the treatment, and the king had endorsed Jenner's controversial theories. But how could cowpox vaccine be transported to the New World? Within Europe, vaccinators ran threads or quills through cowpox sores and stored them in glass vials for delivery to other countries, but the virus would dry up long before a ship could cross the Atlantic.

At last one of the king's advisers suggested a daring and innovative plan. Why not mount an expedition and recruit enough volunteers to assure that the vaccine could be incubated throughout the trans-Atlantic voyage? The king balked at the expense of such a plan until his adviser reminded him of the potentially devastating economic impact of an epidemic in the colonies.

---

* The following poem appeared in the British magazine *Punch* in 1881:
To vaccinate or not, that is the Question!
Whether 'tis better for a man to suffer
The painful pangs and lasting scars of smallpox,
Or to bare arms before the surgeon's lancet,
And by being vaccinated, end them. Yes!
To see the tiny point, and say we end
The chance of many a thousand awful scars
That flesh is heir to – 'tis a consummation ·
Devoutly to be wished. Ah! soft, you, now,
The vaccinator! Sir, upon your rounds
Be my poor arm remembered.

An expedition was born, with the grandiloquent name Real Expedición Maritima de La Vacuna (Royal Maritime Expedition of the Vaccine), headed by the physician Francisco de Balmis. Soon the Spanish ship *Maria Pita* left port with a human cargo of twenty-two boys, aged three to nine, from a nearby poorhouse, as well as a few cows to serve as backup hosts. De Balmis vaccinated five boys before departure; the others would form a human chain to keep the virus alive.

Five days into the voyage, vesicles – small craters with raised edges and sunken centres – appeared on the infected boys' arms. On the eighth day the vesicles reached maximum size: they were rounded and bulging, volcanoes of lymph ready to erupt. The tenth day lymph flowed freely from the mattering sores – it was ready to harvest. De Balmis carefully scraped that valuable lymph into the scratched arms of two uninfected boys. Every ten days two new boys were selected, vaccinated with the live virus, and quarantined until their harvesting time.

(Politics sometimes edges out pure medical rectitude. The royal ship with its cargo of festering sores sailed into San Juan, Puerto Rico, in February, where its proud physician proceeded to boast to local authorities of his life-saving mission. A near brawl broke out when a local physician insisted to de Balmis that his island had already received smallpox immunity from a vaccination source on the Danish island of St Thomas. Incensed that his expedition was being devalued, de Balmis kept his ship at anchor for a month while challenging the physician to prove his population's immunity. The local doctor succeeded and de Balmis, chastened and running out of time, set sail.)

By the time the *Maria Pita* reached Puerto Cabello, Venezuela, the very last boy was keeping the vaccine alive. He represented the only hope for staving off further epidemics. De Balmis selected twenty-eight more boys from the local population and stayed long enough to vaccinate twelve thousand people. From there, the expedition divided. De Balmis's assistant headed for the original destination, Bogotá, now in desperate straits due to the long delays. A moment of panic struck when his ship wrecked on the way, but the carriers of live vaccine survived. Everyone in Bogotá was vaccinated, smallpox soon faded away, and the assistant went on to immunise Peru and Argentina.

Meanwhile, de Balmis himself journeyed to Mexico, where he launched a frenzied vaccination campaign. After crisscrossing the country, he organised a new boatload of volunteers for the dangerous voyage to the Philippines. Those islands, too, eventually received protection from the unbroken human chain that stretched all the way back to the orphanage in La Coruña, Spain. Hundreds of thousands of people lived because of those original twenty-two orphans.

I have stood at the foot of the great bronze memorial to those young boys, in modern Bogotá, and reflected on their stirring sacrifice. History books, which devote pages to petty wars of the time that destroyed human life, rarely mention those twenty-two or the thousands of lives they helped save. Yet the Vacuna Expedición strikingly symbolises the greatest advance in medicine: the capability to recruit defensive properties of one person's blood to help protect another person.

Edward Jenner received the ultimate accolade in the twentieth century when the World Health Organisation decided to use a variation of his procedure in a campaign to obliterate smallpox from the world. Unlike some diseases, smallpox uses no animal hosts; contact must be human to human. Therefore, WHO workers reasoned, if every person proximate to an infected person was vaccinated, smallpox would disappear.

A twenty-year effort saw WHO workers scouring the villages of India and visiting isolated hamlets in South American and Asian jungles, in short, mounting the most extensive public health campaign ever. The African nation of Somalia harboured the last confirmed case in 1977 – workers had to interrupt a border war to track the person down.

Officially, smallpox has vanished. Once the most feared killer, it has become the only disease in recorded history to disappear. What an individual body must do to conquer any disease – destroy every invading microbe – has been accomplished on a global scale. The history of struggle against smallpox has ended in triumph, not because of drugs or advanced technology, but because of the proper application of the skills of human cells. People from every race have learned to share their defenses against it.

As a child in India I experienced the full force of person-to-person transmission because of the relatively unsophisticated manner in which my parents vaccinated for smallpox. My parents had very limited quantities of vaccine, and no facilities for cold storage, so they relied on the same source as did de Balmis: previously vaccinated human beings. Runners would bring the vaccine up mountain paths and hand the precious lymph to my father. Even before the runner caught his breath, Father would break the little tubes of lymph and begin vaccinating the waiting crowd. Later, from one infected arm he would draw enough lymph to vaccinate ten other Indians. Those ten yielded enough to vaccinate a hundred more. The blood of each vaccinated person locked away the memory of the pox virus so that any contact with smallpox alerted an army of defenders capable of overcoming the threat.

This property of blood, which can be shared from person to person, gives meaning to a word used in the Bible that has otherwise seemed puzzling to me: the word *overcome*. In one of the visions in Revelation the apostle John describes a violent confrontation between the forces of good and of evil. Satan is hurled down, and the victors, people who have come into eternal life, are described this way: 'They overcame him by the blood of the Lamb' (Rev. 12:11).

How can such a word be applied in that sense to blood? I have learned to accept blood as a symbol for life, not death, and even learned to appreciate blood's cleansing properties. But this juxtaposition of words, 'overcome by blood', seems at first hopelessly incongruous. 'Overcome' connotes strength and commanding power: a terrorist with a machine gun *overcomes* an aeroplane crew; a huge Japanese sumo wrestler *overcomes* his opponent. On the other hand, 'blood' connotes weakness and failure – a bleeding person has *been* overcome.

Why does the apostle use this jarring combination of words? The answer, I believe, lies in the biological pattern of how blood overcomes. It reveals something of cosmic significance about how God operates in the world and also enriches my understanding of the symbol of blood. To grasp the meaning, we must look at a few biblical uses of the word *overcome*.

At a very tender moment, during his last evening with the disciples before his crucifixion, Jesus said this: 'In this world you will have trouble. But take heart! I have overcome the world' (John 16:33). At that time the declaration with its heady ring of victory did seem heartening. To those of us who read those words in retrospect, however, His words have a strangely hollow tone. For even as Jesus spoke them, Judas was sealing the fateful contract and Pilate's soldiers were buckling on their swords. Upon reflection, Jesus' timing, mere hours before His arrest and execution, seems almost bizarre. Those triumphant words must have soured for the disciples as they cowered in the darkness watching his pale body glimmer on the cross. 'We had hoped that he was the one who was going to redeem Israel,' two of them would later report with great sadness (Luke 24:21).

When the power of God confronted the power of men, Jesus, who could have called on angelic reinforcements, chose to yield to a handful of soldiers with their whips and nails. The distinction between overcoming and being overcome has blurred.

Later, in the book of Revelation the image of a Lamb appears again and again to represent Christ. We too easily miss the irony of the weakest, most helpless animal symbolising the Lord of the universe – and not only that, but a lamb 'looking as if it had been slain' (5:6). This, then, provides the background for the strange phrase 'overcome by the blood of the Lamb'.

God's visit to our planet is primarily remembered not for its display of raw power but for its example of representative suffering. A pattern emerges through the refining fire of suffering: God responds to evil not by obliterating it, but by making evil itself serve a higher good. He overcame evil by absorbing it, taking it on himself, and, finally, by forgiving it. Jesus overcame as the One who goes before, by going right through the centre of temptation, evil, and death.

Think of a scientist, staring through his microscope's eyepiece at a microbe population gone berserk and threatening the world. He longs for a way to remove his lab coat, shrink down to micron size, and enter that microbe world with the genetic material needed to correct it.

In the context of our own analogy, imagine God, after looking with great sadness on the virus of evil that has infected His creation, casting aside His own prerogatives to take on the shell of a victim cell of that abhorrent virus in order to vaccinate humanity against the death and destruction that are sure to follow. An analogy points to truth weakly; nothing could have more force than the simple assertion, 'He became sin for us.'

The profound symbolic meaning of blood as an agent of overcoming must filter down from this kind of abstract theological discussion to a personal application I can reflect on while receiving the Eucharist. That ceremony is, more than anything, a personal reenactment of the theological reality of Christ's life and death.

I come to the Lord's Table directly and without the elaborate form specified in the Old Testament. Jesus Christ made that change possible, and the author of Hebrews summarises what He accomplished:

> Since the children have flesh and blood, he too shared in their humanity so that by his death he might destroy him

who holds the power of death – that is, the devil – and free those who all their lives were held in slavery by their fear of death. For surely it is not angels he helps, but Abraham's descendants. For this reason he had to be made like his brothers in every way, in order that he might become a merciful and faithful high priest in service to God, and that he might make atonement for the sins of the people. Because he himself suffered when he was tempted, he is able to help those who are being tempted (2:14–18).

Somehow, by drawing on the resources of Christ, I become better equipped to meet temptation. Let me explain what happens, using the analogy of blood.

Some years ago an epidemic of measles struck Vellore and one of my daughters had a severe attack. We knew she would recover, but our other infant daughter, Estelle, was dangerously vulnerable because of her age. When the paediatrician explained our need for convalescent serum, word went around Vellore that the Brands needed the 'blood of an overcomer'. We did not actually use those words, but we called for someone who had contracted measles and had overcome it. Serum from such a person would protect our little girl.

It was no use finding somebody who had conquered chicken pox or had recovered from a broken leg. Such people, albeit healthy, could not give the specific help we needed to overcome measles. We needed someone who had experienced measles and had defeated that disease. We located such a person, withdrew some of his blood, let the cells settle out, and injected the convalescent serum. Equipped with 'borrowed' antibodies, our daughter fought off the disease successfully. The serum gave her body enough time to manufacture her own antibodies. She overcame measles not by her own resistance or vitality, but as a result of a battle that had taken place previously within someone else.

There is a sense in which a person's blood becomes more valuable and potent as that person prevails in numerous battles with outside invaders. After antibodies have locked away the secret of defeating each disease, a second infection of the same type will normally do no harm. A protected person has 'wise blood', to use a term Flannery O'Connor originated. Could this process cast light on the description of Christ being 'made perfect through suffering' (Heb. 2:10)? Recall the just-quoted passage from Hebrews: 'Because he himself suffered when he was tempted, he is able to help those who are being tempted' (2:18). And again, 'We do not have a high priest who is unable to sympathise with our weaknesses, but we have one who has been tempted in every way, just as we are – yet was without sin' (4:15).

The blood of Jesus Christ has overcome. It is as if He went out of His way to expose Himself to temptation, to encounter the stress and strain you and I will meet – to gain wise blood for our benefit. Beginning with His personal struggle with Satan in the wilderness, Jesus declined to use naked power to overcome temptations toward success, power, and an escape from the limitations of humanity. In the Garden of Gethsemane those temptations put Him to the ultimate test, but 'for the joy set before him [he] endured the cross, scorning its shame' (Heb. 12:2).

Today, when we partake of Communion wine, it is as though our Lord is saying to us, *This is My blood, which has been strengthened and prepared for you. This is My life which was lived for you and can now be shared by you. I was tired, frustrated, tempted, abandoned; tomorrow you may feel tired, frustrated, tempted, or abandoned. When You do, you may use My strength and share My spirit. I have overcome the world for you.*

An overwhelming, sudden temptation can catch even the strongest Christian off guard. We need to be prepared, and the symbol of the blood reveals how: by relying on the wise and powerful blood of the One who goes before.

8 Transfusion

Wilt Thou forgive that sin where I begun,
  Which is my sin, though it were done before?
Wilt Thou forgive those sins through which I run,
  And do run still, though still I do deplore?
    When Thou hast done, Thou hast not done,
      For I have more.

Wilt Thou forgive that sin by which I won
  Others to sin? and made my sin their door?
Wilt Thou forgive that sin which I did shun
  A year or two, but wallowed in a score?
    When Thou hast done, Thou hast not done,
      For I have more.

I have a sin of fear, that when I have spun
  My last thread, I shall perish on the shore;
Swear by Thyself, that at my death Thy son
  Shall shine as He shines now, and heretofore;
    And, having done that, Thou hast done,
      I fear no more.

John Donne
'A Hymn to God the Father'

The history of blood transfusion, like that of so many other medical techniques, began perilously and quickly sped toward disaster. In 1492, the same year Columbus set sail, a Jewish doctor in Italy tried transfusing blood from three young boys into ailing Pope Innocent VIII. All three donors died of haemorrhaging, while the thrice-punctured pontiff barely outlived them.

Two centuries later, interest in transfusion resurged, especially in France under the leadership of Jean Baptiste Denis, personal physician to Louis XIV. After successfully transfusing blood from one dog to another, Denis went on to restore a dying boy with an eight-ounce injection of lamb's blood. A second blood recipient, spirits revived, headed to a tavern to celebrate and promptly dropped dead. Denis' mixed results merely confirmed what every reputable physician already believed: withdrawing blood, not injecting it, offered the best hope for recovery. After all, M. Cousinot, the royal physician who immediately preceded Denis, had been cured of rheumatism after sixty-four blood-lettings in eight months. And one eminent physician had gained renown all over France by overseeing the letting of a total of twenty million pints of blood. Thus, the nation quickly adopted a law forbidding the heresy of transfusion; this law would stand for a century.

Italian and English physicians did not give up so easily. One Italian physician puzzled over a set of Siamese twins who shared circulatory systems: food swallowed by one of them somehow nourished the other. Could he not similarly borrow the blood of one person for use by the body of another? In those days, blood was viewed not only as an agent for nutrition but also as a vital essence, brimming with 'humours' or soluble personality traits. Some suggested using transfusions to inject sanity into an insane person or to modify personality types. Indeed, would marital strife end forever if the blood of quarrelling spouses could be blended through transfusion?

Not until the nineteenth century did medicine achieve

some success with the mysterious procedure of transfusion. In England, Dr James Blundell saved the lives of eleven of fifteen women who were haemorrhaging after childbirth. Extant etchings record the dramatic scene: a solemn Blundell looks on as one woman, standing, delivers her blood through a tube directly into the vein of a dying woman. Those etchings poignantly capture the human-to-human essence of shared life which today gets lost in the formality of computer-matched blood banks and sterile containers.

Despite their evident value, for many years blood transfusions involved horrible risks. Sometimes, perhaps a third of the time, the recipient's body inexplicably decided not to accept a donor's blood; a violent reaction often killed such patients. Decades of bewilderment passed before researchers sorted out the crucial vagaries of blood typing and Rh factors, along with proper techniques for storage and the prevention of clotting.

Finally, during World War I, the benefits of blood transfusion began to outweigh its risks. Medics carried a wooden box containing two large jars of the precious juice onto the battlefields. Word spread rapidly among the troops: 'There's a bloke who pumps blood into you and brings you back to life even after you're dead!'

An American black man, Charles Drew, solved many problems of blood storage and shipping, making possible a nationwide Blood for Britain campaign during the second great war.* Since then a labyrinthine network of blood supply depots, refrigerated blood banks, trucks, and planes has grown up – in ironic technological mimicry of the body's own circulatory system.

---

* Some barriers to transfusions, however, lay beyond the scope of medical science: in one of the cruelest twists of medical history, Charles Drew died after being refused a blood transfusion in a North Carolina hospital because of his race.

The dramatic experience of watching a blood transfusion at London's Connaught Hospital had drawn me into medicine. Twelve years later, with medical and surgical training behind me, I found myself back in India amid people who still reacted with fear and revulsion to the prospect of giving blood.

I arrived as an orthopaedic surgeon at the Christian Medical College in Vellore just as the college was recruiting specialists from all over the world. Among these was Dr Reeve Betts, from the Lahey Clinic in Boston, who was to become the father of thoracic surgery for all of India. When Betts first arrived, he ran up against an immediate roadblock: the lack of a blood bank. In some surgeries we had been relying on a Rube Goldberg device I designed to suction out and recirculate a patient's own blood. But chest surgery required a prepared supply of five or more pints of blood which in turn entailed an efficient collection and storage procedure. Betts had the experience and skill to save the lives of patients who began streaming to Vellore from all over India, but he could do nothing without blood.

Thus, in 1949, a blood bank became my number one priority. I had to learn the skills needed for typing, cross-matching, and screening of donors for health problems. We had to develop ways to provide pyrogen-free water and to sterilize all our reusable equipment. In the hot, dusty atmosphere of Vellore, where so many people were afflicted with parasites or a hidden virus of hepatitis, we had to struggle constantly to make our system foolproof. Time after time we suffered heartbreak when a transfusion intended to bring health damaged the patient. Those accustomed to the smooth efficiency of blood banks today should pause and be thankful for the pioneers who tackled the many hazards of the transfusion process.

However, the attitudes of Indian people themselves offered the biggest challenge. To them, blood is life, and who can tolerate the thought of giving up lifeblood, even to save someone else?* I have vivid memories of scenes that transpired again and again as Reeve Betts collided with ancient prejudices. 'How could anyone refuse to give blood that would save his own child?' he would mutter darkly after emerging from a lengthy family council.

Usually a whole tribe of relatives would accompany a patient facing major surgery, so there was never a lack of family to consult with, but the prolonged dialogue through a translator into a local dialect took endless patience. It went like this in the case of a twelve-year-old girl with a very bad lung. Reeve first informed the family that the lung must be removed to save the patient's life. The family members nodded with appropriate gravity. Reeve continued: The surgery required at least three pints of blood, and we had only one, so the family must donate two more. At that news, the family elders huddled together, then announced a willingness to pay for the additional pints.

I watched Reeve flush red. The veins in his neck began to bulge, and his shining bald head was an excellent barometer of his remaining tolerance. Working to control his voice, he explained that he had no other source of blood – it could not be purchased. They might as well take the girl home and let her die. Back to the conference. After more lively discussion the elders emerged with a great concession. They pushed forward a frail old woman weighing perhaps ninety-five pounds, the smallest and weakest member of the tribe. The family has decided to offer her as a transfusion donor, they reported. We could bleed her.

Reeve fixed a stare on the sleek, well-fed men who had made the decision, and then his anger boiled over. His bald pate blazed. In halting Tamil he blasted the dozen cowering

---

* Only one category of Indians responded eagerly to our call for donors. Rickshaw drivers, often of the untouchable caste, saw blood donations as an easy way to earn the equivalent of a day's wages. As our regular donors showed up weaker and weaker, we investigated and discovered some had been donating blood at other hospitals also – sometimes up to a pint each week! Ultimately, to prevent them from harming themselves, we had to institute a skin tattoo system to keep track of how often they gave.

family members. Few could understand his American accent, but everyone caught the force of his torrent of words as he jabbed his finger back and forth from the husky men to the frail woman.

Abruptly, with a flourish Reeve rolled up his own sleeve and called over to me, 'Come on, Paul – I can't stand this! I won't risk that poor girl's life just because these cowardly fellows can't make up their minds. Bring the needle and bottle and take my blood.' The family fell silent, and watched in awe as I dutifully fastened a cuff around Reeve's upper arm, swabbed the skin, and plunged the needle into his vein. A rich red geyser spurted into the bottle and a great 'Ahhh!' rustled through the spectators.

At once there was a babel of voices. 'Look, the sahib doctor is giving his own life!' Onlookers called out shame on the family. I reinforced the drama by warning Reeve not to give too much this time because he had given blood last week and the week before. 'You will be too weak to do the operation!' I cried.

In this case, as in most others, the family got the message at last. Before the bottle was half full, two or three came forward and I stopped Reeve's donation and took their trembling, outstretched arms. Ultimately I had to end the routine Reeve had developed in full sincerity because, although he never lost much blood at one time, he gave with such regularity that his blood-forming cells strained to keep up. Nevertheless, his reputation spread: if a family refused blood, the great doctor himself would contribute.

As I ponder the ancient symbolism behind the word 'blood' in the Christian religion, especially as suggested in Jesus' statements, I keep returning to the modern procedure of blood transfusion. Obviously, Jesus and the biblical authors did not envision a Red Cross blood supply depot when they used the word. And yet out of my experience blood transfusion has emerged as a kind of summary image of the Christian symbol, incorporating all of the meanings we have explored.

In a time when blood transfusion was unknown, Jesus chose the perplexing figure of drinking His blood. Ever since, Christians have wrestled with the theology of the Eucharist. Who can describe the process by which Christ's body and blood become a part of my own? We are brought near to Him; we participate in Him; He feeds us – any of these phrases only hints at the mystery. Jesus used the analogy of branches attached to a vine. The more contemporary metaphor of blood transfusion opens the way for me to grasp the intended meaning.

I will never forget the night I saw a woman resurrect before my eyes when connected to a bottle of donated blood at Connaught Hospital. My experiences with blood transfusion, the purest example of shared life, call up for me the life-giving power of blood. The Communion service reminds me that Christ is not dead and removed from me, but alive and present in me. Every cell in his Body is linked, unified, and bathed by the nutrients of a common source. Blood feeds life.

The infusion of fresh blood also helps explain the process of cleansing. I focus on the toxins accumulating in scattered cells of my body and the happy relief that comes when blood washes away those poisons.

And finally, I imagine the furious intercellular warfare within my body and the climactic effect of a serum injection on that struggle. Jesus, the One who went before, earned 'wise blood' which He freely shares.

Thus, the Lord's Supper has become for me, not an embarrassing relic from primitive religion, but an image of startling freshness. I can celebrate the sensation of coming to life through the symbol of Christ's blood transfused into me. The Connaught woman escaped death because of the shared resources of a nameless donor; Reeve Betts' patients gained new hope through the contributions of individual family members; similarly, I receive in the Eucharist an infusion of strength and energy by availing myself of Christ's own reserves.

Some have asked, 'The meaning, yes, but why the ceremony? Why must we repeat this ritual?' Robert Farrar Capon answers such an objection against formality with his own questions. 'Why go to a party, when you can drink by yourself? Why kiss your wife, when you both know you love her? Why tell great jokes to old friends who've heard them before? Why take your daughter to lunch on her birthday, when you're going to have supper together anyway?' The real question, Capon concludes, is 'Why be human?' Or, as one British theologian put it, sex is to marriage what the sacraments are to Christianity: the physical expression of spiritual reality.*

Under the old convenant, worshippers brought the sacrifice – they gave. In the new, believers *receive* tokens of the finished work of the risen Christ. 'My body, which was broken *for you* . . . my blood which was shed *for you* . . .' In those phrases, Jesus spans the distance from Jerusalem to me, cuts across the years separating His time from mine.

When we come to the table we come with light breath, a

---

* Lady Helen Oppenheimer's *Incarnation and Immanence* is helpful here. In it, she says: 'The physical rite, the partaking of bread and wine, is not a magical spell nor a kind of psychological pressure, but a material vehicle for the presence of God, His "real presence" indeed. How after all can any personal relationship be effectively carried on without some such material expression? One needs to utter words, aloud or on paper, to smile or frown, move or keep still; but more than that, one practically needs the handshake or the kiss, the formal standing up, comfortable sitting or perhaps reverent kneeling, to express oneself or understand what other people are trying to convey. It might be possible to define a sacrament as "a point of intersection of the personal and the material", and if so human life is sacramental through and through; and frequently material things are used as "elements". Wedding rings and badges of rank, prizes, medals and birthday presents are not just attractive objects wanted for their own sake, nor "merely" symbolic like a souvenir "of sentimental value only"; but when given in the approved context are truly a sort of human "means of grace", properly conferring the reality they symbolise, whether a change of status, goodwill, affection, honour or whatever it may be. . . .

'But what authenticates the continuing gift of Christ's presence in the bread and wine is his death and resurrection. He could give his body and blood because he did give his body and blood, and he could give them by his chosen material means of a sacramental meal because by rising from the dead he had shown himself Lord of the created universe.'

weakened pulse. We live in a world far from God, and during the week we catch ourselves doubting. We muddle along with our weaknesses, our repeated failings, our unconquerable sins, our aches and pains. In that condition, bruised and pale, we are beckoned by Christ to His table to celebrate life. We experience the gracious flow of His forgiveness and love and healing – a murmur to us that we are accepted and made alive, transfused.

'I am the Living One,' Christ said to the awestruck apostle John in a vision. 'I was dead, and behold I am alive for ever and ever!' (Rev. 1:18). The Lord's Supper sums up all three tenses: the life that was and died for us, the life that is and lives in us, and the life that will be and will come for us. Christ is no mere example of living; He is life itself.

Jesus Christ did not convey Himself genetically. If He had, His offspring would have been one-half Christ, one-fourth Christ, one-sixteenth Christ, on through His distant descendants of modern times when faint evidence of His bloodline would remain. Rather, He chose to convey Himself personally and nutritiously, offering to each one of us the power of His own resurrected life. No other New Testament image, such as shepherd, building or bride, expresses the concept of 'Christ in you' so well as does blood.

Recall the words that scandalised His followers. 'Whoever eats my flesh and drinks my blood has eternal life, and I will raise him up at the last day. For my flesh is real food and my blood is real drink. Whoever eats my flesh and drinks my blood remains in me, and I in him. Just as the living Father sent me and I live because of the Father, so the one who feeds on me will live because of me.'

He is real food and real drink.

Who knows not Love, let him assay
And taste that juice, which on the cross a pike
Did set again abroach; then let him say
   If ever he did taste the like.
Love is that liquor sweet and most divine,
Which my God feels as blood; but I, as wine.
           George Herbert 'The Agonie'

HEAD

9 Pathways

Earth's crammed with heaven,
And every common bush afire with God;
But only he who sees takes off his shoes,
The rest sit round it and pluck blackberries.
                    Elizabeth Barrett Browning

I am sitting in my cluttered office, leaning back in my chair, gazing vacantly out the window. Supposedly, five trillion chemical operations are occurring in my brain at this second. It certainly does not seem so on this lazy day.

I decide to concentrate on my senses, starting with my eyes. Around me, stacks of journals, notes for future books, and unanswered correspondence collect in ragged, top-heavy piles. They oppress me, so I pad over to a window. I glance at my vegetable garden and pangs of guilt remind me I have not watered and fertilised it recently. But over to the right, the plant I take greatest delight in, a fig tree, is bearing fruit in full glory.

Pendulous figs in velvety shades ranging from green to purple dangle so thickly off every branch that the entire tree bows down. Each year when the figs ripen an enormous population of admiring butterflies suddenly appears, all of one species, wearing bars of black, orange, and white in a design not unlike the monarch's. Thousands of them encircle my fig tree in a shifting corona of colour. Outdoors, you can actually hear the papery sound of their beating wings.

I watch as the butterflies test each tempting fruit with a 'tongue' smaller in diameter than a thread. They light on the unripe fig momentarily, linger a few seconds at those just turning red, and settle in to gorge themselves on the figs two days past perfect ripeness. I have learned a foolproof method of selecting perfect figs: pick the ones butterflies loiter on but do not penetrate.

Various trivial sounds reach my ears: my dog snuffling around in a corner, the soft throb of a ship on the Mississippi River, the distant chatter of a lawnmower, classical music wafting in from the living room.

The lawnmower sound accompanies a pungent, vernal aroma of cut grass. If I tilt my head a bit and sniff, I can also smell the sweet fermentation of figs on the ground. Both these scents are partly spoiled by a more pervasive, sulphurous odour from the petro-chemical factory just down the river.

On one level, nothing much is happening today. Yet, as I

attend to it, I realise very much is happening. My nose, eyes, and ears had been recording all those sensations even before I consciously tuned in to them. These senses are so significant in forming my view of the world that each deserves a brief summary.

'God gave man two ears,' observed Epictetus the Stoic, 'but only one mouth, that he might hear twice as much as he speaks.' Compared to some animal protuberances, human ears seem small, and underdeveloped. They capture a smaller share of the auditory range than a dog's or horse's ear, and offer no competition to those animals' talents for ear expressiveness – we move ours only as a party trick.

Even so, the human faculty of hearing is impressive. Ordinary conversation causes air molecules to vibrate and move the eardrum a mere ten-thousandth of a centimetre, but with enough precision for us to differentiate all the sounds of human speech. The eardrum membrane has the flexibility to register the drop of a straight pin as well as the noise of a New York subway one hundred trillion times louder. It could hardly be more sensitive; if ear sensitivity increased by a tiny amount, we would hear the movement of air molecules as a constant whishing sound (this affliction actually plagues some people, with disastrous hallucinatory effects).

Survivors of high-school biology should know what happens after the eardrum vibrates: three tiny bones, informally known as the hammer, anvil, and stirrup, transfer that vibration into the middle ear. I have worked with most of the bones in the human body, and none are more remarkable than these three, the body's smallest. Unlike every other bone, these do not grow with age – a one-day-old infant has them fully developed. They are in constant, unrelieved motion, since every sound that reaches us causes these bones to swing into action. Working together, they magnify the force that vibrated the eardrum until it is twenty times greater than when it entered.

Inside an inch-long chamber known as the Organ of

Corti, the force that began with molecules of air and was converted to a mechanical pounding finally ends up as a turbulent fluid force. The action of the three bones sets up pulsating waves in the viscous liquid inside the sealed Organ of Corti. Everything we know as sound depends on this seismic chamber.

How do I distinguish two different sounds, such as the buzz of a fly droning about in my room and the rumble of the lawnmower a block away? Every distinct sound has a 'signature' of vibrations per second. (A tuning fork shows the process clearly; when struck, its tines visibly move back and forth.) If you hear a wave of molecules oscillating 256 times per second, for example, you are hearing the musical 'middle C'. The average person can detect vibrations from 20 to 20,000 cycles per second.

Inside the Organ of Corti, 25,000 sound receptor cells line up to receive these vibrations, like strings of a huge piano waiting to be struck. Seen through a scanning electron microscope, the cells resemble rows of baseball bats standing upright together. Each cell is designed to respond to a certain pattern of sound. A few of these cells will fire off signals to the brain when a 256-cycle vibration reaches them, and I 'hear' a middle C. The others will await their own programmed frequency. Imagine the moiling chaos of cell activity when I sit in front of a full orchestra and hear twelve different notes at once, as well as the variety of musical 'textures' from the different instruments. In all, the human ear distinguishes some 300,000 tones.*

In considering the brain, the most important fact about hearing is that the vibration itself never reaches the brain.

---

* In nature, survival needs take precedence over aesthetics, and animals that rely on sound for acquiring food exhibit an even greater range of specialisation. A bat emits and receives radar at 50,000 to 100,000 cycles per second. Even the family dog can hear better, and with wider range, than its master. An owl has the unique feature of omni-directional sound: one ear points forward, the other backward, giving it a 360-degree locater sense so accurate that a blindfolded owl can easily pinpoint a mouse rustling in the straw of a large barn.

The process resembles a cassette tape which absorbs sound not as mechanical vibration but as a series of electrical and magnetic codes. Once the vibration excites its appropriate sound receptor cell, the force inside the head changes from mechanical to electrical. Thousands of wires, or neurons, lead from the patch of 25,000 cells into the auditory part of the brain. There the frequencies are received in a sequence of on-or-off blips. Our experience of sound depends on which of these cells transmits its signal, how often, and in cooperation with what other cells. The brain pieces together these messages and we 'hear'.

After receiving the electrical code from the sound receptors, the brain makes its own contributions of meaning and emotion. I experienced this in a most poignant way in 1983 when my wife and I celebrated our fortieth wedding anniversary. The phone rang, and Margaret and I picked up extensions simultaneously. 'Hello, Mom. Hello, Dad. Congratulations!' we heard. It was our son Christopher in Singapore. Then, to our surprise, we heard the same words again, this time from our daughter Jean in England. And then again from Mary in Minnesota, and Estelle in Hawaii, and Patricia in Seattle, and Pauline in London. Our six children had conspired to place a globe-girdling conference call.

I had not experienced such intense emotion in years. It transported me back to scenes around the dinner table when we had laughed and teased together. The sounds of their voices instantaneously brought tears to my eyes and filled me with joy. Though separated by thousands of miles, we felt like a family again. All the warmth of my love for them and the history of our shared experiences somehow surged up at once in my brain. The sounds, that began as mechanical forces faraway, had touched the 'I', the person inside the computer, the 'ghost in the machine'.

I look with even greater amazement on a further phenomenon of the brain. If I let my mind drift I can 'hear' in my mind the four crashing chords of Beethoven's Fifth Symphony, the melodious voice of my daughter Pauline, the piercing tones of a London air raid siren complete with its unbidden sense of anxiety. There is no force, no vibration of molecules, no firing of sound receptor cells, but still I can hear them. My mind creates sounds out of what exists only in the complex of nerve cells jammed into every cubic inch of white matter.

I write of hearing with a sense of wonder but of smell with near incredulity. Smell leaves the world of quantifiable physics and approaches mystery.

Consider a moth who comes across just one molecule of a pheromone emitted by a mate three miles away. He will not eat or rest until he finds the female who tantalises him, and one molecule a mile gives sufficient clues to track her down. Or consider a salmon who leaves a river near Portland, Oregon, as a mere fingerling and voyages far into the ocean, thousands of miles from home. Without a map, without visual signposts, without any clues other than its sense of smell – its receptors bizarrely scattered in random sites all over the fish's squamous body – the adult salmon will find its way back to the stream of its birth. A pig will excavate earth like a bulldozer in pursuit of a truffle; a bear will rip down a tree and brave a hundred stings for a drop of honey. A boll weevil will attempt to mate soft fields of cotton all day long, passionately, when those fields are sprayed with his female's scent. Like no other sense, smell impels.

We moderns have devalued smell, and, alas, a large portion of our brain atrophies. We forget that smell (and its companion sense, taste) played a leading role in human history. Were it not for a European craving for spices and Columbus's brave quest for more, America might have lain undiscovered for another century. Most of us have far more capacity for smell than we ever exercise (except those few professionals whose livelihoods depend on their tasting of wine or coffee or tea or smelling of incense or perfume). Were we forced to live in the wild and depend on smell for survival, that dormant portion of our brains would awaken, directing the relentless search for food and warning of the nocuous odours of putrefaction, bitter poisons, and vile, smoky vapours.

Smell operates by direct chemical action: tiny olfactory receptors perform eleborate chemical tests on any stray molecules that float by. In flies and cockroaches, these receptors harbour disgustingly on the creatures' feet; in moths, fuzzy smell antennae work similarly to TV antennae, by increasing the reception capability; in humans a penny-sized patch of receptive tissue lies at the top of our nasal cavities. For a good analysis we must sniff in, forcing the molecules up to the sensitive spot and then trapping them in the sticky moisture of the nasal lining. Even with our more primitive systems, we can detect one garlic molecule in the waftage of fifty thousand other molecules.

The amount of substance needed to trigger smell defies belief. No DuPont laboratory can perform an analysis with one-hundredth the speed and accuracy of a bloodhound's nose. A detective holds a sock before the baleful dog. He sniffs deeply a few times, sorting out stale cigarette smoke, the artificial odour of Dr Scholl's footpads, the complex history of a piece of leather, traces of bacterial action and, somewhere, pieces of the man himself, the criminal. He finds a trail through the woods and shuffles along, snorting and evaluating. Suddenly a yelp. He has sniffed in another piece. The pine needles, the dust, the men around him, the thousand smells of the forest floor – none of these interfere with his singular determination to follow the one molecular structure imprinted on his brain. He will follow that spoor through creeks and swamps, across logs, down city side-walks, up apartment stairs – wherever it leads – one day, two days, even a week after the criminal has left the telltale bits.

I know of no laboratory in the world that would agree to distinguish one human from another analysing bits of two socks, let alone track that smell through such conditions.

The nose also is an organ of nostalgia. The smell of coffee, a whiff of briny seashore, the faintest lingering trace of a certain perfume, or the etheric odour of a hospital corridor can stop you like a bullet. You relive that former moment in a flash, jerked backward in time by the fragrance locked away in your brain. I experience this whenever I visit India, a country that appreciates the sense of smell (Columbus's original destination, after all). In 1946, as a young doctor I sailed into the Bombay harbour after a twenty-three-year absence. A tremendous surge of long-neglected childhood memories swept over me as the fantastic scents of that country drifted across the sea. The steam-powered trains, bazaars, exotic people, spicy food, sandalwood, Hindu incense – all these rushed through me as the air of India reached my nose. Something similar happens today whenever I step off a plane and inhale India.

Yet just a few days later these overpowering sensations fade into a barely noticeable background atmosphere. The brain faithfully squelches odours after an initial heightened period – 'nasal ennui' Richard Selzer calls it. Smell is primarily a sentinel warning and, once warned, why should the brain be troubled with redundancy? Fish merchants, tanners, garbage collectors, and paper mill employees gratefully accept this mercy of habituation. 'You get used to it', they say with total accuracy.

Certain phrases keep recurring in textbook descriptions of smell: 'difficult to explain', 'not yet determined', 'it is still not understood precisely how'. We humans possess baffling powers capable of discriminating some 10,000 different odours, yet is there any sense we attend to less or take for granted more?* We have foundations and self-help groups for those who have lost hearing or sight, but I know of no National Foundation for Olfactory Deficiency.

---

* One person did not take the sense lightly. Helen Keller wrote: 'Smell is a potent wizard that transports us across thousands of miles and all the years we have lived. The odours of fruit waft me to my southern home, to my childhood frolics in the peach orchard. Other odours, instantaneous and fleeting, cause my heart to dilate joyously or contract with remembered grief. Even as I think of smells, my nose is full of scents that start awake sweet memories of summers gone and ripening fields far away.'

Taste deserves mention, of course, as one of the five great senses. 'Gastronony rules all life', wrote nineteenth century French epicure Jean Anthelme Brillat-Savarin. 'The newborn baby's tears demand the nurse's breast, and the dying man receives, with some pleasure, the last cooling drink.' But taste suffers in comparison to smell and, in fact, relies mostly on smell, as any chef or any eater with a stopped-up nose can confirm.

An electron microscope scan of the tongue's dense mat of taste buds reveals splendid structures: dramatic cliffs and caverns, cactus flowers, clusters of tall, waving stalks, exotic leaves. They work well enough to afflict most of us with lavish appetites and insatiable cravings. But it takes twenty-five thousand times as much of a substance to register on a stubby taste bud as it does to register on a smell receptor. And for some mysterious reason, taste buds live a mere three to five days, then die off, so the only 'experienced' taste exist in the fortress of the brain.

Lest taste and smell appear mere flourishes without a strict utilitarian function, consider this startling fact: when a patient is receiving food directly into the stomach or intravenously, the body will absorb more nourishment if the patient 'primes' it by tasting food first. The experience of taste stimulates the gastric juices in the same way the smell of sizzling steak or frying bacon can awaken in us a sudden, unexpected hunger.

My brief survey of the senses and their connections to the brain would be incomplete if I omitted sight, the sense which more than any other shapes our understanding of the world (the sense of touch was covered in *Fearfully and Wonderfully Made*). As the husband of an eye surgeon, I hear daily of the virtues of the eyes, which take up a mere one percent of the weight of the head, and of the tragedies resulting from their malfunction.

'Who would believe,' asked Leonardo da Vinci, 'that so small a space could contain the images of all the universe? O mighty process . . . what talent can avail to penetrate a nature such as this? What tongue will it be that can unfold so great a wonder? Truly none!'*

The human eye's characteristic colouring comes, of course, from the iris, comprising radial and circular muscles that assist in opening and closing the pupil, thus increasing or decreasing the amount of light permitted by a factor of sixteen. A camera f-stop shutter duplicates this mechanical function, but nothing duplicates the lovely texture of those exquisite muscles that ripple and flute like the gills of a tropical fish. Inside, a precision lens, made of living tissue, is slung with transparent protectors and kept in position by a clear liquid that renews itself constantly to nourish the cells and kill stray germs. In children, the lens has a startling crystalline transparency. Later, protein deposits accumulate, harden, and scumble the clear lens, causing a condition called 'Cataracts', because the effect reminds one of looking out through a waterfall.

The complexity of perceptual cells beggars the imagination. In humans, 127,000,000 cells called rods and cones line up in rows as the 'seeing' elements that receive light and transmit messages to the brain. Rods, slender and graceful tentacles that reach out toward light, outnumber the bulbous cones 120,000,000 to 7,000,000. These rod cells are so sensitive that the smallest measurable unit of light,

---

* Even the sceptic David Hume, one not given to expounding the argument from design, said, 'Anatomise the eye, survey its structure and contrivance; and tell me, from your own feeling, if the idea of a contriver does not immediately flow in upon you with a force like that of a sensation!' No doubt Hume was referring specifically to the human eye. I equally enjoy studying other prototypes in nature: the sea urchin with vision-sensitive spots scattered about its body, or the scallop with bright blue ones rimming its shell like a row of landing lights; the crayfish which scrapes along the mud-flats with eye-spots studding the surface of its abdomen, or the Copilia, with its single-celled roving TV camera; the common fly with thirty-thousand autonomous eye units. A nautilus eye functions like a primitive pinhole camera, whereas a high-flying kestrel has four times as many eye cells as humans do – with that much greater acuity, useful for spotting prey. Every animal possesses some component of vision, if only the amoeba's and earthworm's instinctive tropism away from light.

one photon, can excite them. Under optimum conditions the human eye can detect a candle at a distance of fifteen miles. Yet with rods alone, we would see chiaroscuro, only shades of black and grey, and would not get the focal resolution allowed by the more complex cones.

Squeezed into the dense forest of rods, the larger cones tend to concentrate in the precise spot in the eye where focusing is most acute.* Although cones are one thousand times less sensitive to light, they make possible all perception of colours and fine details. (The diversity of animal vision depends largely on the distribution of these two cells. Owls have far more rods to allow for superb night vision. In contrast, a chicken has only cones, for detecting tiny insects; beyond a certain range, a chicken is nearly blind.) Our assortment of rods and cones lets us see objects at the ends of our noses and also stars light-years away.

Plato mistakenly believed that vision consisted of particles squirting out of the eye and falling on external objects. We now accept the reverse: light of a given wavelength – whether particles or waves of energy the physicists are still debating – streams through the sky and bounces off external objects, then enters the eye. To that extent, the eye does operate like a camera, with precise shutter and focusing mechanisms to admit and record the light. A variable pinhole lets in mountains, fig trees, a skyscraper, a giraffe, a flea. But at the back of the eye, in a coin-sized patch called the retina, the camera analogy becomes obsolete, for the actual physical image stops with the retina. From there on, everything is electricity. In effect, we do not actually see with the eye, but rather with the help of it.

For a more accurate analogy, we could look to the spacecraft that rockets off our planet and hurtles across our solar system to circle Venus or Jupiter or Mars. We have all

---

* The centre of our eye focuses on only about 1/1000 of the visual field. We see clearly an angle of only four degrees – less than the angle at the point of a pin. Stare at a single word on this page. Other words around it trail off into a blur, and the rest of the page and surrounding room are mere background shapes.

seen the remarkable pictures with their details of satellites and rings and planetary landscapes. Yet as we read the accompanying article we learn that we are not seeing an image recorded on film, but rather a translation of an image. The spacecraft takes a picture and converts it by computer programme into thousands of bits of information about shading, shape, and colour. That data comes back to earth in the form of radio messages: blips and bleeps broadcast across the solar system. On earth, scientists receive and translate those codes, electronically enhancing the messages, and produce a photograph that looks as if the spacecraft had pointed a camera at the planet and snapped a picture on high-contrast film. We have 'seen' not Jupiter, but a reconstruction of bits of information about Jupiter.

Similarly, our brains do not receive photographic images of anything. Rather, some of the 127,000,000 rods and cones get 'excited' by light waves and fire off messages into the 1,000,000 fibres of the optic nerve, which coils like a thick television cable back into the recesses of the brain. Impulses from the retina race along the fibres of the optic nerve, fan out in the brain, and finally slam into the visual cortex, stimulating the miracle of sight.

The cortex has no easy task, since one billion messages a second stream in from the retina. Only in the last few years have scientists gained a glimpse into how the visual cortex sorts out these electrical signals, by observing the process in anaesthetised animals, usually cats or monkeys.

A researcher opens up a cat's head, locates the visual cortex in the brain, and attaches an unimaginably slender microelectrode to a single brain cell. Then the researcher places a variety of shapes and patterns of light and movement before the animal's eye and meticulously records which objects or patterns cause that particular cell to fire. The 'receptive field' of a given cell is so specific that it may only fire when the cat is presented with a horizontal bar at a thirty-degree angle. Some cells are excited by a large spot, some by a small spot. Some fire only in the presence of a bar of light in the centre region of the field; if the bar is tilted ten or twenty degrees, they will no longer fire. Some record a bright line moving on a dark background, and others only record the boundary regions between light and dark. Some cells respond only to motion.

The Nobel laureate who first charted these patterns in the brain cortex states with resigned humility, 'The number of neurons responding successively as the eye watches a slowly rotating propeller is scarcely imaginable.' As I read reports from such scientists, who spend their lives mapping out the visual cortex cell by cell, I am most impressed by this fact: when I see, I am totally unconscious of the process of cells encoding data and firing, then uncoding and re-assembling it within the brain. The fig tree outside my window with its swirl of butterflies comes to my consciousness not as a series of dots and light flashes, but as a fig tree, whole and intelligible and complete with meaning.

This ability to tranpose units of messages – whether from the ear, the nose, the tongue, or the eye – into ever-higher strata of meaning is only possible because of the inner functions of the secluded brain. Cells inside that ivory fortress have no immediate experience of light, sound, taste, or odour. Yet every bit of data transmitted by sense organs terminates there. Indeed, no sensation truly registers until the brain has taken hold of it, translated it, and made sense out of it. The pathways of the senses now lead us inside that brain.

10   The Source

All bodies, the firmaments, the stars, the
earth and its kingdoms are not equal in
value to the lowest mind; for mind
knows all these and itself too; and these
bodies know nothing.

Blaise Pascal
Pensées

We have torn away the mental fancies to
get at the reality beneath, only to find
that the reality of that which is beneath is
bound up with its potentiality of
awakening these fancies. It is because
the mind, the weaver of illusion, is also
the only guarantor of reality that reality
is always to be sought at the base of
illusion.

Sir Arthur Eddington
Nature of the Physical World

In all of medicine, there is no more shocking procedure than brain surgery. It seems a violation, as terrifyingly sacrilegious as bursting into the Holy of Holies. No one who opens a human skull escapes this grim sense of defilement. For centuries the human brain remained undrawn, or sketched only in rough caricature – the mysterious organ daunted even the brave pioneer da Vinci, as shown by his hesitant and inexact studies. (His successor Vesalius had to plead with executioners for heads severed in decapitation, still warm, to produce the first good anatomical drawings of the brain.)

I was first given a human head containing a brain during my medical training, when I chose as my senior project the task of exposing the major nerves in a human head. I wanted to trace the pathways of sense organs to their source.

Two years of medical school had not steeled me sufficiently for the experience of getting my own cadaver head, whole and perfectly preserved though shrunken slightly by the chemicals. It had belonged to a middle-aged man with plentiful hair and bushy eyebrows. When I slid back his eyelids with my thumbs, he stared out with gimlet eyes. What is the appropriate way to transport a cadaver head? Hold it by the ears? Grasp the scalp as you would pick up a kitten? Textbooks did not mention such things.

During the next month I spent most of my waking hours with the head of my nameless friend. I planned to do a complete dissection of the major nerves in his face, tracing them from the ear, the eye, the tongue, and the nose through the skull into the brain. 'That skull had a tongue in it, and could sing once,' Shakespeare wrote, and I had to push from my mind images of this hunk of wrinkled tissue on the table singing, talking, winking, smiling. I felt almost grateful for the pungent odour of the formaldehyde that had seeped through my skin and was affecting the taste of food, toothpaste, and everything else in my life during that month. It reminded me I was carving away not on a man but on a specimen of preserved tissue, a face that had fully served its time.

I knew how authentic brain surgeons proceeded. I had seen them slice through layers of scalp, muscle, and membrane and peel these back to reveal the gleaming bone inside. I had watched in amazement as those surgeons huffed and puffed, leaning heavily some twenty degrees off the vertical to force a whirring drill bit through the quarter-inch sheath of bone. A cloud of fine bone dust would sometimes form and float through the room. By the time they drilled and sawed through enough skull to lift a trap door into the brain, perspiration beaded their faces.

Nothing so well-fortified can be entered without a twinge of foreboding. My cadaver's skull was a nearly impregnable orb of granite that had sealed off its owner's brain from every nuance of sensation, temperature, moisture, or other disturbance in the outside world. Yet, paradoxically, that same brain had contained within it all his knowledge of the outside world, thanks to the frail white nerves leading to it, the nerves I now sought to uncover.

I began my exploration with the parts I knew best, the familiar shapes of eye, ear, nose, and tongue. I sliced away, peeling back skin, fat, and muscle until I found the inner structure with its nerves leading to the brain. Then I worked inward, like an explorer searching for the source of the Nile, following a small sliver of white through increasingly dense territory into the penetralia of the brain itself. Nerves resisted exposure: the fifth nerve, for example, began conveniently enough in the chin, but meandered wickedly through the jawbone before disappearing into the base of the skull.

Unlike the brain surgeon, I could not simply draw a cutting plan with a marking pen and start sawing. I had to chisel the facial skeleton in thin layers, coaxing out slivers of bone while taking care not to cut too deep and sever the nerve. Fortunately, I had worked as a stone mason for a full year, and after a little practice with a mallet and chisel the process of shaving away layers of bone the thickness of tissue paper seemed natural and even artistic. I strove to expose the nerves intact in their settings, leaving behind no obvious signs of forced entry.

The orbit of the eye consists of seven bones fused together in a protective socket. I had to slice through each of these, unsheathing the full depth of the glossy eyeball, then gently trace the optic nerve along its tunnel back into the brain. I remember being most impressed by the vast range of textures. I would pick up a scalpel to make a satiny slice through muscle and fat, holding my breath and keeping the blunt edge toward the nerve – one quiver of my finger and that nerve would snap. Then I would lay down the scalpel, pick up a mallet and chisel and attack the bone, hard as masonry, with all my force.

After I had spent several arduous weeks dissecting, one-half of my cadaver's face was unrecognisable. Fine streams of white led from the ear, eye, tongue, nose, larynx, and facial muscles and disappeared into the cavity that contained the brain. Finally, I was ready to enter the brain itself. After slashing through hairy scalp and sawing through bone, I reached the three membranes, or meninges, that sheathed the brain. I slit each one, remembering with a smile the arcane Latin names I had learned in anatomy class: *dura mater* (hard mother), *arachnoid* (cobweb), and *pia mater* (tender mother). The innermost membrane fit like cling film over the convolutions of the brain, and when I punctured it a small piece of the brain bulged through the opening like a tiny fist. I stared at it a full five minutes before continuing.

At first sight the brain, coiled extravagantly and pinkish-grey in colour, uncannily resembled the lowly intestines. It had the consistency of paste or cream cheese, making the actual brain encountered quite different from what one would expect after studying the solid-looking renditions in anatomy texts. The brain's walnut-shaped appearance held endless fascination for me as I kept on dissecting. Its landscape dipped and rose and turned in on itself – a topographical map of all the mountains on earth compressed into a tiny space. (Those folds increase the surface area thirty-fold.)

Red and blue lines crisscrossed the topography, and I breathed a prayer of thanks that I was practising on a dead brain. A surgeon operating on a living patient spends much time avoiding those vital channels of blood and stanching the vessels severed by his scalpel. In addition, formaldehyde had strengthened the brain tissue and, though it was softer than any tissue I had yet encountered, I could prod it and move it with my hands without tearing it. A living brain laid on a flat surface would sag and perhaps rupture under its own weight.

I had hoped to trace sensory nerves to their ultimate sources, but the brain does not yield easily to map-making. Nerves there, ensconced in the ample armour of skull, have the doughy consistency of the rest of brain matter and will break at the slighest push or pull. Following a soft thread of white into a white mush devoid of surgical landmarks was like trying to track a river's confluence with the ocean: after a certain point, the river becomes the ocean. In only a few cases did I succeed in finding the final destination of nerves. In the others, I labelled the source from what I had seen in the textbooks, not from my own tedious exploration. The pathways of thought and sensation were unmarked by signposts and indiscernible by dissection, almost as if the frequent passage of a thought had left invisible footprints that only thoughts could follow.

Professor West took tutorial delight in my ambitious undertaking, insisting he had not seen a head dissected in quite that way before. He awarded the completed cadaver head a prize and ordered that it be pickled and put on display in the Welsh National School of Medicine Museum. As far as I know, a certain jar is still gathering dust there, its contents leering out at tourists with a naked, Cyclopean stare. I, of course, had schoolboy fantasies of becoming a pioneer brain surgeon. Years later, when of necessity I attempted a few hazardous ventures into neurosurgery, I thought with gratitude how wise I had been in *not* pursuing that enormously challenging field.

In some surgeries on living brains, the patient stays awake in order to cooperate with the exploring surgeon. As a result, the atmosphere in the operating room crackles with unspoken tensions. The patient's consciousness serves to edit the normal prattle of surgery, and any mild emergency is met with suppressed anxiety. Standing on the sidelines, watching such procedures, I notice the sounds. The faint electronic beeps of monitoring machines and the deep sighs of the respirator give a percussive accompaniment to the more interruptive sounds of medicine at work: the shrill whine of the drill, a popping sound from the electric cautery, and the clinking of instruments being passed around like dinnerware. The object of all this attention glistens in the bright lights, and if you look close enough, you see it heaving gently. The brain is alive.

Brain surgeons face the relentless threat of uncontrolled bleeding. When other bodily tissues bleed, vessels can be clamped and tied off, but the brain is too soft to hold a clamp or to tie off. Even a slight tear can unleash enough blood to flood the site and make further probing impossible. A suction nozzle follows the surgeon's knife like a meticulous housekeeper, slurping up blood to clear the view.* Sometimes the surgeon will put forceps to the bead of blood and touch a cautery to that instrument. Zzzt – the blood coagulates and bleeding stops. Other times, an assistant will drop small squares of cotton lint called 'pledglets' onto the bleeding vessel. A quick application of the suction nozzle will pull blood into the pledglet, encouraging clotting. After an hour of surgery, fifty or sixty of these used squares, attached to long black threads for easy removal, may dot the landscape of the brain.

Even the most experienced surgeon has difficulty with orientation in the brain, for everything appears soft and white, like a blizzardy Arctic landscape. Brain surgery would still be in a primitive state were it not for one remarkable discovery of science. When a surgeon inserts

---

* All suction must be regulated carefully; otherwise, pieces of brain tissue will disappear forever into the central refuse disposal. 'Oops, there go the piano lessons!' a surgeon may joke if the patient is unconscious. Fortunately, the brain rarely notices a small loss.

a needle-like electrode into a portion of the brain and switches on the current, the brain responds, indicating what functions that area controls. The brain itself has no sensation of pain or touch, so the patient will say something like 'I feel a tingling sensation in my left leg' if the surgeon lightly stimulates the surface of a particular lobe.

Wilder Penfield, a brain surgeon in Montreal, has recorded bizarre results from such stimulation. While trying to locate the source of epileptic seizures, he found that in certain portions of the brain he could electrically stimulate specific memories in sharp detail. One young South African patient began laughing, reliving second by second an incident on a farm in his native land. A woman recalled every note in a symphony concert she had heard long before. The memories surged up in such vivid detail for one patient on the operating table that she remembered sitting at a train crossing years before and could verbally describe each train car as it went by. Another counted aloud the number of teeth of a comb used in childhood. Often these memories from early childhood precede the patient's first conscious memory.

By drawing on such techniques and by studying stroke victims, anatomists have been able to develop a fairly reliable map of the brain. Most brain research centres on the top layer of the brain, the cerebral cortex, which is far more advanced in humans than in any animal. The thickness of the sole of a shoe, the cortex contains neurons that sift, sort, collate, and process the information we perceive as sight, sound, touch, conscious behaviour, and the higher activities of learning and memory. The bulk of nerve cell population lives in that layer of grey matter, the fertile topsoil on the brain.

Eminent neurologist Sir Charles Sherrington neatly divided certain brain nerve cells into two groups: 'the way in', or *afferent* cells which carry impulses from the organs of the body to the brain, and 'the way out', *efferent* cells which carry instructions from the brain out to the extremities. In the entire brain, only one in one thousand cells reports in from the extremities: all visual images, all sounds, all touch and pain sensations, all smells, the monitors of blood pressure and chemical changes, the sensations of hunger, thirst and sex drives, muscular tension – all the 'noise' from the entire body – occupy only one-tenth of one percent of the brain's cells. Each second those fibres bombard the brain with a hundred million messages. Of these, a few hundred at most are admitted above the brain stem.

Another two-tenths of one percent of cells control all motor activities: the motions involved in playing a piano concerto, speaking a language, dancing a ballet, typing a letter, or operating a video game. In between these two groups, the Way In and the Way Out, lie all the others: enormous numbers of cells cooperating in a vast network of intercommunication to allow the processes we know as thought and free will.

Brain biologist J. Z. Young likens the network to ten billion bureaucrats constantly phoning each other about plans and instructions for keeping a country running. Sir Charles Sherrington, more poetically, rhapsodises about an 'enchanted loom' with lights that flash on and off as messages weave their way through the brain.

Unlike a telephone switchboard that connects single subscribers indirectly through a central switching station, *each* nerve cell in the brain has up to ten thousand of its own private lines. All along its length dendrites reach out and form connections with other neurons, in effect linking each cell with wires from an entire city. It 'listens in' for the patterns of impulses and their average rate of arrival and decides whether to continue the message by firing off chemicals along its thousands of other connections.

Physiologically, the whole mental process comes down to these ten billion cells spitting irritating chemicals at each other across the synapses or gaps. The web of nerve cells defies description or depiction. One cubic millimetre, the size of a pinpoint, contains one billion connections among cells; a mere gram of brain tissue may contain as many as four hundred billion synaptic junctions. As a result, each cell can communicate with every other cell at lightning speed – as if a population far larger than earth's were linked together so that all inhabitants could talk at once. The brain's total number of connections rivals the stars and galaxies of the universe.

Even in sleep the nerve cell community never stops chattering. The brain is a turbulent cloud of electrical potentials. During each second of life it performs about five trillion chemical operations. When we are awake, only a few reach our level of consciousness, and those so quickly we are hardly aware of the process. I decide to write the next sentence; in a flash my brain computes first the thoughts and then the words I will use, then the elaborate coordination of muscles, tendons, and bones required to type the words. Before I finish typing, my brain begins composing the sentence to follow.

Steven Levy recorded this reaction when he came across a jar containing Albert Einstein's brain: 'I had risen up to look into the jar, but now I was sunk in my chair, speechless. My eyes were fixed upon that jar as I tried to comprehend that these pieces of gunk bobbing up and down had caused a revolution in physics and quite possibly changed the course of civilisation. There it was.'

I have a similar reaction to any human brain I have ever seen. Solzhenitsyn once referred to a man's eyes as 'sky-blue circles with black holes in the centre and behind them the whole astounding world of an individual human being.' I will never forget the sensation that washed over me the first time I chipped through bone and exposed the cadaver brain in my laboratory room in medical school. Even with all the blood vessels, membranous linings, fluid-filled cavities, and billions of specialised nerve cells, the organ weighed barely three pounds. Yet that fragile, greyish jelly once contained a whole life.

In a biological sense a whole body had existed just to keep that brain nourished and protected for forty years. The brain had used up one-fourth of all the oxygen its owner had breathed in – its lack of oxygen for five minutes had caused his death.

One nerve had controlled all the subtle movements of his lips that made speech and eating and kissing possible. Another had brought in every nuance of colour and light to form his visual construct of the world.

The brain contains imagination, morality, sensuality, mathematics, memory, humour, judgment, religion, as well as an incredible catalogue of facts and theories and the common sense to assign them all priority and significance. In the human head, concludes Nobel laureate Roger Sperry, 'there are forces within forces within forces, as in no other cubic half-foot of the universe that we know.' There is nothing on the earth so wonderful.

And yet nothing on earth is so fragile. One bullet may destroy it, or one spill from a motorcycle. One dosage of a powerful drug can upset the delicate balance inside a brain forever.

I have been inside a human brain on maybe a half-dozen occasions. Each time I have felt humble and inadequate, a trespasser entering where no man was meant to. Who am I to invade the holy place where a person resides? Perhaps if I worked on brains daily I would grow more callous and unimpressed. But I think not – the brain surgeons I know still talk of their subject in hushed, almost worshipful tones.

In the analogy of the Body of Christ used in the Bible, Christ Himself is said to take on the role of the Head. In the next chapters we will explore some parallels that do apply and also sense the limitations of that analogy, of any analogy, to convey the essence of God in the world.

If you have been inside a human brain, as I have, and held the quivering substance in your hand, if you have gazed through a microscope at a tiny section of the unimaginable network of nerve cells, if you have watched brain wave machines record a minute sampling of the communications between cells, if you have pondered the interwoven mysteries of brain and mind and human personality, then I think you should be prepared, if not for the concept of the analogy, at least for its emotional force. A whole person lies inside the bony box, locked in, protected, sealed away for the indispensable duties of managing one hundred trillion cells in a human body. The Head of the Body is the seat of mystery and wisdom and unity. He is the Source.

11 Confinement

That glorious form, that light unsufferable,
And that far-beaming blaze of majesty,
....
Forsook the courts of everlasting day,
And chose with us a darksome house of mortal clay.
John Milton
'On the Morning of Christ's Nativity'

He whom the world could not inwrap
Yonder lies in Mary's lap.
Martin Luther

Although it seems as if nothing much is happening when I sit in my cluttered office and gaze vacantly out the window, as we have seen, the apparent stillness deceives. My brain is humming and crackling, performing five trillion operations each second.

The common catalogue of five senses – sight, hearing, touch, taste, and smell – hardly covers all that is taking place. Other vital senses inform me of muscle tension and the pressure on joints and tendons; I know instinctively the tilt of my head, the bend of my elbow, the position of my left foot. Different sensors inform me of lunchtime; my stomach 'feels empty'. Below the conscious level, automatic systems adjust the chemical components of blood, control air pressure in my lungs and blood pressure in my arteries, and monitor organ stretch receptors. My brain, isolated in its thick ivory box, receives all these signals in a kind of electrical Morse code.

It appears the brain needs this ceaseless turmoil. When a person reduces the number of sense impressions, for example by lying in a dark tank of warm water cut off from most sensations, before long the brain begins to hallucinate and fill the void with sensory content of its own devising. And during sleep billions of cells spark through the night, their level of activity barely diminishing from daytime levels.

Often the interplay between the sense organs and the brain's fund of memories is so subtle that the two cannot be easily distinguished. Consider, for example, a Beethoven piano sonata. In the totally deaf state of his later years, Beethoven never 'heard' the music he composed – that is, the eardrum, three bones, and sound receptor cells never participated in the experience. Yet somehow by the extraordinary ability of his brain to reconstruct tone and harmony and rhythm, he did hear it. No molecules danced their tarantella; all took place in silence, cerebrally, in code.

Today, if my musically talented wife picks up a written score of Beethoven's *Sonata Pathetique*, she recognises it almost at once. She can hum along as she reads, relying on her own mental file of sounds. She 'hears' it in her mind. Or, if we merely sit at home and select a radio station, after hearing just a few measures we can recognise the sound as part of that same sonata.

How many billions of brain computations are required to recognise a piece of music? Yet how long does it take – two seconds? Or, what process of neuronal communication instantly convinces me that red globe hanging in a tree in my garden is not a balloon caught on a branch, but a star located 93,000,000 miles away? All these processes occur with blinding speed and little conscious effort.

When you read this page, you are not conscious of the individual letters forming each word. You do not spell them out one by one, reassemble them into a composite, and then scan a dictionary for the meaning of that composite – and yet in reality your mind does all that, subconsciously. It works so fast that when I speak, using letters, words, grammar, and punctuation, I can concentrate solely on the meaning of what I want to communicate. Neurons with stored knowledge freely supply the individual elements, and my central nervous system arranges the glottal puffs and slides to create intelligible sounds.

My brain presents the world to me not in data banks and reductionist blips, but wholly, conceptually, meaningfully. And herein is the great mystery. The mind that coordinates all this profound activity lies locked away. The brain itself never 'sees': if I opened one up to light, I would likely harm it irreparably. It never 'hears': the brain is so sheltered and cushioned that it feels only the most reverberant sensations. The brain does not experience touch: there are no touch or pain cells there. Its temperature varies no more than a few degrees; it has never felt hot or cold. It never sustains a mechanical force; upon meeting up with one, it would quickly lapse into unconsciousness.

Everything that forms me, Paul Brand, reduces down to a sequence of dots and dashes (-.–.-..–) reporting from millions of remote stations into a bony box that has never directly experienced those sensations. The taste of chocolate, the prick of a pin, the sound of a violin, a view of the

Grand Canyon, the smell of vinegar – all these reach my consciousness via signals that are virtually identical. I perceive them because tiny, flower-shaped neurons have shot chemicals at each other.

The brain, floating in its ivory box in a pool of cerebrospinal fluid, contains the person I am. Every other cell in my body ages and is replaced at least every seven years. My skin, eyes, heart, even bones are entirely different today from those I carried around just one decade ago. In all respects but one I am now a different person – the exception being my neurons or nerve cells. Never replaced, these maintain the continuity of selfhood that keeps the entity of Paul Brand alive.

From the darkness and loneliness of that bony box I reach out to reality with millions of living wires. They extend from my brain like tendrils of a plant, stretching desperately toward impulses of smell, sight, sound, and touch into the world of light and matter.

First through a glimpse at the sense organs, then through my dissection of a cadaver head, and now through the individual elements that conspire to give me a total experience, I have been pointing toward the summary function of the amazing lump of cells we carry around in our skulls. I have extended this biological survey in order to lay the groundwork for the analogy of Christ as Head of the church, a title the New Testament applies to Him seven times. We customarily think of power and authority when we envision someone in the role of Head. The biblical metaphor applied to Christ expresses some of that meaning, surely, but the actual physiological working of the brain sheds light on the style in which Headship is exercised.

The analogy from the body hints at a fundamental choice God has made in interacting with this world. The parallel we will explore, in short, is this: God, a Spirit untrammelled by space and time, first humbled Himself by taking on the confinement of matter and time. He enfleshed

Himself. Later, Christ's body departed (or, more accurately, was transformed) and He withdrew into the position of the Head. Today, Christ's Body consists of millions of individual cells in His church. As the Head, He establishes His presence in the world through people like us. In a mysterious way He has chosen to make our prayers, our actions, our proclamation of His truth and justice His chief means of communicating Himself into the world of matter.

Why? Why would a God who is pure Spirit take on matter? And why, in fact, did He choose to rely on ordinary human beings while He receded to the isolated 'ivory box' role of Headship? He could, if He wanted, express Himself again through the flash and smoke of Sinai. His presence on earth could again ignite a bush or cause a terrifying glow of light, as it sometimes did in the Old Testament. Instead, He has chosen a self-limiting way.

Questions are often raised about God's style of involvement with His created world. For the agnostic, those questions take on a shrill tone of accusation: 'If there is a God, let Him prove it somehow! Let Him step in and straighten out the royal mess of this world!' For me as a Christian, the issue is not so much 'Is God really there?' as, 'Why has He chosen such an indirect, hidden style of activity? Why doesn't He show Himself more clearly?'

The term 'self-limiting' may help explain this world. If we can accept God limiting Himself to the extent of relying mainly on human agents, then we understand dimly why He does not, and must not, brazenly interfere with what He has made. 'God has, so to speak, imprisoned Himself in his own resolve,' said Kierkgaard.

I gained some insight into the issues behind self-limitation when my one-year-old daughter Pauline discovered the electrical outlets in our Indian home. The outlet boxes, conveniently mounted six inches off the floor, carried a 220-volt current and were designed for metal plugs that were round rather than flat – exactly the shape and diameter of Pauline's tiniest fingers. Pauline had a habit of sucking her fingers two at a time. Like any normal infant of that age, she was inquisitive and loved to poke her fingers into things.

My wife and I were naturally alarmed by Pauline's interest in the enticing paired holes. We tried covering the outlets with adhesive tape, but Pauline quickly learned she could peel off the tape. She looked mischievously over her shoulder at us, removed her wet and slippery fingers from her mouth, and waited for us to leave the room.

What could we do as parents? We could tie her to her crib or attempt to control her every movement. Or, we could somehow convince her of the danger. But how?

'Pauline, now listen to me! Inside those holes, electrical terminals are producing a potential difference of 220 volts. You have wet fingers, which decreases the resistance of your skin to electric current. If you touch those terminals, the current will travel up your arms, destroying your nerves and denaturing the protein of your muscles. . . .' That explanation, albeit true, would have meant nothing to my gurgling daughter.

I grasped at something that had already entered Pauline's experience. 'Pauline!' I began in my most threatening voice, 'If you touch those holes, fire will come out! You will be burned!' She looked at me sceptically, certain I was merely denying her access to fun. But I sounded earnest. And she had learned one very painful lesson about burns from the floor-level fire our Indian cook had been using. Was it worth the risk?

'And, Pauline, if you touch those holes I will smack you.' This warning struck home. She retreated. She knew that threat and had learned to fear it. The dark holes suddenly lost their intrigue.

Pauline has now graduated from college and could probably teach me about ohms and volts and resistance. When she reflects on that experience, if she ever does, I rather doubt that she questions her father's honesty or wisdom. She realises now that in the most literal sense those dark holes contained no fire. But she also knows the ignorance then was in the child, not the father. To communicate with her, I had to use a language and concept she could understand.

In my work with various cultural groups, I have similarly had to accommodate my language. I explain an electron microscope to an eager student in the Tamil language by analogy, using approximations of concepts that he or she can understand. And if I someday learned that a nuclear device was about to explode in remote Somalia, I would warn the nomads there to dig for cover not by expounding the mutability of matter and principles of nuclear fission, but by saying something like 'Fire in the sky!' or 'Poison dust!' I must use words that mean something to the person who hears them.

Is this not the problem God faces in communicating with human beings? How can infinitude express itself to finite beings? The analogy of language is enlightening. A concept exists in the mind but has no reality until distilled into a thought, and has no communication potential unless it can be expressed in language. Only as the concept – mysterious, spirit-like – wraps itself in the clothing of language and enters the material world of vocal chords and puffs of air and pen scratchings, does it exist in a way anyone else can recognise.

Jesus, appropriately, was called the Word of God. Infinite, ineffable, inexpressible God became a man. God spoke in as articulate a way as humans could possibly bear: He became one of us and 'tabernacled among us'.

'It was much, that man was made like God before/ But, that God should be made like man, much more,' said John Donne. For thirty-three years Jesus gave us an image; we can now look back upon it to perceive the true image of God. Through Christ, God softened language to His hearer's ears. One example: If you had said to Isaiah, 'God is going to touch you today,' he would have fled in terror. For him, touch was not a quality of communication between God and man. With Jesus, all that changed.

Yet the Incarnation, as great as it was, did not complete God's purposes on earth. Christ receded to the role of

Head in order to create a new Body, this one composed not of living cells but of millions of men and women all cohering in Him. 'As you sent me into the world,' Jesus said to His Father, 'I have sent them into the world' (John 17:18). The profound change could hardly be expressed more succinctly.

In one sense Christ's departure was an ascension – it is called that on every church calendar – but in another sense it was a further condescension. Now God 'tabernacles' neither in a Most Holy Place, nor in one perfect body, but in millions of ornery, frail, bodies – some short, some tall, some smart, some dull, some steady, some volatile. Christ withdrew into the ivory box.

God does not, it is true, 'need' anything to be done by finite agents. He need not work indirectly, in the role of Head. In Omnipotence He could find a way to nourish bodies without food, to fuel the brain without red blood cells, to convert people without missionaries. But for some reason He has chosen the terrene stuff of soil and vegetables and chemistry and words and human will to carry out His own plan on earth.

Today, we are God's medium, His Body. When you look at me, you never see the whole Paul Brand; rather you see a thin layer of skin cells stretched across my frame. The real Paul Brand resides inside, especially centred in my brain, locked away from the outside world. The same is true with God. We cannot 'see' God; we have no perceiving organs adequate for that. Rather, we see God in a comprehensible form in the shape of each other as members of His Body. God could not accommodate His language to human ears and His shape to human eyes more fully than by dwelling inside men and women.

Dorothy Sayers lists three great humiliations God has willfully undergone. In the first, the Incarnation, He stripped off the prerogatives of deity and stooped to become a man. In the second, the Crucifixion, He became sin for us, suffering the ignominy of death. The third humiliation, she says, is the church. God humiliated Himself by choosing to live within a Body comprised of people like us.

From one standpoint, she is absolutely correct. The Head working through us involves a sort of shrinking, an abdication wherein God chooses to lay aside His omnipotence and take on an invisible, behind-the-scenes role in human history. In so doing, God again self-limits Himself. He invests His own reputation, His name, in imperfect human beings. Once a nation bore that name, and bore it to disgrace. We who are His Body have similarly stained God's reputation by galloping off on bloody crusades, cracking bones and joints on torture racks, christening a slave ship *The Good Ship Jesus*, furthering racism in His name. God in Christ, in human form, is one thing; God in us is quite another.

The church, His Body, is indeed a humiliation. And yet, counterbalancing that humiliation, a kind of exaltation shines forth, a hint that perhaps from the very beginning God planned for His Body and name to be carried by people exactly like us. For the deliberate shrinking of Omnipotence into the role of Head allows us as members of His Body to participate in the restoration of the universe. 'The whole creation,' says Paul, 'is on tiptoe to see the wonderful sight of the sons of God coming into their own. . . . And the hope is that in the end the whole of created life will be rescued from the tyranny of change and delay, and have its share in that magnificent liberty which can only belong to the children of God!' (Rom. 8:19, 21 PHILLIPS).

A reward will come, to be sure. C. S. Lewis suggests it: 'As mere biological entities, each with its own separate will to live and to expand, we are apparently of no account; we are crossfodder. But as organs in the Body of Christ, as stones and pillars in the temple, we are assured of our external self-identity and shall live to remember the galaxies as an old tale.'

Because God has risked entrusting His kingdom to bumblers such as us, we gain by becoming the sons and daughters of God. The image of God is being restored. 'Even angels long to look into these things' (1 Peter 1:12).

As a teacher, I have at times experienced the peculiar satisfaction of work done through others.

If I were to review my years in India and try to calculate the number of hands that I personally operated on, I might come up with a number around 10,000. In some ways that number seems overwhelmingly large to me, and it points up my advancing age with a rude jolt. But as I reflect further, I realise how negligible that number is. We estimate 15,000,000 people in the world suffer from leprosy, a quarter of whom have hand damage. In a lifetime of surgery, putting in as many hours as I can muster, I have personally only been able to help a fraction of one percent of the people with needs.

But again and again I have visited a tiny rural clinic in a place like Borneo and watched a young doctor perform procedures that derive from those we developed at Vellore. In Japan, Singapore, Hawaii, Ethiopia, or virtually anywhere a leprosy work thrives, you can find students who were trained at Vellore or Carville. Nothing – absolutely nothing – fills me with more joy than to see the seeds of ideas and disciplines I taught now sprouting in peoples' lives. It seems almost a miracle when I see it in action. My work done in a classroom can multiply a hundred times what I could possibly achieve on my own.

When I leave this world, the number of hand surgeries I have performed will not increase; no other patient will be helped by my own hands. But the students I have left behind will continue to multiply the original mission we adopted at Vellore. That realisation gives me additional insight into God's way of working in the world.

A teacher extends his or her work through students left behind. A brain expresses itself through cells obedient to its command. And God expresses Himself through a Body in which He serves as Head.

'He who listens to you listens to me; he who rejects you

rejects me,' Jesus once told his followers (Luke 10:16). The identification of the Body with its Head is that complete. A little later, on the night before He died, Christ explained His imminent death for the confused and sombre disciples. 'It is for your good that I am going away,' He said (John 16:7). They did not know it at the time, but the era of Headship was about to begin.

12 The Way Out

In 'The Happy Hypocrite' Max Beer-
bohm tells about a regency rake named
Lord George Hell, debauched and
profligate, who falls in love with a
saintly girl, and, in order to win her
love, covers his bloated features with the
mask of a saint. The girl is deceived and
becomes his bride, and they live together
happily until a wicked lady from Lord
George Hell's wicked past turns up to
expose him for the scoundrel she knows
him to be and challenges him to take off
his mask. So sadly, having no choice, he
takes it off, and lo and behold beneath
the saint's mask is the face of the saint he
has become by wearing it in love.

Frederick Buechner
Telling the Truth

The television camera was merciless. It never blinked, not when the teenage girl's tongue lolled over to the side, not when her eyes rolled wildly, not when she drooled and sputtered and fought off gagging on her own saliva. For this science programme devoted to cerebral palsy, the camera recorded every extreme manifestation of the disease.

Another person with cerebral palsy, a young man, entered the girl's room, brought there by the television programme's producers. He had made astonishing progress in rehabilitation, and he demonstrated his skills for the bedridden girl. He spelled out words, one alphabet letter at a time, with wide scraping arcs of his feet, so fast that an accompanying 'interpreter' had trouble keeping up. He also typed with his toe, using a metal connection to complete a circuit on the keys. He had even learned to use a machine that amplified his clicking, glottal speech enough to make it intelligible to a trained ear.

In contrast, the girl had received no rehabilitation therapy. An Ohio state agency, unable to care for her medically, had placed her in an insane asylum. The television programme pointed out the stark irony: everything was wrong with this girl *except* her mind. Behind the wild expressions, the drooling, and the catalepsy was a beautiful and intelligent mind, imprisoned.

Workers at the hospital had drawn a large chart divided into eighty squares of key phrases such as 'I want' or 'I need'. The girl communicated by looking at a square with the appropriate phrase, whenever she could make her eyes hold steady long enough. Someone asked her if she had any questions for her 'progressive' cerebral palsy visitor. She twitched and shook, and her eyes darted and weaved and danced. A volunteer watched her eyes carefully for tell-tale clues. It took about five minutes for the girl to look at three squares coherently enough to ask a question: 'Were . . . you . . . angry?'

For anyone who watched that television programme, the lesson would last forever: a mind is not enough. To express itself and to communicate with others the mind needs a cooperative body.

People afflicted with diseases such as acute cerebral palsy face the constant frustration of disobedient cells. Some of the victims possess magnificent minds: Englishman Stephen Hawking, for example, one of the world's premier astronomers, suffers from spasticity caused by ALS, or 'Lou Gehrig's disease'. And yet often these people are dismissed as ignorant or even retarded. They have an obvious dissension between mind and body.

A healthy body relies on proper channels from the brain to body parts, as well as a commitment from individual cells to do the will of the head. In a spastic disease or paralysis, somewhere, often in the descending fibres to the cells (The Way Out), communication breaks down. A paraplegic can lie in bed all day and plot how to move her toe, and then *will* to move it with her full mental energy, but if the connection is broken the toe will not move.

In the spiritual Body, The Way Out describes the descending aspect of the Head's channels to each cell. As we have access to God, He also has access to us. There is a sense – a guarded, mysterious, ineffable sense that the next chapter will explore – in which God Himself relies on bursts of messages from His fibres in the world. But there is a blatant, life-preserving, absolute sense in which we individual cells must rely on the messages streaming down from the Head to each of us. One quality affects whether a cell will do its job effectively: a willingness to follow the messages from the Head. Only the Head can determine the needs of the whole Body. And obedience alone determines our individual usefulness in His Body.

The Body of Christ, like the spastic patient's, can be judged by its disobedient body parts. When Dorothy Sayers made her comment about the church being God's third great humiliation, no doubt she was thinking of the soiled 'reputation' we have given our Head in historical demonstrations of selfishness, greed, intolerance, and spiritual pride. The flaw is not in the Head, to be sure, but the humiliation is there.

God continues to work through blundering human agents. He does not interfere to correct impaired perception or overrule an awkward movement, but limits His activity to such flawed representatives as David the murderer and adulterer, Jonah the insubordinate, Peter the traitor, Luther the Jew-baiter, Calvin the executioner. God has taken up people like them – and these five represent some of the best of the lot – into Himself. He has given us His name and His Spirit, incorporated us into His Body and contented Himself to serve as Head. If the Incarnation is a mystery, how much more this?

I have searched the four Gospels to observe how Jesus prepared for the new phase of Headship, and a trend does emerge: during His three years of ministry Jesus increasingly turned His work over to His disciples. At first He did all the healing, exorcising, ministering, and evangelising. But as the time for His death neared, He concentrated more on training those who would be left behind. A few key events stand out.

'I am sending you out like lambs among wolves,' He warned one of the first groups of His followers to go forth on His behalf (see Luke 10:1–24). Thus He began to entrust sacred tasks to a ragtag group of six dozen novices. Despite the stern warnings, the seventy-two met with great success on their mission. 'Lord, even the demons submit to us in your name,' they reported exuberantly. Jesus responded with unparalleled enthusiasm – I know of no other scene that shows Him so full of joy. He burst into prayer and then pronounced these ringing words, 'For I tell you that many prophets and kings wanted to see what you see but did not see it, and to hear what you hear but did not hear it.' The work of the kingdom had advanced, but this time while Jesus Himself was serving in an indirect role. His exclamation underscored the significance of that step of progress.

Later, at the very end of His earthly life, Jesus took a further step: He turned over the entire mission. The transfer occurred in a gathering, The Last Supper, that has no equal in the New Testament for its emotional intensity. 'I confer on you a kingdom, just as my Father conferred one on me,' Jesus said that night (Luke 22:29). From that point on, He has mainly relied on The Way Out, the indirect way of working through human 'cells'.

Incredibly, God now depends on us to do His will in the world. He allows us to do awkwardly and sluggishly what He could do perfectly and instantaneously. In a manner full of mystery, Christ has put Himself at our mercy; our lack of faith can paralyse His action.* Clearly, He seems to prefer delegating His authority to His creatures.

Errors inevitably creep in – spastic movements, if you will. It cannot be easy for Omnipotence to endure the humiliation we bring on. (Is there a divine counterpart to the frustration a paraplegic feels?) But before we become too concerned about what the church has dragged God through, we should remember that the great, soaring Pauline words about the church – Body of Christ, Bride of Christ, Temple of God – were addressed to actual, visible, and decidedly sinful congregations. God welcomes sinful human beings as His children; likewise, He depends on flawed members to accomplish the work of His Body.

Even if the mind-body connection is severed completely, utterly eliminating The Way Out, death does not always follow. Surprisingly, animals can stay alive and function at some level with their higher brains removed. The lower cells, in this event, do not follow voluntary orders, but merely respond to localised instincts. Sir Charles Sherrington studied a brainless frog swimming easily across a pond. You can, he said, get the impression the injury is trivial until you examine the behaviour closely and see that the frog is swimming randomly, with no purpose, just kicking its legs in reflexive patterns. There can be no 'purpose' with a brain removed.

---

* 'He could not do any miracles there, except lay his hands on a few sick people and heal them. And he was amazed at their lack of faith' (Mark 6:5,6).

Higher animals are more affected by the removal of a brain. A decerebrated dog stands in a rigid, statuesque posture. Although it can be propped up on all fours, like a stuffed animal, it cannot adjust its stance to maintain balance and will topple over at the slightest touch.

Human beings also may experience an interruption in the links between brain and body. One test for damage to those channels is simple: a gentle tap on the knee with that ubiquitous rubber hammer. Normally that tap, as we all know, brings on a reflex response from the patellar tendon. When the hammer blow reaches the tendon, the reflex loop has the momentary impression that the knee is bending. In quick response, the *local* neurons (the message reaches the higher brain only later) tighten the muscle that straightens the knee. In normal life, that reflex keeps us from falling if we stumble.

However, if a spinal injury has destroyed the connection between a person's brain and leg, a tap with a hammer will produce a radically different reflex, and the doctor who taps the hammer will need fast reflexes of his own. The patient's muscles will jerk violently, his leg shooting forward with enormous force. It may then flail back and forth, the muscles in spasm.

Such leg muscles and tendons are healthy – they are exhibiting their power spectacularly – but have lost contact with higher orders from the head. The brain normally constrains involuntary reflexes (in Sherrington's words it 'has a civilising influence on primitive parts'). When this vital pathway is severed, the body part can still act, but autonomously, disconnectedly, irrationally, overreacting to local parts of the body.

Analogies to the spiritual Body apply only partially, for dysfunction there never results from brain damage. But many nervous disorders – cerebral palsy, for example – occur when synaptic channels below the level of the brain somehow clog up. Poisons, such as cocaine, botulinus, and atropine, can also jam the chemical transmission across synapses.

We have a theological word for such poisons in the Body: sin. Sin steals into the intimate channel between Head and member, interrupting communication and separating the cell from the higher authority that directs and coordinates its actions. The usefulness of a single cell requires unimpeded communication from above and an obedient response from below.

The apostle Paul, master of metaphor, gives a precise description of a person suffering from a sort of disconnection, in his letter to the Colossians. The person he describes had erred by legalistically judging other members of the Body; he had focused on his neighbouring cells rather than on receiving individual orders from the Head. 'Such a person goes into great detail about what he has seen, and his unspiritual mind puffs him up with idle notions. He has lost connection with the Head, from whom the whole body, supported and held together by its ligaments and sinews, grows as God causes it to grow' (Col. 2:18–19). Once severed, new pathways linking the mind and body do not reestablish themselves easily.

The normal brain assigns a specific area to govern each finger, each toe, each significant body part. If, for instance, the assigned area represents my ring finger, that portion of the brain will contain all the associations of my finger. Can it play the guitar? Steady my hand in writing? Does it bear a scar from a prior injury? The brain stores these memories and abilities. If my finger is used prominently, as in playing the guitar, the brain will have an increasing richness of association with the finger.

As a surgeon, I sometimes get involved in disrupting these associative pathways and trying to establish new ones. For example, we give some leprosy patients new eyebrows (for cosmetic purposes) by cutting a swatch of hairy scalp and tunnelling it under the forehead to the eyebrow area. It comes still attached to the scalp's original nerve and blood supply, and so the patient's new eyebrow still 'feels like' part of his scalp. If a fly crawls across the transplanted eyebrow, the patient will likely respond by slapping his crown.

Or, in a tendon transfer procedure I may move a healthy tendon from the ring finger to replace a weak or useless one on the thumb. To the recuperating patient, orders from the brain still feel like the ring finger should respond. 'Move your thumb,' I will say, and nothing happens. The patient just stares at his hand. 'Now move your ring finger,' I say, and the thumb springs forward.

Over time, the patient must repattern his or her brain to interpret the sensation of ring finger motion as activity by the thumb. It can take months to reestablish smooth patterns, and many patients over the age of forty never fully adjust to the change.

The image of thumb cells struggling to receive a strange new set of orders from the head helps in visualising Paul's injunction to be transformed 'by the renewing of your mind'. He urged fellow-members, cells in Christ's Body, to learn God's 'good, pleasing and perfect will' (Rom. 12:2).

Elsewhere, Paul drew specific applications of how God's will should express itself in our lives. He exhorted the Philippians to 'Let this *mind* be in you which was in Christ Jesus' (Phil. 2:5 KJV), and then defined what the mind or attitude should be:

> Who, being in very nature God,
>   did not consider equality with God
>   something to be grasped,
> but made himself nothing,
>   taking the very nature of a servant,
>   being made in human likeness.
> And being found in appearance as a man,
>   he humbled himself
>   and became obedient to death –
>   even death on a cross!

I envision this renewing process as the intensive effort to develop a smooth, steady stream of transmission between the cell and its Head, both on ascending and descending fibres. By examining the image or model set down by Christ, and by forming a relationship with Him, I am, in fact, learning the mind of Christ. I have seen the biological process at work in hundreds of my patients, and the spiritual process in many committed Christians.

Some Christians are now rediscovering ancient disciplines of faith. In such acts as meditation, fasting, prayer, simple living, worship, and celebration, we can build proper communication between ourselves and the Head. Even the simple practice of repeating prayers from the Book of Common Prayer can help discipline the mind. In neurophysiology as well as spirituality, repeated acts of obedience strengthen the connections. A concert pianist does not consciously think through the motions involved for each finger to strike a note. Rather, a performer's mind dwells on mood and timing and interpretation; the fingers follow pathways laid down through hours of practice long before.

Just as musicians and athletes develop skill through the repeated exercise of the brain-to-cells pathways, members of Christ's Body can develop an ever-increasing richness of association between themselves and the Head. For the beginning Christian, the process of learning Christ's mind may seem mechanical and ungainly. The Christian 'walk', as does the infant's walk, begins with hundreds of false starts and stumbles and missteps. (Paul alludes to 'another law at work in the members of my body, waging war against the law of my mind' Rom. 7:23). Gradually, though, those muscles and joints in knee and leg and foot learn to cooperate together so concertedly that the infant runs across the room without giving a single conscious thought to the process. Each attempt at a new skill or a sport will begin in a fumbling, error-prone way until movements become fluid and dependable. Daily, we adults take these motions for granted unless we are shocked into gratitude by someone handicapped with paraplegia or cerebral palsy.

On long walks outdoors, I have been watching a pair of orchard orioles build their nest. The birds are young, and this is undoubtedly their first nest. Just a few branches away hangs another nest, built last year by older orioles; it has survived a winter storm that tore branches from the tree. Yet these young birds never go over to inspect the old nest or study it for design innovations. They know exactly what to do. They neglect eating in the urgency of their task.

First they spend time selecting the best location. They need a branch with a well-spaced fork on which to weave the nest. The branch must be so thin as to droop a little from the mere weight of the leaves, in order to protect the nest from squirrels. Foliage must surround the site to conceal the young from hawks and other predators flying high above.

Once a prime location is agreed upon, the birds search for individual blades of grass, of one type only, that must conform to a certain length and consistency. One of the birds stands with a foot perched on each branch of the fork. It holds a blade of grass under one foot against the twig. Then, using only its beak, it ties a half-hitch knot around that twig, leaving a long end dangling. After flying away for another blade, it ties a half-hitch on the other twig, pulling the blades under its body. Then it plaits other hanging strands into a thick cable. The nest itself will swing between these cables. After several days of selecting, weaving, plaiting, and wattling, the two birds will have a neat, spherical home, strong enough to withstand gale-force winds.

Inside my house, at the same time, my wife is knitting a pullover sweater for me. I can see her through a window. She is a good knitter, and I will wear the sweater with pride. The wool demanded the skill and experience of shepherds and shearers and spinners and dyers. Margaret keeps glancing down at a printed pattern that combines the artistry and calculations of master knitters. Reading those instructions requires education, and following them employs a skill she has learned over the years. The sweater will finally emerge, a result of the shared intelligence of many brains over many years. Given a live sheep and told to create a sweater with no outside help, my wife would probably fail.

I know that I, even with full concentration and the manual dexterity developed in years of surgery, cannot weave strands of grass into a hollow globe that will cling to a branch in a storm. I tried to once, and it fell apart, limp and useless. Yet I have ten fingers while an oriole has only a beak and feet.

Instinct is the key, of course.* A kindred species, the bunting, follows another imprinted code that guides it across the Gulf of Mexico to a new land five hundred miles away. I have watched migrating birds take off. They sit on a reed in the swamp and look out across an expanse of water that must appear endless. Fortunately the birds, unencumbered by reason, take off every time. Their wisdom predates the egg they came from.

I sometimes think of the bunting and the oriole as I struggle with spiritual decisions. Messages from God reach me along the pathways of The Way Out. With my reason, even as I contemplate what the Bible says, I can easily rationalise my way to other conclusions. The commands are hard; they require love and sacrifice and compassion and purity when I have excuses that make those seem unattainable for me at any moment.

At such times, as my own selfishness and pride surge up, I need a force more dependable than reason. Just such a force comes built into each of us: the conscience or subconscious, a law written in our hearts (see Rom. 2:15). This instinctive sense of our responsibility to God can be encour-

---

* But how blithely we dismiss phenomena as 'mere instinct'! A genetic code built that oriole's brain, cell by cell, directing neurons to line up with appropriate synapses so that the arrangement would inevitably, one day, direct its feet and beak to accomplish these intricate manoeuvres. Even the wisdom of what grass to select and what site to choose was included in the instructions of the genetic code that preceded the brain. The oriole's brain is the product of the need for thought, but a prior thought anticipated the requirements of that brain and built in a genetic code that would instruct all the bird's cells to cooperate obediently, without debating the commands.

aged and nurtured by the disciplines of faith. Hiding God's Word in my heart and meditating on it help to strengthen this force and thus to renew my mind.

When the moment of critical choice arrives, there is often little chance for conscious reflection, and all that has gone before enters into the result. I think of those tiny birds, the oriole and the bunting, and ask that in renewing my mind God would imprint His instructions into me as if they were put there genetically. I ask for an uninterrupted flow of messages from Him and for an obedient response.

13 The Way In

I was a stricken deer that left the herd
Long since; with many an arrow deep infixed
My panting side was charged, when I withdrew
To seek a tranquil death in distant shades.
There was I found by One Who had Himself
Been hurt by the archers. In His side He bore,
And in His hands and feet, the cruel scars.
With gentle force soliciting the darts,
He drew them forth, and healed, and bade me live.

William Cowper
The Task, Book III

To God, as God, it belongeth to express
Himself, and to know and love Himself,
and to reveal Himself to Himself; and all
this without any creature. . . . And
without the creature, this would lie in
His own Self as a Substance or well-
spring, but would not be manifested or
wrought out into deeds. Now God will
have it to be exercised and clothed in a
form . . . and this cannot come to pass
. . . without the creature.

Theologia Germanica

At a precise time in each of our lives, normally around the age of twelve months, a profound change takes place. A person's perception of the world moves from a predominant reliance on touch to a reliance on sight. Touch precedes and teaches sight, until the sight cells gain dependable notions of shape and distance and solidness. This learning process occurs in everyone – everyone, that is, except the blind.

Sightless people never make the transition unless their sight somehow is restored. And early in this century that dramatic event occurred often, thanks to the just-perfected miracle of cataract surgery. People blind from birth, who had always lived by a tactile conception of the world, suddenly could see. When their eyes opened, they encountered a world far different from what they had imagined. (In some cases of long-term blindness central vision had atrophied, but peripheral vision gave these patients a first look at the world).

One prescient author, Marius von Senden, sensed an unrepeatable opportunity to observe adults coming to terms with a perceptual revolution that most of us experience as inarticulate infants. He recorded what took place among sixty-six patients in his startling book *Space and Sight*.

Basic notions of space, motion, and shape are incomprehensible to the newly sighted, von Senden concluded. For example, sighted people have learned certain assumptions about spatial distance. A building 'within sight' is nearby, within walking distance; a destination that requires a bus, train, or plane is obviously farther away. The sightless, in contrast, judge distance by its effect on their muscle tension. To them, reaching a building a mile away requires the taking of many steps, but a destination involving a train, bus, or plane ride seems nearby because getting there uses little muscle tension.

Once these patients could see, a bewildering world of size and perspective confronted them. Previously they had a firm conception of size: an orange was about the size of a cupped hand, a face two hand-widths. In a shocking reversal, after surgery none of these rules applied. 'How big is your mother?' a researcher asked a sixteen-year-old girl. The girl held her index fingers a few inches apart, the same distance she had estimated for the size of a book. Her mother, standing across the room, took up about that much of her field of vision. And the sun? Obviously, it was about the size of a penny – who could believe the sun was larger than the earth?

Gradually, over a period of months these patients had to learn the meaning of space, distance, and perspective. Vertical distances remained unfathomable for a long time, for the newly sighted had no prior conception of space beyond what they could feel by touch. Skyscrapers and trees loomed high, but how could they gauge height over ten feet, the height reachable with a cane? One patient, observing some interesting activity on the street below, stepped off the balcony of a tall apartment building and was killed. A plane in the sky, or an elevator that moved them with no muscular effort were mysteries defying explanation.

The blind also had learned motion in terms of muscle changes and could not readily perceive it with their eyes alone. A doctor waved his hand in front of the face of an eight-year-old boy. 'Can you see it is moving?' he asked. The boy, confused, stared intently straight ahead. He 'saw' interludes of light and darkness, but his eyes made no attempt to follow the moving hand. 'He was clearly trying to grasp the meaning of this phrase [moving] in relation to the gesture', reported the doctor, 'but without success. His eye failed to follow the long swinging motions of the hand.' Finally, allowed to touch the hand, the boy cried out joyfully, 'It's moving!'

Even common shapes proved totally undecipherable to those who had known the world only through touch. A researcher arranged a row of fruit on a table before a woman patient; the row corresponded exactly to the row of six different fruits before him. 'Pick this up,' he said, selecting an apple from his row. The patient stared intently at the objects before her, trying her best to distinguish the six shapes visually. Finally, hesitantly, she reached down only to choose a plum – easily one-sixth the size of the apple. When allowed to touch the researcher's apple, she instantly succeeded in choosing an apple, but the strange world of different sizes, confusing colours, and blurry shapes was simply too much to take in visually.

An alert twenty-year-old-patient usually required four intensive weeks of training to learn to distinguish visually between round, square, and triangular shapes. One patient mistook an apple for a key, a loaf of bread for a hand. Another, grasping for some clue to please the teacher, seized on colour. She learned a matchbox was yellow; from then on everything yellow she called a matchbox whether it was an apple, a banana, or a book jacket.

If it took weeks of trial and error to differentiate a circle from a square, imagine the obstacles to recognising just one face. A newly sighted husband required four months of practice to distinguish his wife's face from anyone else's, unless she spoke or he could touch the tiniest patch of her cheek.

One young girl played with a pet cat for twenty-one days, four hours each day. Then, upon seeing a hen in a garden she squealed with delight, 'My cat!' After all, the thing was small and somewhat grey and it moved. The same girl mistook a bookcase for a stove and called a fountain a tree 'because it is big and round'. The simplest sights provoked great alarm in her: a black coat on the floor looked like the mouth of a well, a column of smoke from the chimney appeared to crack the sky in two, and the spots on her dog Muffy seemed like holes through him.

'How is it that I now find myself less happy than before?' one distraught woman wailed in the midst of her training. 'Everything that I see causes me a disagreeable emotion. Oh, I was much more at ease in my blindness!' She could not cope with a baffling world in which she was expected to distinguish between a knife, spoon, and fork without touching them. (Eventually, to her pleasure, she went blind again.) Virtually all patients muddled through such despondent periods for a time. They were being asked to relearn the world, like persons abruptly deposited on another planet where the laws of physics do not apply.

The newly sighted had even more difficulty mastering such advanced concepts as spatial wholeness, or two-dimensional depth perception (a quality that stumped artists until five centuries ago). After receiving sight a girl realised she had never conceived of her dog as a whole, made up of a head, ears, and legs joined together to make one animal. Like the proverbial blind men feeling an elephant, she had never touched all the parts at once and thus had not pictured the dog as a whole being.

In order to explain depth perception, the researchers led patients to heights. A landscape held no meaning for them at first. A band of green (forest) or a strip of blue (river) gave no clues to the newly sighted about actual identity. They had never touched anything so faraway; how could they comprehend it? It took even more months of effort to train such patients to recognise objects from paintings or photographs. The image of a face, hard enough to distinguish in flesh and blood, did not transfer well when pressed onto a two-dimensional square of light and shadow.

Eventually, of course, most of these people adjusted to the world of light and colour and shape and size, and discovered levels of perception and beauty that previously had eluded them. But the process involved great anxiety in every case. For months, sometimes years, the patients shut their eyes for critical manoeuvres, such as walking around a cluttered part of a house near a staircase. The new world had betrayed them; it was not at all what they had expected. Or, more accurately, their other senses had betrayed them by giving them an incomplete conception of what the world is like.*

---

* Brain researchers have further demonstrated that our picture of the world depends largely on all sensory input from the environment we are exposed to. Kittens raised in boxes painted with horizontal stripes do not even notice vertical stripes at first: their brain cells have not yet developed a category of 'verticalness'. And, bizarrely, kittens raised in a painted cylinder with constantly rotating sides can not readily cope when exposed to a non-moving environment. They start spinning in circles to duplicate the effect of the cylinder!

Within the analogy of this book, von Senden's accounts illustrate how the brain, shut off in its ivory box from the actual stuff of matter, must interpret reality based on partial clues from the rest of the body. When a condition such as blindness restricts those clues, the entire body is affected.

I hasten to admit that the perception analogy cannot be pushed too far. The Mind or Head of this Body – God Himself in the person of Christ – is not dependent on or limited by perceptions gained through the members of His Body. His knowledge encompasses all; He does not need our frail fibres to increase His wisdom. Yet in another sense, because of the awesome fact of God's self-limitation, the analogy of the lonely mind does apply.

We have seen already that God self-limits His activty (The Way Out) by relying primarily on bumbling human agents. In ways beyond our comprehension God also has chosen to make His presence on earth dependent on The Way In, the communication from the members, or cells, of His Body.

Of all the marvellous aspects of the human body, I know of no greater wonder than that every one of the hundred trillion cells in my body has access to the brain. Many cells, such as those used in sight, have direct neuronal connections; others have channels immediately available to them to report in on their needs or current states. And in the Body of Christ, I know of no greater wonder than that each one of us has direct contact with Christ Himself, the Head. Amazingly, He listens to our input, considers our requests, and quite literally uses that information to influence His direction of activities in the world. 'The prayer of a righteous man is powerful and effective' (James 5:16).

Through us who serve as His hands and ears and eyes and pain cells, God stays 'in touch with' this world and the people in it. His activity takes into account the communication we give Him. There is also a 'benefit' for God, so to speak. In varied and striking phrases, the Bible expresses the awesome truth that God takes pleasure in His church:

we are 'peculiar treasures', 'a pleasing aroma', 'gifts that He delights in'. And more than thirty times the New Testament reminds us that we are His Body, joined to Him so fully that what happens to us happens to Him as well. As astounding as it may seem, the conclusion is inescapable: God wants fellowship with us. He longs for communication from His Body: The Way in. He created us that He might receive our love.

Do we somehow miss the revolution that has taken place in the universe? In ancient religions, the actions of the gods in the heavens above were believed to affect the earth below. Gods cavorting in the skies brought forth rain and and earthquakes and thunderbolts. Like kids dropping rocks off highway bridges onto the cars below, they dropped judgment and cataclysm onto the earth. Now Christ reverses the ancient Hermetic formula: 'As above, so below,' becomes 'As below, so above'. Human action, such as prayer, affects heaven. The conversion of one sinner causes all of heaven to rejoice.

Prayer is the central channel, of course, a way for us to 'participate in the dignity of causation', in Pascal's phrase. Prayer itself can be a full-time occupation; for centuries cloistered mystics have adopted it as that. Again and again, so often that writers unavoidably repeat the same words, the Bible reminds us in the strongest terms that God hears our prayers, Incredibly, it seems that God yearns for contact with the disparate members of His own Body. The lack of such contact and the absence of human faith limit the spiritual Body as surely as the lack of a sense like sight limits the entire physical body.

The intimacy, or open channel, we now have with God traces back to the reconciliation won for us by Christ. In the Incarnation He took on a role like that of a 'cell', stepping into His own creation. And throughout His time on earth Jesus felt the need to slip away and commune with the Father. God talking to God – the mystery of the Trinity. By His example the Son of God showed us the vital pattern of sending a ceaseless stream of communication to the Father.

In his reflections on the Incarnation, the author of Hebrews tied together in three stages the progression of intimacy between God and people: the Old Testament approach to God through a priest, Christ's personal visitation, and the more intimate Body that resulted. He concluded, 'For we do not have a high priest who is unable to sympathise with our weaknesses, but we have one who has been tempted in every way, just as we are – yet was without sin. Let us then approach the throne of grace with confidence so that we may receive mercy and find grace to help us in our time of need.' (4:15–16).

Later, that same book hints at profound truths that we cannot fully understand: Jesus 'learned obedience from what he suffered', Hebrews says (5:8). It is a disquieting concept, to say the least, that God, omniscient and self-complete, learned through suffering. And yet the Incarnation was a form of learning, a direct experience of confinement within matter. Jesus felt the joy of a wedding and the grief of a funeral; the love and then betrayal of close friends; and finally the lash of a whip and the sting of spittle.

Today, God's tendrils of activity in this world of matter mainly reach out through members of His Body. And, most significantly, because of the Incarnation God hears our prayers in a new way, having lived here and having prayed Himself. We now have a high priest who is able to sympathise with our weakness . . . let us then approach Him with confidence.

The Body of Christ has a clear advantage over the physical body, for in it the Head remains totally accessible and receptive to the faintest communication from an extremity. The Head never needs to be awakened or enlightened. No lack of wisdom or power limits the activity of God on earth. Rather, the only limitation is the participation of member cells in relating to the Head. Individual Christians need only learn to refer every emotion, every action, every experience of their lives to God.

David is an example of a flawed human, a murderer and an adulterer. Nevertheless, he found favour with God, so much so that he was called 'a man after God's own heart'. Reading the poems attributed to him, I can see why David deserved that appellation. His poetry contains anger and despair, but also joy and praise; helplessness and sorrow, but also strength and confidence; pain and vengeance, but also humility and love. Blatantly contradictory moods butt up against each other. His emotions welter. David hid nothing from God, neither the bad nor the good. That, I think, is what God loved. The 'cell' named David took God seriously. He gave a daily, sometimes minute-by-minute reporting of every situation in his life, and expected – sometimes demanded – that God respond to him.*

The Way In and The Way Out: both are essential for a healthy body. The entire Body of Christ may be harmed if one part of the Body does not communicate with the Head. If a prophetic cell refuses to discern truly and to warn the rest of the Body, we may all stumble off course. Like von Senden's blind people, we may go through life unaware and uninformed. A silent intercessory cell will surely take its toll. And if one part of the Body becomes insensitive to pain in a finger or a limb, that part will gradually deteriorate.

Through The Way In the cells in the sense organs, extremities, and other vital parts send in a flood of data, informing the head about the condition of cells themselves and the sentient world outside. Likewise, brain cells coordinate a stream of ordered instructions along The Way Out. To walk, we need a 'feedback loop' of muscle and joint cells reporting in tone and position and pressure and also receiving instructions on proper movement. Motion requires a dynamic equilibrium of the ascending and descending messages. If The Way In is accurate and complete, and the cells

---

* Many of the Psalms by a variety of authors show this divergent quality. As an example, consider the full range of human response shown in just five psalms, 21–25.

receiving messages along The Way Out are obedient and responsive, only then will the body work.

One scene more than any other symbolises for me the role of the head in the human body, and of the Head in the spiritual Body. It involves a blind person, a patient I will call José.

José's body had suffered much damage from leprosy by the time he came from Puerto Rico to Carville for treatment. His insensitivity to touch was so great that, when blindfolded, he could not even detect whether someone had entered the room and held his hand. Touch cells and pain cells had fallen silent. As a result, scars and ulcers covered his hands, face, and feet, bearing mute witness to the unintentional abuse his body had endured without any sensation of pain. Mere stubs on his hands marked where fingers used to be.

Because pain cells in his eyes no longer alerted him when to blink, gradually José's eyes dried out. That condition, aggravated by severe cataracts and glaucoma, soon made him blind. My wife Margaret (who is an eye surgeon) told him surgery might correct the cataract problem and restore some vision, but she could not operate until inflammation of the iris went away. A terrible misfortune cut off José's last link with the outside world. In a desperate attempt to arrest the sulphone-resistant leprosy, doctors tried treating him with a new drug, and José had a rare allergic reaction. He lost his hearing.

Thus, at the age of forty-five José lost all contact with the world. He could not see nor hear if a person spoke. Unlike Helen Keller, he could not even use tactile sign language – the leprosy had dulled his sense of touch. Even his sense of smell had disappeared as the leprosy had invaded the lining of his nose. All his inlets from the world, except taste, had been blocked off. Weeks passed and we watched the effect on José as his mind began to accept the reality that it had lost all meaningful contact with a world of flowers and rivers and islands and people.

José's body responded with a pathetic reflection of what was happening inside: his limbs pulled inward toward his trunk, and he began curling into a foetal position on the bed. He would wake up from sleep and forget where he was. He did not know whether it was day or night, and when he spoke, he did not know if anyone heard or answered. Sometimes he would speak anyway, bellowing because he could not hear the volume, pouring out the inexpressible loneliness of a mind condemned to solitary confinement.

In such a world, thoughts go in circles and spirals, stirring up fears and suspicions. Is not madness the loss of perception of the real world? José's body coiled tighter and tighter on the bed. He was preparing for death in the same posture as his birth. Those of us on the staff would pass his room, pause for a moment at the door, shake our heads, and continue walking. What could we do?

Margaret faithfully visited José. Unable to bear watching this otherwise healthy man self-destruct, she felt she must attempt some kind of radical treatment to restore at least part of his sight. She waited impatiently for the infection in his eye to improve enough to schedule surgery.

Trying to follow government rules, Margaret faced a nearly insurmountable problem. Naturally, she must obtain 'informed consent' forms for the surgery. But who would sign for José? No one could penetrate through his isolation even to ask him for permission to help. After painstaking research, the hospital staff finally located a sister in Puerto Rico, and the police department there visited her with a surgery release form. The illiterate sister marked an X on a paper, and surgery was scheduled at last, with faint hopes for success.

José, of course, did not comprehend what was happening as he was moved to a stretcher and wheeled to the operating room. He lay passive throughout the eye surgery. After a two-hour procedure, he was bandaged and sent back to his room to wait.

Margaret removed the bandages a few days later, an experience she will never forget. Although José had sensed some gross movement, and had probably reasoned someone was trying to help him, nothing had prepared him for what actually did happen. He got use of one eye back and could see again. As his eye struggled against the bright light and slowly focused on the medical people gathered around the bed, the face that had not smiled in months cracked into a huge, toothless grin. Contact had been restored.

During that long period of isolation, José's brain had floated intact inside his skull, complete with memory, emotions, and instructions for directing his body. But it stayed useless because The Way In had been blocked.

I think of José when I think of what God endures by electing to serve as Head for a Body comprised of human beings. The most magnificent organ in the body can lie isolated and useless without the cooperation of informing senses and obedient cells. God chose that very position for Himself, working not despite or in opposition to us, but through us. That is the humiliation.

But there is also a triumph, and it comes to light when communication is restored. When José's sensory channels were reestablished, suddenly all that had been isolated and useless was free to express itself to the world outside. José made it known to us that he wanted his wheelchair parked at the door to his room all day long. He would sit there quietly, every few seconds glancing up and down the long corridors of the leprosarium. When he saw another person coming, his face would break into that irrepressible smile.

Today, José has contact with the world. He insists on coming to our small church every Sunday, even though he can hear nothing of the service. With stubby fingers, he can barely grasp the control knob of his electric wheelchair, and his narrow tunnel vision causes him to bump into objects up and down the long corridors. But still he comes, regardless of the weather outside. Other attenders have learned to greet him by stooping down, putting their faces directly in front of his, and waving. José's wonderful smile invariably breaks out, and sometimes his bellowing laugh. Although he cannot see well, and cannot hear or feel at all, somehow he can sense the fellowship of that church. It is enough for him.

José's mind is no longer isolated and alone, but united with the other cells in his body. All that is in his powerful brain now has an outlet to the rest of us outside. He can express the image that had been sealed inside.

SPIRIT

14 Breath

When a prospector first strikes oil there is often a violent eruption of the oil which sometimes bursts into flames and burns for many days before it is brought under control. Later on there will be no room for such displays. The oil will all be pumped through pipes and refineries to its destination, and a desire to go back to the early fireworks will be rightly regarded as infantile. But the early displays did at least prove something; they proved that oil was there, and without this all the pipes and refineries in the world are merely futile.

Lesslie Newbigin
The Household of God

What tree rivals the banyan in extravagance? It drops roots not only from its trunk but also from its branches, dozens and soon hundreds of thewy stalks wending toward the ground to sprout root systems of their own. Uninterrupted, a banyan tree will grow forever, renewing itself in the radial extremities even as the inner core dies of old age. A single tree may cover acres of land, becoming a self-perpetuating forest spacious enough to shelter a full-scale bazaar (its name comes from the Hindi word *banian*: a caste of merchants).

You can see a majestic example of a banyan in Calcutta today, preserved in the Botanical Gardens. The Great Banyan Tree there covers ground 1,251 feet in circumference. It looks like a giant, bushy tent supported by colonnades of wooden poles. Somewhere in the middle of that velutinous thicket of trunks and branches the central trunk began growing two hundred years ago. After sustaining damage from a fungus and a cyclone the inner core was finally removed in 1925, but the outer tree grows on.

For a child who likes climbing and swinging from vines, the banyan tree provides endless amusement. As a six year old, I found myself free to explore one for several days when my parents camped under a banyan during a missionary venture. As they went about their medical and spiritual work, my sister and I played Swiss Family Robinson inside the great tree. The stalks that fell like stalactites from upper branches made for ideal climbing. Even better, some helpful people had looped and knotted various vines to form low swings and high swings and trapezes.

I was swinging on one such loop through a corridor within the tree, calling on my sister to push me higher and higher. As the height of my arc increased, I felt another loop of tendril brush against the back of my neck on my back-swing. I ducked to avoid it, but failed to duck again as the swing lurched into its downward descent. The high loop caught right under my chin and held me by the throat. The swing abruptly stopped. Fortunately, my main weight still rested on the seat, but my windpipe was totally clamped shut by the vine and I could not breathe or speak or scream.

I hung suspended there like a puppet tangled in its wires. My sister, on the ground, made a few frantic efforts to pull me off, and then must have run for help.

I woke up sometime later with my mother stooping over my camp cot pleading with me to speak to her. When I said her name, she burst into tears. She had feared brain damage, and my first word came as a welcome relief to her.

Other than a sore neck and a slight skin abrasion resembling a rope burn, I carried no physical scars from the experience, but for many years I harboured a primitive terror of breathlessness. Anything that covered my mouth and nose, even immersion in water, brought back that terror, and I would fight as if for my life. I learned starkly that lack of breath does not feel like anesthesia or sleep; it is like death.

Since that afternoon in the banyan tree, I have seen many medical situations that confirm the terror I felt that day. Emergencies of all types produce panic: heart attack victims clutch their chests; people with brain damage may thrash violently; soldiers in war gape, unbelieving, at a severed limb. But I know of no human experience that produces such a spasm of uncontrolled panic as does breathlessness.

We have all seen film clips of the marathon runner staggering across the finish line with mouth agape, his ribs heaving, his head bobbing like a rooster's, his whole body jerking in a bellows motion until gradually the oxygen floods in and the emergency subsides. Yet the marathoner feels no panic, for he has planned to end the race in a critical oxygen debt. His gestures underplay those of a person who *must* have oxygen: eyes bulge, hands grasp frantically at empty air, and the heart races. Oxygen shortage kicks into motion a vicious cycle: the accelerated heartbeat, trying to distribute faster what oxygen is there, consumes energy itself and requires even more oxygen. The downward spiral begins.

We are, all of us, five minutes from death. Life depends on our ability to stay in contact with the vital element of oxygen around us. When deprived of air for any length of time, the patient actually turns blue, first around the finger-nails, tongue, and lips, projecting the internal drama onto the visible screen of skin. High school biology students learn what causes the colour shift: blue blood has not got the supply of oxygen from the lungs that normally turns it a rich scarlet. The animal kingdom lives in utter dependence on this one element, oxygen.

Some lower animals' devices for gathering oxygen are inexpressibly beautiful: the jewellike fronds of marine worms, the fluted gills of tropical fish, the brilliant orange skirt of a flame scallop. Our own lungs come down on the side of function, not form, but they work well enough to make an engineer drool. The beginning medical student who first cuts into a corpse's torso gets graphic evidence of the lungs' importance. He has studied the vital heart and kidneys and pancreas. But the lungs!* They crowd all the rest, spilling into every crevice and cranny. When air is pumped in to simulate breathing, they seem to want to burst out of the chest cavity.

Bronchial tubes from the throat bisect, narrow down, divide again, and fan into a tree of tubes that culminate in three hundred million sacs called alveoli. The sacs, only one cell thick, are caught like dewdrops in a spider web of blood vessels that channel blood around the alveoli for the all-important oxygen transfer. The folds and convolutions of the lungs result in a surface area forty times larger

---

* The medical student is in for another shock when he compares lungs of different patients. The lungs of a non-smoker from the country have a gorgeous pink sheen of health. Tiny blood vessels show clearly against their light background. In dramatic contrast, the lungs of a city-dwelling smoker are dull charcoal in colour, almost as dark as those of a coal miner. Perhaps if the skin on our chest were transparent membrane like a tropical fish's so that every person could see for himself that contrast, as well as the fungoid ugliness of lung cancer, our society might undergo some major changes.

than the skin's, an area large enough to carpet a small apartment.*

We need the space. On an average day our lungs move enough air in and out to fill a medium-size room or blow up several thousand party balloons. Each breath sucks in about a pint of air, and if we don't think about it we take around fifteen breaths a minute. Any slight change, such as going up stairs or running for a bus, can double the capacity of air per breath and also double the intake frequency. Receptor centres scattered around the body constantly take oxygen and carbon dioxide measurements to determine the ideal rate. The entire process continues uninterrupted during sleep, without conscious control, or we would die. And the utilitarian body makes us borrow the same air flow system for such acts as speaking, singing, laughing, sighing, and whistling.

My own love affair with breath began after my young body hung from the banyan tree. I breathed with even more gratitude after I studied the mechanisms involved. Since then, I have watched a whole series of patients live out the drama of breathing.

Shortly after arriving in India as a doctor, I received two telephone calls on the same day, one from Calcutta and one from London. Both concerned the medical predicament of a young polo player in Calcutta. He was British, the only

---

* We could, theoretically, carry around sufficient oxygen dissolved in blood plasma and avoid red cells entirely – one icefish in the Antarctic lies around in 34° F water with his huge mouth open gulping in oxygen for his blood plasma, with no red cells at all. But a human so outfitted would need seventy-five gallons of plasma and would likely resemble a jellyfish with four floppy limbs and a head attached. Even so, the dissolved oxygen would only suffice for two and a half seconds; a long sneeze would probably prove fatal. Fortunately, a complex molecule called haemoglobin permits twenty times as much oxygen to be ferried around in our blood. The chemical molecule looks like this, $C_{3032} H_{4812} N_{780} Fe_4 O_{872} S_{12}$, and gives blood its characteristic red colour. In all, 9,508 atoms hook up in intricate formation around four crucial atoms of iron. Haemoglobin grabs passing oxygen atoms like a magnet, and the red cells' biconcave shape assures the maximum exposure to oxygen in the lungs. Each red cell carries 280,000,000 haemoglobin molecules.

son of a wealthy lord, and had come to Calcutta to learn and practise international banking on behalf of his father's global network of banks. The doctors in Calcutta and his relatives in England urged me to take the very next flight to Calcutta to examine him, because the day after a strenuous polo match he had become suddenly paralysed with poliomyelitis.

Over the phone I shouted instructions for the hospital to prepare an iron lung and to perform a tracheostomy, if he developed breathing difficulties, to prevent fluid buildup in his throat. Then I dashed to the Madras airport to catch the night flight. When I arrived in Calcutta, a car sped me to his hospital bedside.

I have a lasting impression of the figure I found inside that hospital room. A life of good nutrition and much leisure time on the rugby and polo fields had given the young man a superb physique. He was large in stature, and his arm and leg muscles bulged even in repose. All four limbs and trunk, however, were paralysed. He had built up an enormous lung capacity, now virtually useless on its own, so useless he had been placed inside the iron lung. The machine worked on a bellows principle, pushing his chest in and out in order to force respiration.

The cruel irony of the scene struck me: that marvellous body shoved inside an ugly metal cylinder that noisily forced air in and out of his lungs. I thought briefly of a series of sculptures I had seen, *The Captives*, by Michelangelo. In these works magnificent bodies seem trapped in marble despite their efforts to free themselves. Now before me, this man's Herculean body lay locked in steel. Nurses told me he had felt symptoms of 'influenza' on Friday, but had gone ahead with a polo match on Saturday in order not to disappoint his teammates. Exertion at the onset of polio can prove deadly.

To my dismay, I learned that the hospital had not performed the tracheostomy, so I immediately ordered up an anaesthetist. I worried about the fluid that can collect when muscles for coughing or clearing the throat no longer operate. I explained to the young athlete what we planned to do. An aide who stood beside him assured me that money was no object and we should attempt whatever might help. The young man responded, just two sentences. He could only say one word per breath, and that with great effort. Every sound came in a clicking, wheezing, almost choking expulsion of air. 'Give . . . me . . . breath . . .' he said, and paused. I leaned closer to hear him over the rhythmic pumping of the iron lung. And then, 'What . . . is . . . the . . . use . . . of . . . money . . . if . . . you . . . can't . . . breathe?' I looked at his face with great sadness.

After reassuring him we would do all we could, I stationed a nurse with a throat suction by him and went downstairs for a cup of coffee and bite of breakfast. The anesthetist had not yet arrived and I, having missed a full night of sleep, sought a little nourishment to improve my concentration. I had not finished my coffee when a nurse came with the news that the patient had died. Evidently, he had regurgitated some fluid which obstructed the flow of oxygen. The suction device could not keep up. His breathing stopped, and with it his life.

In English we describe breathing as a succession of two acts: inspiration, expiration . . . inspire, expire. 'I have expired' means I have breathed out, or, in the ultimate sense, I am out of breath and therefore dead. 'I have inspired' means I have breathed in; if changed slightly to 'I am inspired' it could mean I am filled with an enlivening breath from the artistic muses or, in a religious context, filled with the Holy Spirit. The writers of the Bible claim to have been inspired, or in-breathed.

I have mentioned already the tendency of languages – Greek, Hebrew, German, Latin, and English among them – to fall back on words for 'breath' or 'wind' to express the mysterious mode of contact between God and man. Thus in the Bible the Greek or Hebrew word for spirit, even when referring to the Spirit of God, is exactly the same word used for biological breathing or even the wind gusts from a storm.

Linguists love to speculate on double meanings, guessing why the ancients borrowed *that* word to express *this* concept. The relationship between breath and spirit is obvious. Jesus referred to one parallel in His conversation with Nicodemus: 'The wind blows wherever it pleases. You hear its sound, but you cannot tell where it comes from or where it is going. So it is with everyone born of the Spirit' (John 3:8). An invisible force from far away, whether wind or Spirit, has visible manifestations. A person of faith sitting alongside a dying person would likely notice another relationship. As a dying person breathes his or her very last breath and *expires*, life departs. Although the body remains intact, breath and spirit leave hand in hand.

Books have been written exploring each of these conceptual links, but I will limit my discussion to an aspect of breathing I deal with daily. I must stay close to the biological fact of breath that impressed me first as a six-year-old dangling limply from a tree, and then again as a doctor watching my patients' last few expulsions of life. For me, breath represents the fuel that sustains living matter. Any break in the fuel supply means instant death (the fastest poisons, like curare and cyanide, work by interrupting the transport and use of oxygen).

Life depends on an organism's ability to relate to its environment. On the desk before me rests a bowl of nuts: walnuts, pecans, cashews, Brazil nuts. They serve as decoration and provide an occasional snack. Each nut has within it the potential to grow into an organism far larger and more impressive than I, but none will do so unless I place it in the environment of soil and water that will stimulate life. Kernels of corn trapped inside a glass jar in our kitchen will not sprout and yield without a similar process.

Animals depend on oxygen for life, but each animal also needs organs specifically adapted to obtain that oxygen from the right environment, either water or air. The earth offers an atmosphere we can relate to, and if our physical bodies leave earth we must somehow reproduce that atmosphere.

I labour the point somewhat because, analogously, our entire faith begins here. We are told in so many words that eternal life cannot consist of mere oxygen and soil and water and nutrients. For eternal life we need contact with a new environment where oxygen will not suffice. Jesus affirms, 'I tell you the truth, unless a man is born of water and the Spirit, he cannot enter the kingdom of God. Flesh gives birth to flesh, but the *Spirit gives birth to spirit*' (John 3:5–6). In the alien atmosphere of earth, a person's spiritual nature resembles a clumsy astronaut on the moon who must rely on a link to another oxygen source for his very survival. The breathing process of spiritual life will fail unless we establish correspondence with a spirit like the wind, the Holy Spirit.

'Blessed are those who hunger and thirst for righteousness,' said Jesus – a picture comes to my mind of a runner gasping for breath, or an athlete in an iron lung – 'for they will be filled' (Matt. 5:6). An Old Testament psalmist used the image of a deer panting for streams of water; 'So my soul pants for you, O God,' he cried (Ps. 42:1). The Holy Spirit offers the only adequate solution to the 'oxygen debt' hinted at in these phrases.

I must confess a hesitance to write even a paragraph on Spirit, let alone several chapters. I have sympathy for the apocryphal Japanese gentleman cited by Dorothy Sayers who said, 'Honourable Father, very good; Honourable Son, very good; but Honourable Bird I do not understand at all.' Has any doctrine of our faith become more muddled? The word Spirit itself, taken from a metaphor as common as the air outside, remains nebulous and imprecise. It tends to foster extremism of all kinds and a slide toward mystagogy. As one trained in scientific disciplines, I find it much easier to write of the material world that I can touch and see and experiment with. And yet there is no Christian faith without Spirit. Because God is Spirit, only Spirit can convey the image of God in the church, Christ's Body on earth.

He was there in the original act of creation, the Spirit of God hovering over the waters as matter came into existence. He inspired God's spokesmen through the spiritual droughts and famines of Old Testament history. He anointed Jesus at the beginning of His ministry and was transferred to the apostles when Jesus *breathed* on them (John 20:22). The Spirit is essential, said Jesus, for the new birth required of each one who wishes to enter the kingdom of God.

At Pentecost the Holy Spirit ('with a sound like the blowing of a violent *wind*') dramatically invaded and transformed a tiny band that was to become the church. This event more than anything forced the church leaders to formulate the doctrine of the Trinity and include the Spirit as a separate person within the God-head. They could not exclude Him: evidence for Him seemed as real and convincing as evidence for another Person whom they had seen and touched.

The Holy Spirit, then, allows the reality of God Himself to establish a presence inside each one of us. God is timeless, but the Spirit becomes for us the present-tense application of God's nature. He is the personalised God, the Go-Between God, in Bishop John Taylor's wonderful phrase. Correspondence with Him keeps us alive in a spiritual environment.

God does not dwell in a temple or tabernacle, or off in the heavens, or even in a physical body in Nazareth, but rather inside us, as vital to our spiritual lives as breath is to our physical lives. In the Spirit we have the indwelling contact point between heaven and earth across which run connections with the sustainer of the universe.

Unfortunately, the breathing response in the spirit is not so instinctive and urgent as that in the physical body. We can get out of breath and yet not sense it. Breath may choke off slowly, unnoticed at first, until a constant state of energy shortage sets in. I saw the physical parallel to this spiritual process in a patient I treated in London.

She came to me – a middle-aged woman, a widow and a hard worker – complaining about her recently noticed tendency to drop things. 'My hands tremble,' she said, 'and just this week two of my best china cups broke when they slipped out of my fingers.

'I must be getting old,' she said with a deep sigh and a shaky voice. 'I get so tired, and now I can't seem to control my hands or my nervous disposition.' In strong terms I told her that fifty was certainly not old, and that I would do my best to locate physical causes for her condition. As she described a variety of symptoms of nervousness, I began to suspect thyrotoxicosis, a disease of the thyroid gland that can cause such problems.

First I checked manually for a thyroid swelling, but found none. When a chest x-ray showed a shadow behind the upper end of her breast bone, I examined her neck again, this time probing with my fingers down into the base of her neck while she swallowed. Indeed there was an obstruction – I felt a rounded lump rise up out of her chest and touch my fingers. It seemed also that her windpipe may have bent over to one side.

Another x-ray of her upper chest revealed that the rounded shadow had compressed her windpipe, constricting it severely. I asked, 'Don't you have trouble breathing?'

'No, not at all,' she replied to my surprise. 'I just get tired.'

I explained that I believed her problem stemmed from a lump that had grown in an unusual place in her thyroid gland, causing thyrotoxicosis. The lump had extended into her chest, and because of the danger of cancer we needed to remove it. If we did not, I emphasised, she might soon find it difficult to take a breath.

I assisted at the surgery conducted by my chief. We were prepared to saw through bone to open up her upper chest, but after some gentle pulling the lump popped into view. It was fibrous and well-nourished, the size of an orange. It had indeed bent the windpipe, constricting it from both sides. We removed the tumour and closed the wound.

I next saw the woman a few weeks later when she

returned for a checkup. She rushed up to me, and even before I had time to greet her she almost shouted, 'I can breathe!'

I was puzzled. 'Were you afraid the operation would stop your breathing?' I asked.

'No, no, you don't understand,' she said with great excitement. 'Now I can *breathe* for the first time in years and years. I can run up stairs! I feel like a teenager again. I can breathe!'

Her story came out bit by bit. That lump must have been growing slowly for fifteen years or more, gradually compressing her trachea, like a boa constrictor tightening its grip. The woman had adapted even without thinking about it. She had learned to stop and catch her breath frequently. It bothered her at first, but having known old people who became breathless and unable to climb stairs, she assumed she too had an aging heart. She restricted herself to walking very slowly and taking steps one at a time. She had become, in her eyes, prematurely senile. The hand tremors corroborated this image of herself.

Now, however, she could take great gulps of air and run up steps. Over fifteen years she had forgotten how good it felt to breathe deeply and freely. Her breath had all come back, she reported enthusiastically.

Since treating that woman early in my career, I have observed similar reactions among asthma patients recovering from a brief spell of breathlessness or among smokers who have quit the habit and regained their breathing. But I will never forget the near-miraculous change in the posture, facial expression, and total attitude toward life of this woman with the retrosternal thyroid lump. Absolute ecstasy spread across her face as she swelled her chest and announced loudly, 'I can breathe!'

Occasionally I try to savour the pleasure of God's good gifts, like breathing, by imagining for a moment that I have lost them. I hold my breath and pretend my trachea is blocked. I sense the rising panic spreading throughout my body. I envision my red corpuscles turning blue. I hear a drumming in my head. Then suddenly I open my mouth and suck in a gulp of air. I blow out carbon dioxide and vapour and then distend my chest and let the air rush in. I feel a short burst of the relief and ecstasy experienced by the woman with thyrotoxicosis.

The cells of my body need the breath of oxygen to survive. Herbert Spencer expressed the scientific principle: whatever amount of power an organism expends in any form equals the power that was taken into it from without. The same principle holds true in the spiritual world. Christ's Body needs breath, the inspiration of His Spirit. We need the stream of life that comes from God, and only His Spirit can provide that. 'Do not put out the Spirit's fire,' warned the apostle (1 Thess. 5:19).

15   Belonging

We cannot follow the movement of our own eyes in a mirror. We can, by turning our head, observe them in this position and in that position with respect to our body, but never in the act of moving themselves from one position to the other, and never in the act of gazing at anything but the mirror. Thus our idea of ourself is bound to be falsified, since what to others appears the most lively and mobile part of ourself, appears to us unnaturally fixed. The eye is the instrument by which we see everything, and for that reason it is the one thing we cannot see with truth. The same thing is true of our Power of response to a book, or to anything else . . . this is why books about the Holy Ghost are apt to be curiously difficult and unsatisfactory – we cannot really look at the movement of the Spirit, just because It is the Power by which we do the looking.

Dorothy Sayers
The Mind of the Maker

There are few hermits, in humanity or in nature. At the smallest observable levels cooperation prevails, and we could neither breathe nor eat without it. Producing the oxygen we live by requires colonies of bacteria to aid the photosynthesis process, and nutrition relies on similar colonies to help break down all that we ingest.

In the insect world species cooperate to such a degree that even the most prudent observers come away muttering strange phrases such as 'a common mind'. Listen to Lewis Thomas's description of a termite colony at work. 'When three or four termites are collected together in a chamber they wander about aimlessly, but when more termites are added, they begin to build. It is the presence of other termites, in sufficient numbers at close quarters, that produces the work: they pick up each other's faecal pellets and stack them in neat columns, and when the columns are precisely the right height, the termites reach across and turn the perfect arches that form the foundation of the termitarium. No single termite knows how to do any of this, but as soon as there are enough termites gathered together they become flawless architects, sensing their distances from each other although blind, building an immensely complicated structure with its own air-conditioning and humidity control.'

These termite structures, conical rococo castles of red dirt, decorate the deserts of India and Africa. In the towers you would look in vain for a mastermind, an architect with blueprints who semaphores orders with his front legs or antennae. The cooperation occurs at a deeper, more primeval level than simple hierarchy.

Wherever we look, it seems, community is the order of the day. Our earth is not the centre of the universe, but rather a speck of dust in a boundless community of planets, stars, and galaxies, all of which interact with and affect each other. The tiny atom, once thought indivisible, now appears as a universe of its own, with whirring electrons and mesons and quarks and glimmers of reality that last a scant nanosecond.

Living matter ushers in new levels of unpredictability.

The smallest living unit, the cell, comprises a nucleus jammed with chromosomes as well as an Irish stew of various organelles: mitochondria, sacs, tubules, cilia, all squirming around in near-chaotic freedom. And this book concerns a community of such cells, one hundred trillion in all, which must cooperate together to produce a functioning human body. In short, each system of reality yet disclosed – atom, cell, organism, universe – forms a sub-unit in a higher system. We can only understand any of them through a study of group behaviour.

What makes the joint ventures possible? How do the termites or the electrons or the mitochondria communicate? What mysterious force unites the cells in my body so that they all act like Paul Brand (with a few rebellious exceptions)? No question of modern science provokes such a mixed response. Eminent scientists (Agar, Dobzhansky, Thorpe, and Heisenberg) see an 'awareness' in the very primary particles of matter, whereas the sociobiologists don't even admit to freedom in human behaviour. As Sir Arthur Eddington said some years ago, 'We often think that when we have completed our study of *one*, we know all about *two*, because "two" is "one and one". We forget that we have still to make a study of "and".'

The study of the Holy Spirit concerns that 'and'. As Creator He seeks, in Paul's words, to liberate 'from its bondage to decay' a creation that 'has been groaning as in the pains of childbirth right up to the present time' (Rom. 8:21–22). Perhaps the Spirit of God Himself is at work at the molecular level as the dynamic force that reverses decay and holds together the fabric of existence. The Bible hints at such a role, but only briefly. It does, however, comment explicitly on another 'and': the current of communication that runs between God and all cells in His Body. In 2 Corinthians 13:14, one of the few verses to name all members of the Trinity, Paul gives this benediction: 'May the grace of the Lord Jesus Christ, and the love of God, and the fellowship of the Holy Spirit be with you all.' In a neat summary of the essence of the triune God, he does not say 'the power of the Holy Spirit' or 'the wisdom of the Holy Spirit', or 'the purity of the Holy Spirit', but rather 'the fellowship', the communion, the in-betweenness.

In my body some remarkable systems orchestrate the hundred trillion cells, applying the will of the head to the multifarious parts below. Similarly, the Spirit applies the infinite God to His people on earth. We do not commune with the Spirit; rather, He *is* the communion between God and us.

We cannot imagine the invisible. We need a symbol, something thrown across from our world of sight and touch, and the human body provides that symbol. Breath fills in only one aspect of the role of the Spirit. Perhaps the characteristics of a healthy, co-ordinated body described in the next few chapters will take us further into the mystery of a Body controlled by the Spirit of God.

Cells that form the human body share one most basic feature: a near-infallible sense of belonging that links each cell to every other one. All cells in my body know, through their DNA, that they belong to Paul Brand, and the body maintains constant vigilance against intruders. Teams of transplant surgeons go to great lengths to thwart that early warning defence. They bombard transplant sites with x-rays and immuno-suppressant drugs to lull the guards, hoping to sneak in a kidney or heart or skin graft from someone else. They know, painfully, that as soon as the body realises it has been invaded, the foreign cells will be thrown out.

Occasionally children are born without an immune system. You see their photos in the newspaper: they spend their lives in a plastic tent, untouched by humans, breathing purified air. NASA rigged up a bulky spacesuit for one such child, and he tugs behind him a clicking golfcart-size contraption that scrubs the air of impurities. This unfortunate boy's cells lack the sense of belonging. They welcome invaders, even bacteria and viruses that would kill them. (A related problem is spreading fear among adults: the condition known as AIDS, for auto-immune deficiency syndrome).

At its most basic level, the image of the Body of Christ expresses this shared sense of belonging. We members take on His name and identity, and He asks of us the same kind of loyalty and unity that my own body's cells give to me. The Holy Spirit acts as His agent to accomplish that identity transfer. The Spirit lives in those, and only those, who belong to Christ's Body – the New Testament unmistakably assumes that fact (Rom. 8:9; Acts 15:8; 1 John 3:24; 4:13). He provides the fundamental mark of belonging to Christ.

Drawing on a variety of figures of speech, Paul explores how the Spirit applies God Himself to the lives of individual believers. It is the Spirit, he says in Romans 8:15–16 who gives us a sense of sonship so that we approach God not as cringing slaves, but freely, as His children. 'By him we cry, "Abba, Father". The Spirit himself testifies with our spirit that we are God's children.' The Book of Ephesians uses the word 'seal' or 'deposit' to describe the Spirit as a down payment God has given us to guarantee the future redemption to come (1:13; 4:30). Do not undervalue that seal of God's presence, Paul warns, for the power behind it is the very same as that which raised Christ from the dead (1:19–20).

All these varied references to the work of the Spirit assume a unity among the scattered and diverse members of His Body. It is a unity guaranteed by the Spirit's presence, and no artificial labels or doctrinal boundaries can alter the fact. Calls for 'unity in the church' that get bruited about periodically have no meaning unless they begin with the fundamental sense of belonging determined by the Spirit of God. We *are* Christ's Body. Whether we accept the fact or act in a manner in keeping with the new identity is left up to us.

The term 'Spirit' appears sporadically throughout the Old Testament, but Paul's letters make clear that something new occurred with Pentecost. God now establishes His Presence by knitting together the members of His Body by His Spirit. Bishop John Taylor noted this historic change by counting only 126 references to the Spirit from Genesis through Luke, but 196 from that point onward. 'In other words, it is only in the epistles and the gospel of John that the Spirit appears in that fullness in which the Christian church has always known Him. . . . In a disturbing flash of insight the Gospel of John says with reference to the death and resurrection of Jesus: "the Spirit had not yet been given, because Jesus had not yet been glorified", which R. P. C. Hanson suggests might be better rendered: "it was not yet Spirit", as one might say, "it was not yet spring". That is exactly how it must have appeared to anyone looking back from the end of that prodigious first century. There had never been anything like it before, and it had all stemmed from Jesus.'

As the Incarnation gives way to Pentecost, the departure of God in the flesh opens the way for the presence of God in Spirit to live inside many bodies. 'It is for your good that I am going away. Unless I go away the Counsellor will not come to you,' Jesus said. The Holy Spirit brings with Him that quality of communion or inbetweenness that defines Christ's Body as decisively as DNA defines my own body by imprinting itself in each of my many cells.

In the human body, the sense of belonging extends two ways: every cell attunes to orders from one brain, and every cell recognises an inherent bond with every other cell in that body. So too, in Christ's Body, the Spirit establishes a connection not only between each cell and the Head but also among all the cells of His body. The very word 'church' in Greek means *called-out ones* and from His initial choice God calls us into a community. The Spirit does not approach me in the solitude of my own soul, for that would leave me alone and unreconciled to my neighbour. Rather, He calls me to join a Body that binds me in love with a community of diverse cells. Each individual cell awakens to the conscious reality of the larger whole.

In human society, we approach such unity only rarely.

Families achieve it sometimes – it is the tug of loyalty that binds me to my children scattered around the world. In a crisis, a town or even an entire nation may join together spiritedly in common cause.

Jesus prayed for an even richer experience of unity in His Body. He asked 'that they all of them may be one, Father, just as you are in me and I am in you. May they also be in us so that the world may believe that you have sent me' (John 17:21). Do we catch a glimmer of the wonder of that unity in the church, a unity based not on social class or interest group or kinship or race, but on common belonging in Jesus Christ? I have seen it, rarely, in small outposts of His Body. Those few scenes give me a lasting vision of the image of God at work in the world. I will mention only one example.

John Karmegan came to me in Vellore, India, as a leprosy patient in an advanced state of the disease. We could do little for him surgically since his feet and hands had already been damaged irreparably. We could, however, offer him a place to stay and employment in the New Life Centre.

Because of one-sided facial paralysis, John could not smile normally. When he tried, the uneven distortion of his features would draw attention to his paralysis. People often responded with a gasp or a gesture of fear, and so he learned not to smile. Margaret, my wife, had stitched his eyelids partly closed to protect his sight. John grew more and more paranoid about what others thought of him.

He caused terrible problems socially, perhaps in reaction to his marred appearance. He expressed his anger at the world by acting the part of a troublemaker, and I remember many tense scenes in which we had to confront John with some evidence of stealing or dishonesty. He treated fellow-patients cruelly, and resisted all authority, going so far as to organise hunger strikes against us. By almost anyone's reckoning, he was beyond rehabilitation.

Perhaps John's very irredeemability attracted my mother to him, for she often latched onto the least desirable specimens of humanity. She took to John, spent time with him, and eventually led him into the Christian faith. He was

baptised in a cement tank on the grounds of the leprosarium.

Conversion, however, did not temper John's high
dudgeon against the world. He gained some friends among
fellow-patients, but a lifetime of rejection and mistreat-
ment had permanently embittered him against all non-
patients. One day, almost defiantly, he asked me what
would happen if he visited the local Tamil church in
Vellore.

I went to the leaders of the church, described John, and
assured them that despite obvious deformities, he had
entered a safe phase of the arrested disease and would not
endanger the congregation. They agreed he could visit.
'Can he take communion?' I asked, knowing that the
church used a common cup. They looked at each other,
thought for a moment, and agreed he could also take
communion.

Shortly thereafter I took John to the church, which met
in a plain, whitewashed brick building with a corrugated
iron roof. It was a tense moment for him. Those of us on the
outside can hardly imagine the trauma and paranoia inside
a leprosy patient who attempts for the first time to enter
that kind of setting. I stood with him at the back of the
church. His paralysed face showed no reaction, but a
trembling gave away his inner turmoil. I prayed silently
that no church member would show the slightest hint of
rejection.

As we entered during the singing of the first hymn, an
Indian man toward the back half-turned and saw us. We
must have made an odd couple: a white person standing
next to a leprosy patient with patches of his skin in garish
disarray. I held my breath.

And then it happened. The man put down his hymnal,
smiled broadly, and patted the chair next to him, inviting
John to join him. John could not have been more startled.
Haltingly, he made shuffling half-steps to the row and took
his seat. I breathed a prayer of thanks.

That one incident proved to be the turning point of
John's life. Years later I visited Vellore and made a side trip

to a factory that had been set up to employ disabled people. The manager wanted to show me a machine that produced tiny screws for typewriter parts. As we walked through the noisy plant, he shouted at me that he would introduce me to his prize employee, a man who had just won the parent corporation's all-India prize for the highest quality work with fewest rejects. As we arrived at his work station, the employee turned to greet us, and I saw the unmistakable crooked face of John Karmegan. He wiped the grease off his stumpy hand and grinned with the ugliest, the loveliest, most radiant smile I had ever seen. He held out for my inspection a palmful of the small precision screws that had won him the prize.

A simple gesture of acceptance may not seem like much, but for John Karmegan it proved decisive. After a lifetime of being judged on his own physical image, he had finally been welcomed on the basis of another Image. I had seen a replay of Christ's own reconciliation. His Spirit had prompted the Body on earth to adopt a new member, and at last John knew he belonged.

16   Go-Between

If a man carry treasure in bullion, or in a wedge of gold, and have none coined into current money, his treasure will not defray him as he travels. Tribulation is treasure in the nature of it, but it is not current money in the use of it, except we get nearer and nearer our home, heaven, by it. Another man may be sick too, and sick to death, and this affliction may lie in his bowels, as gold in a mine, and be of no use to him; but this bell, that tells me of his affliction, digs out and applies that gold to me, if by this consideration of another's danger I take mine own into contemplation, and so secure myself, by making my recourse to my God, who is our only security.

John Donne
Devotions

It is a familiar route, Interstate 10 linking New Orleans and Baton Rouge. I have just flown in from another city and reclaimed my car at the airport. I concentrate more intently than usual because a heavy downpour has spread a sheet of water across the macadam, and the headlights and line markers tend to play tricks on the eyes. Without warning, a small dark shape scurries out onto the road – probably an armadillo or opossum. But before I can even think that thought, my foot has instinctively tapped the brake pedal.

I can feel the sickening, out-of-control sensation of a skid coming on as the rear of the car planes off to the right. My hands grip the steering wheel more tightly. In response to a few quick jerks of my wrist, the car fishtails and finally straightens out. Once I have steering back under control, I breathe deeply and slow down until my anxiety subsides.

The entire incident has lasted maybe three seconds. When I arrive home, I will recount to my wife what happened: an animal crossed a rain-covered highway and I arrested a dangerous skid just in time. Those are the external events, simple and matter-of-fact. But the rest of the way home, still keyed up from the adrenaline pumping through my body, I think back on a few of the internal events.

It all started in the brain. When the sight of the animal reached my visual cortex, a trained reflex response directed my foot onto the brake pedal. After that, my hypothalmus ordered up chemicals to launch with lightning speed a series of reactions designed to put me in prime condition to cope with the alarm.

Few parts of my body went untouched by the crisis. First, my vision intensified as my pupils dilated. All my muscles went on alert. Stress hormones affected my entire circulatory system. My heart beat faster, contracting more forcefully, and even in the extremities vascular muscles relaxed in order to allow blood vessels to widen and carry a greater blood flow. Blood components themselves changed: more blood sugars surged in, providing emergency reserves for working muscles, and clotting materials multiplied in preparation for wound repair. Bronchial tubes flared open to allow faster oxygenation of the blood.

On my largest organ, the skin, blood vessels contracted, bringing on a pale complexion ('white as a ghost') but lowering the danger of surface bleeding in case of injury. A reduced volume of circulation in skin also freed up more blood for the muscles' urgent need. The electrical resistance of skin changed as a protective mechanism against potential bacterial invaders. 'Goose-pimples' bulged up all over my body, holding erect millions of hair shafts. Sweat glands poured out assistance to increase the traction of my palms on the steering wheel.

Meanwhile, nonessential functions slowed down. Digestion nearly came to a halt – blood assigned to that and to kidney filtration was redeployed for more urgent needs.

In an external sense, not much happened. I avoided the animal, corrected the skid, and drove on with a racing heart, dilated pupils, and a slight tremor in my muscles. Yet inside my body a full-scale battle was fought and won to equip me for the classic alternatives of 'fight or flight'. A single unifying chemical messenger, adrenaline, managed to coordinate an entire galaxy of select cells.

We experience the effects of adrenaline every day: we are startled by a loud noise, we hear a bit of shocking news, we drive through a dangerous neighbourhood, we stumble and nearly fall. Adrenal reactions occur so smoothly and synchronously that we rarely, if ever, stop to reflect on all the elements involved. And yet adrenaline is just one of many hormones at work in my body coaxing a cooperative response from diverse cells.

The incident on the highway offers a clear illustration of two types of communication that unite the body. My first response, applying my foot to the brake, resulted from a direct command of the nervous system. Long ago, when I first learned to drive, my brain sorted out the sequence of nerve firings required for me to lift my foot and slide it to the left, and to turn the steering wheel with short, jerky motions. Unlike a novice, I did not have to think, 'Where's the brake pedal?' In a moment of stress, my brain relied on a memory bank of programmed responses and sent high speed orders along nerve pathways. The orders were, so to speak, 'foot-specific' and 'wrist-specific'.

However, the other complex reactions – the heart rate, skin changes, respiratory adjustments – occurred because of the hormonal system. My brain initiated an order to a gland, in this case the adrenal, to secrete a chemical messenger into the bloodstream. The hormone does not deliver a message as immediate, precise, and definite as the nerve's, but in a few seconds it can reach every cell in my body.

Fear, relief, heightened awareness – I felt all these sensations, and for the next twenty miles they made me a much better driver. All my muscles, not just my foot and wrists, were poised for action. I saw better and concentrated more on the hazardous driving conditions.

These two types of communication, the nervous and hormonal systems, have a parallel in the spiritual Body also. At times we may have a direct 'hotline' from the Head, a clear directive for a specific action. In my experience, those times occur infrequently. More commonly, I sense a certain prompting to respond, a heightened awareness, or a pang of conscience about some command of Christ's I have failed to follow.

Christian literature has devoted much attention recently to the 'gifts of the Spirit'. Could such gifts follow alternate types of communication systems within the Body? Some are chosen to be pastors and teachers and prophets and administrators. By ability and by calling, these represent a sort of central nervous system, a direct line of communication from the Head. We cells rely on them to teach and interpret and to direct us in our various functions within the Body.

But in addition the Spirit moves as a go-between force among all cells, gently bringing to mind the will of the Head and thus permeating and mobilising the entire Body.

Until recently anatomists believed that glands such as the adrenal and pituitary sent out their hormonal instructions independently. New discoveries point to reliance on the brain at virtually every point. Instructions on growth, on deployment of resources, on how to meet a crisis all originate in the head, which senses the needs of the entire body. The glands and enzymes and prostaglandins act as agents for the will of the head, carrying the message to each independent cell. And so in the spiritual Body, 'We will in all things grow up into him who is the Head, that is, Christ. From him the whole body, joined and held together by every supporting ligament, grows and builds itself up in love, as each part does its work' (Eph. 4:15–16).

Besides the communication from the head through nerves and hormones, a third system of communication operates in the body. To me it is the most impressive of all. It determines the needs of individual cells and informs the rest of the body. In my adrenaline response to the skidding car, messages went from my head to cells, quickly arousing each cell in my body. Intracellular communication reverses the flow: an alarm sounding in individual cells works its way to neighbouring cells and outward until finally the message reaches the brain itself.

Medicine has coined a wonderful word to describe the state that results from such cooperative behaviour: homeostasis. A noble physician and fine writer, Dr Walter Cannon, introduced the term in his classic study *The Wisdom of the body*. He viewed the body as a community that consciously seeks out the most favourable conditions for itself. It corrects imbalances in fluids and salts, mobilises to heal itself, and deploys resources on demand, all in order to maintain a dependable *milieu interieur*, as the French like to say.

Even the most common acts rely on elaborate confederacies. Already I have referred to the monitors that measure oxygen intake and regulate breathing. Oxygen requirements also trigger changes in the heart rate, and the chain of cells serving as the pacemaker of my heart is far better attuned to the needs of the body than any electronic wizardry inserted to replace it. The natural pacemaker listens to instructions from the vagus nerve, factors in readings of oxygen requirements, and also takes note of any special conditions that might call for increased heart-beat as indicated by the presence of adrenaline. (Walter Cannon found in a series of experiments that the pacemaker of a cat could detect the presence of 1 part of adrenaline in 1,400,000,000 parts of blood. A quantity that minute would make the cat's heart beat faster.)

You can see evidence of homeostatis on vivid display in modern hospitals where constant digital readouts report a patient's pulse and other vital functions. I visit a woman patient who suffers from high blood pressure. When I enter the room, the red numerals glow a steady 82, her resting pulse. She notices my presence and greets me; the flurry of emotional responses shoots her pulse up to 91. She reaches over to shake my hand; and the rate surges past 100. During my thirty-minute visit, the numbers rise and fall in concert with her moods and actions. A sneeze causes the most violent reaction of all, a pulse of 110. That kind of ceaseless monitoring and adjustment goes on in all our bodies each moment in order to keep oxygen supplies in balance.

Similarly, cells communicate other needs. From the viewpoint of the body, taste and appetite are mere techniques to compel us to provide nourishment. Inside our bodies, sophisticated chemical sensors measure which minerals and salts are lacking and, in an utterly mystifying way, communicate a desire for them to our appetite. A mountain goat travels five miles to lick a block of salt; a pregnant woman feels strange cravings for the taste of certain foods that just happen to contain the specific vitamins and minerals she needs.

The body's relentless search for homeostasis never stops. The delicate kidneys increase or decrease the level of fluid that goes out based on the body's need for reserves. They may halt the excretion of sodium while unloading a surfeit of potassium. If the person has exerted himself or herself to an unusual degree, kidneys may stop excretion altogether to prevent dehydration. Thus a marathon runner may not urinate for twenty-four hours after a race.

Sweat. I could write an entire chapter on that remarkable aspect of homeostasis. What a lizard wouldn't give for warm blood and sweat glands! In the morning that reptile must somehow wriggle over to the sunlight and warm up before it can start climbing trees and catching flies. If the lizard overheats, it frantically scuttles towards shade. In humans, however, an efficient cooling system uses sweat to cool our bodies to a constant internal temperature so that sensitive organs can maintain a *milieu interieur*. (Muscle contractions, or shivering, correspondingly warm the body). Were it not so, we could hardly function in a climate where temperatures exceed 80° F.

Japanese physiologist Yas Kuno spent thirty years studying sweat, and in 1956 published the authoritative 416-page book *Human Perspiration*. He found human nervous and hormonal systems to be so sensitive that a change of one-twentieth of a degree Celsius may trigger the mechanisms that heat or cool the body. Humans have the finest cooling system of all mammals; most animals will run fevers on a hot day. (Animals compensate variously. A dog or tiger pants, creating its own internal fan. An elephant finds a refreshing-looking waterhole and wades in for a hose-down.)

Over a hundred years ago a meticulous German counted 2,381,248 sweat glands on a human body – he needn't have bothered, since the total varies from person to person. Regardless, we all have enough to get the job done. A marathon runner may shed three to five quarts of fluid in a three-hour race, but inside his temperature will hardly waver.

All these operations – heartrate, fluid control, perspiration – adapt every second as the body seeks the very best environment for its vital functions.* We are barely beginning to understand how cells communicate with each other. Two Swedes and an Englishman earned the 1982 Nobel Prize in Medicine for discovering some of the substances that control these homeostatic activities. They identified substances called prostaglandins (so named because the first was erroneously traced to the prostate gland), and now more than a dozen prostaglandins have been isolated. One lowers blood pressure, while another raises it. One widens bronchial tubes, a second constricts them. One initiates inflammation; another inhibits it. Prostaglandins aid in such processes as clotting, regulating gastric acid, and controlling uterine contractions. These messenger fluids travel constantly from cell to cell, visiting nearly every tissue of the body, linking isolated cells and organs into units of a coordinated response.

This type of cell-to-cell communication has a parallel in Christ's Body on earth. Here, too, the Spirit serves as the Go-Between God who unites each of the members of that Body to each other and to God. It is He who expresses the needs of the Body to the Head and who brings a sense of commonality to individual members.

In several places the New Testament refers to the Spirit's role in conveying and even formulating words of intercession to God. 'The Spirit helps us in our weakness,' says Paul. 'We do not know what we ought to pray, but the Spirit himself intercedes for us with groans that words cannot express' (Rom 8:26). In a play on words that must

---

* Occasionally, something more violent is needed to maintain homeostasis. When an intruder gets in, something irritating or toxic, the body calls on spectacular forces of expulsion. A sneeze produces hurricane-force winds in the nasal passages and sends the heartrate soaring. Coughing or vomiting solicits the combined forces of scores of muscles in the chest cavity and diaphragm, with such vigour it can leave us sore. When homeostasis is threatened, the body does not take chances. Without our conscious cooperation, whether during a pianissimo concert or on a business flight, it protects at all costs.

have been intentional, Paul uses that word 'groan' two other places in the same chapter: once to express the pains of a fallen creation that groans, 'as in the pain of childbirth', for restoration, and again to express the Christian's longing for a fully redeemed body. The Spirit senses those inexpressible, primeval groans of fallenness, separation, and incompleteness and presents them to God on our behalf. 'And he who searches out hearts knows the mind of the Spirit, because the Spirit intercedes for the saints in accordance with God's will' (8:27).

Because we are a Body, it is only natural that God rely on other 'cells' to meet individual needs. A local area in my physical body responds quickly to a call for help; in Christ's Body the Spirit achieves homeostasis by calling on neighbouring parts. The Spirit awakens us to human need in our neighbours and prompts us to shift resources from a section of plenty to a section of want.

Charles Williams uses the phrase 'co-inherence' to describe the mystical way in which all of us cells join together in that Body. Co-inherence sounds ethereal, but in reality the responsive actions can take on such mundane forms as sharing food, sitting with a grieving person, or cleaning a bedpan. A short time after the exuberance in the Spirit at Pentecost, the early church found itself needing guidance on the practical matters of poverty and the distribution of relief supplies.

The word 'another' signifies a kind of cell-to-cell cooperation, and we cannot escape the word in the New Testament. It appears as a relentless leitmotif. 'Accept one another', we are told. 'Serve one another' by 'washing one another's feet'. We are to confess our sins to one another, pray for one another, forgive one another, teach and admonish one another, comfort one another, bear one another's burdens. And, of course, Jesus left us the most inclusive command of all: 'Love one another as I have loved you.' Our obedient response and our openness to one another are the points of contact where the Spirit of God works in us. That intracellular communication is the very sign of His presence. Christ is forming His Body in the world. His Presence, through a Spirit that draws all of us together.

As a surgeon, I have opportunity each day to see cells serving one another in perhaps the body's most beautiful display of working toward homeostasis: healing. In the human body, cells cry out to their neighbours when injured – the chemistry of the wound attracts healing cells – and the body responds on a local level. The process does not depend on instructions from the head, but goes on even if the head has not been informed. My leprosy patients prove that: if one cuts a finger, healing will start even if there is no pain system to inform the head. Healing seems a part of the DNA programme built into each cell and takes place at the cell-to-cell level.

Elsewhere (in *Fearfully and Wonderfully Made*) I have described the thrilling experience of sitting at a microscope and watching what happens at an injury site. Fibroblasts weave their delicate clotting web, white cells rush in to battle infection, blood vessels magically self-repair, inflammation sets in to assist the whole process.

In my medical career I have never felt more helpless and despairing than at one time in India when I treated a patient who lacked the basic mechanism of healing. A young missionary couple brought in their infant daughter who had been vomiting and showing signs of a blocked intestine. I operated immediately, removing the section of impacted and gangrenous bowel. It was a routine surgery and baby Anne came through well. The parents left delighted and grateful, taking Anne home for post-operative care.

A few days later, the couple returned with their daughter. The mother had noticed the dressings were wet. As I unwrapped the bandages, I could detect the unmistakable odour of intestinal fluid, and indeed I could see it seeping out of the wound. Feeling embarrassed, I took the baby back to the operating room and reopened the incision. Strangely, as I cut through the surface stitches, the wound fell loosely apart. It showed no sign of healing. Similarly, inside the abdominal cavity I found the intestine leaking and unhealed. It did not look diseased or infected, just porous. This time I cut away the edges and made a most meticulous closure using many very fine stitches.

A series of operations followed. It soon became clear that the little girl lacked the unifying healing processes that coordinate various cells. Her body failed at achieving homeostasis in its most crucial form. Sewing her intestine was like sewing a rubber balloon: it would always leak, because nothing summoned new living cells to seal up the puncture marks. Repairs lasted a few days, until the stitches ripped through the tissue.

We prayed over Anne's tiny body. I did research on her condition. We gave her nourishment and blood transfusions through her veins, and I even tried wrapping the intestinal junction with the filmy omentum that the body used to heal accidental wounds. But nothing ever healed. The skin flaps refused to adhere, the muscles gaped apart, and intestinal juices sooner or later trickled out between the stitches.

Little Anne would lie there with a sweet and trusting smile as we surveyed the damage, and her face would tear at my heart. She grew thinner and thinner. I don't think Anne experienced much pain; she just quietly faded away.

When her tiny, wasted body was wrapped for burial, I cried in grief and helplessness. Even now as I write these words the little smile in her wrinkled face comes back with a stab of pain.

Anne's body lacked the go-between, the mechanism that responds to a wound by healing it. She had plenty of fibroblasts and new cells – her body was using them for growth all over, weaving fibre for tendons and tissue. Nothing, however, informed them that her body was wounded and that they must rush to the site of injury. No alarms went off alerting one part of the body to another's need.

Fortunately, in medicine we encounter very few patients like Anne; otherwise our entire profession would disappear. Physicians and nurses do not heal; we merely coax the body to heal itself. Without its help, our own efforts prove futile.

The same is true in the spiritual Body composed of diverse members representing different races and statuses and income levels and intelligences and cultures. When we allow the Spirit of God to move in, hovering in-between the differences and disproportions and varied hurts and needs, He can direct the process needed for healing and for growth. Sometimes orders come directly through the central nervous system, sometimes indirectly through hormones, and sometimes through simple cell-to-cell contact. But without that Spirit, regardless of all our methodology, institutions, or techniques, we will all be as helpless as poor Anne.

17 Listening

To insure the greatest efficiency in the
dart, the harpooners of this world must
start to their feet out of idleness and not
out of toil.

Herman Melville
Moby Dick

We doused the burning bush and cannot
rekindle it; we are lighting matches in
vain under every green tree. Did the
wind use to cry, and the hills shout forth
praise? Now speech has perished from
among the lifeless things of earth, and
living things say very little to very few.
Birds may crank out sweet gibberish
and monkeys howl; horses neigh and
pigs say, as you recall, oink oink. But so
do cobbles rumble when a wave recedes,
and thunders break the air in lightning
storms. I call these noises silence. It
could be that wherever there is motion
there is noise, as when a whale breaches
and smacks the water – and wherever
there is stillness there is the still small
voice, God's speaking from the whirl-
wind, nature's old song and dance, the
show we drove from town.

Annie Dillard
Teaching a Stone to Talk

One-half the human population comes equipped with the potential for a major internal upheaval. If the event happens, it will absorb the body's full attention for a long time, usually nine months. I speak, of course, of pregnancy.

Each month certain cells in a woman routinely conspire in a cycle of activity intended to anticipate pregnancy. They strip away the old lining of the uterus if no conception occurs and reline it for the next month. Then one day a fertilised egg settles on the receptive cells of a freshly lined uterus and new life begins. Everything changes.

At first local fluids nourish the fertilised egg, but very quickly the lining cells recognise they have at last encountered what they have been created for. A most remarkable organ, belonging neither to the mother nor the child, begins to develop: the placenta. People who see the placenta only after it has completed its function and been expelled dismiss it with the ignominious name 'afterbirth'. In reality it is one of the most active and discriminating organs in nature. It forges a supreme bond of symbiotic intimacy.

Burrowing deep into the tissues of the mother, the placenta interlaces a web of vessels through membranes so fine that all the chemicals in the mother's blood can diffuse into the child's, and all the wastes from the child can be eliminated through the mother. Yet no open passage joins one to the other, no cells cross the membrane, and the mother remains wholly mother and the child wholly child. (Often, their respective blood types differ, so that any blending of blood might prove fatal.)

The placenta is an organ full of mysteries. It develops soon after fertilisation, and from the mother's immunological standpoint its tissue is foreign matter – yet her body welcomes it for nine months. Furthermore, its nucleate cells fuse together to form what is in effect a single cell, the largest single cell in all of nature.

In addition to nourishing the foetus, the placenta plays a major role in directing the intricate proceedings of pregnancy. From it, as well as from the ovary and the brain, come hormones to organise and induce each stage of response. Very little distinguishes these messengers from a host of similar hormones that maunder through the bloodstream, and only an expert chemist can differentiate them. Even when the chemical formulas are written out, one must look carefully to notice the placement of a few atoms that distinguish, for example, between the hormone that makes a male from that which makes a female.

Chemists may have problems discriminating, but not the cells themselves. Chemicals that previously have never provoked more than a mild reaction suddenly, after conception, foment revolution. Cells seem to listen to hormonal messages with a new alertness and receptivity. The hormone progesterone, for example, visits the uterus regularly in small concentrations, sometimes irritating the lining and indirectly causing the noxious reaction of menstrual cramps. But after the onset of pregnancy, it and estrogen launch a series of ventures that galvanise millions of cells in remote sites.

Inside the uterus, those hormones prompt uterine cells to begin a massive fortifications project, thickening the walls of that organ to prepare for the child it will soon shelter and protect. Cells pile on top of cells, layering, stretching, dividing, crowding each other. Eventually the uterine wall grows to one hundred times its resting size.

The mother's blood likewise increases in volume, by as much as 50 percent during pregnancy. The surplus safeguards against potential heavy loss during delivery itself. Blood also automatically adjusts its clotting properties to prepare for probable vessel breakage. Thus, although the same hormone contacts many kinds of cells, each group interprets the specific message very differently.

These same hormones excite a contrary response in certain joints and ligaments. As the chemical messengers wash through pelvic joints, they leave their imprint on fibroblasts and osteoblasts and osteoclasts, the building blocks of cartilage and bone. Rather than increasing in quantity or strenghthening, these cells begin to reverse their normal construction procedures and slacken up. Fibroblasts, which lay down cells to make ligaments joining bone to bone, lengthen their fibres. Ligaments that have always kept the skeleton taut and stable and strong now defy their heritage. They must: the pelvic bones need to stretch apart enough for a baby's head to pass through. The loosening of connective tissue brings on backaches and a waddling gate that Shakespeare called 'the proud walk of pregnancy'.

Fortunately, not all ligament cells follow these orders. Fibroblasts in other joints, while receiving the same chemical message, recognise that it does not apply to them, and thus pregnant women are spared the problem of a wobbly head, loose knees, and elbows that dislocate easily.

Skin also expands to accommodate enlarging breasts and abdomen (a fact that causes some women consternation if their bodies later retain the stretch marks). Similarly, smooth muscle cells throughout the body slacken, and the pregnant woman notices lessened precision in her urination and digestion. As the smooth muscles relax and the body devotes fewer resources to the production of digestive enzymes like pepsin, nausea may result. More and more, the woman's body reorders its priorities toward creating a new life, not just preserving a familiar one.

Finally, in the fullness of time, the woman's body prepares for parturition. A complex interaction of enzymes and hormones between mother and child convinces the mother's body that the foetus is ready. For months uterine muscles have been gently contracting in waves, practising for the extreme act they were engineered to perform but, in the case of a first birth, have never accomplished.

During birth, everything speeds up violently. Hormones direct a frenzy of sudden contractions and relaxations as dramatic as anything the body will ever know.

A child is born. Even so, those same hormones keep flooding the body, in many cases causing the opposite reactions from those in effect just minutes before. The uterus no longer enlarges, but pulls in. (It is the only organ programmed to grow and then shrink.) Blood vessels torn from the placenta seal up. The placenta itself, masterful orchestrator of much of this activity, exits anticlimactically shortly thereafter and is discarded without a whisper of thanks. The umbilical cord stops pulsing and begins to shrivel. New priorities take over: healing, restoration, and a new bonding between two separate individuals.

The drama of independent life is underway. Air rushes into lungs previously unused but in perfect working order. The entire congregation of bronchial passageways, diaphragm muscles, and all the other components of breathing must simultaneously coordinate. Oxygen filters into blood cells through the lungs now, not through the placenta.

Even the infant's heart must make renovations. Before birth, only one-third of the foetus's blood – the amount needed to nourish developing lung tissue – travelled to the lungs. A separate artery, the *ductus arteriosus*, channelled off two-thirds of the volume into the aortic arch for direct passage to the rest of the body. But from the moment of birth all the blood must pass through the lungs for oxygenation. To accomplish this change, an amazing event occurs. In response to a chemical signal, a flap suddenly descends like a curtain, deflecting the blood flow, and a muscle constricts the *ductus arteriosus*. That muscle had developed, like all other muscles, through an elaborate process of cell division and growth in the embryo. But it is needed only for this solitary act. Once the extra channel is shut off, the heart permanently seals it and the body gradually absorbs the *ductus arteriosus*.

The foetus is now a baby, free and independent but still incapable of supporting its own life. Happily, the woman's body has been readying itself for just this situation since about age eleven. Younger boys and girls have nearly identical cells on the upper parts of their trunk, including similar nipples. Beneath the skin, specific cells related to fat and milk-production rest in a primitive and sedentary state. But at puberty, a certain hormone present only in females begins to secrete at a gentle level. Ninety percent of the body's cells ignore the chemical; breast cells, among others, listen. They irrupt spectacularly and shape the perfect symmetry of a mature breast. Once a certain size is reached, they simply stop mutiplying. For more years, they wait, quiescent. Breast cells grow old, die, and are replaced each year, without ever making the milk they were designed to produce.

During pregnancy progesterone and estrogen, the same hormones that loosen ligaments and firm up uterine walls and indirectly cause nausea, visit the breasts. Cells that have lived in the relaxed contentment of reserve duty receive a summons to active service. Other hormones have floated past these breast cells each day for years, with no effect. They are screened in an indifferent, mildly curious way, much as one might scan a neighbour's mail. But today, the message applies to the tranquil breast cell.

It would be wrong to call what follows pandemonium, because the activity proceeds in a spirit of orderliness. But in nine months a complete factory must take shape, constructed on the foundations laid during puberty. First, each summoned cell gains reinforcements by breeding. It divides and divides again until finally enough cells exist to arrange themselves into a tube. Then the tube begins to ramify and these buds and branches burrow into the surrounding fat of the breast tissue.

Neighbouring fat cells read a different interpretation into the identical hormone message. For them the message says, 'Prepare to decrease. You must give up your fat and your space to make room for new ducts and milk factory cells. Release your substance to be recycled.' Paradoxically, these same hormones also inhibit the production of milk until the proper time.

At the same signal, blood vessels in the breast elongate, skin grows to accommodate a larger shape, and pectoral muscles strengthen to support the new weight. Far away, the cells responsible for appetite and taste respond to the same message by concocting strange and unfamiliar cravings and some revulsions that the body may not understand, but will do well to obey.

After several months new hormones from the departing placenta travel to the breast and circulate among the host of cells that now congregate in the place previously occupied by a lone duct cell. These hormones announce that the time has arrived, and the new factory churns into motion. Cells that line the ducts open up their cell walls to allow secretions to ooze out into the hollow of the tubes. The tubes themselves, having never carried anything before, may clog with material too viscous to flow easily. If so, the mother will feel a soreness that tells her of the distension, and her nurse or perhaps her mother may show her how to milk it out a little.

Into this crisis comes the new living creature. The baby has no experience – it has never been a baby before. It has never seen a breast and may, in fact, have never opened its eyes. But a baby knows what to do upon contact with a woman's breast.

An observing engineer, knowing that fluid flows from an area of high pressure to an area of low pressure, might marvel at the mechanics of suction employed. The baby creates low pressure in the pharynx by closing its mouth over an area of compliant skin and then contracting its superior pharyngeal muscles, while not forgetting to close off the glottis so as to maintain the low pressure vacuum and also avoid drowning in the fluid. A nutritionist would surely marvel at the remarkable broth of vitamins, nutrients, anti-bodies, and macrophages that comprise mother's milk. The baby thinks of none of these, but he knows when and how to suck.

In a beautiful symbiotic feature of nursing, now the mother needs the baby just as the baby needs the mother. The blocked duct and engorged tubes of the breast have no easy alternative to rid themselves of congestion and pain. The breast is designed to serve the baby. The placenta's final messages before expulsion, a sucking force, and even the baby's cry all combine to stimulate the flow of milk.

One can hardly avoid words like 'miracle' when speaking of childbirth. Yet the phenomenon occurs so commonly that four billion proofs of its effectiveness exist on this planet today. Relatively few messengers direct the process, and they elicit utterly different responses from cells in the breast, pelvis, uterus, and blood. Today, in the body of every young woman, millions of cells lie in wait, carefully perusing the molecular structure of every chemical that happens by, searching for the precise signal that will prompt them into action.

As impressive as pregnancy is, the real miracle of cooperation unfolds within the growing infant, whose hormones regulate the development of one hundred trillion cells. What handicaps would result if the kneecap grew 10 percent faster than the tendons, ligaments, and muscles surrounding it, or if the right leg grew slightly longer than the left? (Sometimes, as a result of a genetic defect, one of the two parallel bones in an arm may grow faster than its partner, contorting the angle of the wrist into an odd and almost useless position.) Some body parts double in size, some triple, and some enlarge to hundreds of times their original length. Yet with few exceptions each body part grows in proportion to supporting structures and is well-supplied with blood at each stage of growth. The entire body works together.

I like to imagine myself as one cell in such a body, for analogously that is the position of every Christian in the Body of Christ. I must admit, I sometimes chafe at being one cell. I might prefer being a whole body, or another kind of cell with a more significant role in His Body. But gradually I have learned to view myself as a very minor part of a great enterprise that will only work if directed by the Spirit of God, not by me or any other conjunction of human leaders.

In that Body, I come in contact with diverse messages, similar to the chemical messengers that course through my physical body. Some of them come mediated through human agents: spiritual leaders, my loved ones, the community of faith around me. Some come directly through God's Word in the Bible. Still others, though few, come through the direct contact every cell has with the Head. The messages arrive in code, and I must examine them to determine how they relate to me. They may seem confusing or even contradictory at first. What is my role in such a Body? How do I discern the time for action? Is this specific message for me or someone else?

In the Body of Christ, the Holy Spirit performs the function of prompter. He must coordinate all its members to assure that the work of God continues according to His will. A sensitive member of the Body will hear many stirring calls to action. Some will describe the desperate needs, physical and spiritual, of people in other lands. Some will point to neighbours close by. Others will give emphasis to the contemplative life, or to reform of the justice system, or to the need for high personal ethics. All these calls have merit, are supported by Scripture, and apply in some degree to each of us. But the Holy Spirit will instruct us in our *specific* response, and it is to Him we must listen.

My own response has included spending time in another culture, India, where physical needs are great. Every sensitive Christian should feel stirred by the human and spiritual needs of such countries. We should all respond, but the form of our response will vary. Praying, writing letters to missionaries, lobbying for humanitarian aid, taking a short-term assignment, supporting Christian work financially – all of these constitute appropriate responses, as diverse as the responses of my body's cells to a hormone, but equally valid if the Spirit has given clear instructions.

One chemical messenger instructs uterine cells to contract but cervical cells to relax during childbirth. Likewise, even messages from the Bible may seem at first to contradict. If you read the book of Galatians and then I Corinthians consecutively, you may question whether the same author could have written both. But Paul wisely knew that parts of the Body need different messages at different times. The legalistic Galatians needed the fresh, cool breeze of God's gracious acceptance, whereas the pagan, lawless Corinthians needed a prod towards obedience and righteousness.

I have learned that the first and perhaps most essential

requirement of a loyal cell is learning to listen to the code. I must wait, scrutinise the messages, tune in. The Spirit will employ various means to speak to me and instruct me in the way I should go, but only if I hear his voice.

I can hardly think of a more difficult task than listening for the voice of God. We want to leap into action, to exercise our faith in dramatic ways. Regardless of our motives, unless such actions are prompted by the Spirit, they will not help the growth of the Body, just as a kneecap spurting in growth disproportionately may demonstrate its own strength but will handicap the rest of the body.

Think back to the resurrection of Jesus Christ. In that event, all of history converged. It was, in Tolkien's phrase, a 'eucatastrophe', an event of unimaginable goodness. The disciples and followers of Jesus could hardly contain themselves with the news that their faith in the Messiah had proved right despite the ugly fact of His crucifixion. Yet even in light of that eucatastrophic news Jesus told them to stay in Jerusalem and wait. They sat still for forty days. Something else was needed: the baptism of the Holy Spirit. Counsellor, He is called, and elsewhere Comforter. He is the Guide, the Prompter of what activity is required of each cell.

The great saints and mystics have left us guidebooks on aligning ourselves with 'the mind of God', and some have devoted their lives to the discipline and commitment involved in finding His message for them. Bishop John Taylor refers to two kinds of prayers: the prayer of movement, in which the mind moves from topic to topic, bringing each to God's attention; and the prayer of stillness. The latter is a profound concentration on hearing God's Word for one individual cell. I think of Elijah despondent in the cave: the voice of God he heard came not in the mighty wind, nor in the earthquake, nor in the fire, but in the gentle whisper, the still, small voice. Or I think of Jesus, the Son of God Himself. Even He confessed the need for direct contact with the Father through prayer and fasting.

Mahatma Gandhi, one of the busiest and most famous men in the world, used to set aside Monday as a Day of Silence. He needed the stillness, he said, in order to rest his vocal cords and to promote an inner harmony in his soul amid the turmoil of life around him. I wonder what power would be released if all Christians devoted one day a week to listening to the voice of God to discern His coded message for our lives. The Counsellor can only lead us if we receive His voice.

I have vivid memories of the person who best demonstrated for me this skill of listening to God: my grandmother. Grandma Harris was eighty when I first knew her, and lived to age ninety-four. I never saw her walk unassisted; her health confined her either to bed or to 'Grandma's chair' in her quaint room with its lace curtains and dark Victorian furniture. My sister and I would visit that room for about an hour or so each day. Of Huguenot descent, Grandma had us read the French Bible to her so that we could practise our French while also learning the Bible and hearing her talk about the passage we had read.*

Grandma was bent and wrinkled, and she suffered severe headaches. She rarely laughed and could never comprehend our jokes, but her quiet joy and peace somehow reached even us play-minded children. We never resented our daily visits to her room. She radiated love.

When Grandma had trouble sleeping, she sometimes lay awake half the night quietly reciting chapters from her storehouse of memorised Scripture and praying for her eleven children and scores of grandchildren. My aunts took turns sleeping in her room. Quite often, in the middle of the night Grandma would suddenly call for paper and pen and

---

* Grandma was not above using extrinsic motivation on her grandchildren. Knowing that whatever we committed to memory in childhood would last a lifetime, she rewarded our *word perfect* memorisation of a chapter of Scripture with a bright, freshly minted silver coin. Those half-crowns and shillings were like a fortune to us. To this day, almost all the full chapters of the Bible preserved in my memory are those I was paid for by Grandma Harris.

someone to write down her thoughts. She would say, 'I sense that Pastor Smith in Ipswich is in need of help just now. Please write to him like this. . . .' She would then dictate a letter and ask my aunt to enclose a cheque.

Days later, when the mail brought a letter of reply, Grandma would beam with joy. Invariably, the letter expressed astonishment that she should have known the precise timing and amount of a need. She would laugh with a pure sense of innocent delight. We children marvelled at the conspiracy of intimacy between the Holy Spirit and Grandma.

In the Body of Christ, I picture her as a nerve in the sympathetic nervous system, a sensor that God entrusted with the moment-by-moment responsibility of sensing His will. Pastor Smith had sent cries for help to the Head. My grandmother 'heard' the transmitted impulse from the Head and supplied whatever resources were needed. Grandma had prepared all her life for that role. In her youth she had physical energy and beauty. During those busy years of rearing eleven new lives, despite constant demands on her schedule, she had taken the time to know God. She had saturated her mind with the Word of God, storing away whole books of the New Testament, as well as all of the Psalms, in her memory. Later, when her body grew old and withered, she became a clear channel for the grace of God.

Today, more than fifty years later, much of my own love for the Bible derives from her. She could do little but listen to the Prompter, but her faithfulness is still bearing fruit.

In the human body, a minute quantity of the proper hormone can launch a complex upheaval; the still, small voice of God, if responded to, can change a person, a community, and perhaps a world.

18 The Prompter

*The computer makes us fantastically
more able to calculate and analyse; it
does not help us to meditate. We have
instruments to enable us to see everything from the nebulae to the neutron –
everything, except ourselves. We have
immeasurably extended our gift of sight,
but not of insight. For that we have the
same equipment as the eighth-century
prophets. Potentially the same, but
actually far poorer, for while we have
been so busy extending one aspect of the
knowing and telling self, we have
allowed other aspects to atrophy. We
have built ourselves up into powerful
transmitting stations, but as receiving
sets we are feeble.*

John V. Taylor
The Go-Between God

When I first returned to India as a doctor, in 1946, I travelled by ship. I had learned navigation several years before, when I spent a summer as one of a crew of five sailing a schooner along the coasts of Great Britain and France. On the schooner we had used direct navigation based on sighting lighthouses and buoys and calculating progress from one to another. But on the passenger ship, in the boundless, open sea, we had no landmarks against which to check calculations. How did the Captain know our location with any certainty?

Ships had no radar equipment in those days. The instruments used – sextant, compass, and chronometer – differed little from those used by Columbus and Magellan. I went to the bridge and asked the Captain if I could observe his methods of navigation. He kindly agreed and loaned me a sextant, which I already knew how to use. I looked forward to comparing my own readings with those of the experts.

A sextant consists of two tubes resembling telescopes, joined at a hinge. To measure the height of a mountain, for example, you sight the summit precisely in one tube and line up the second one along sea level. When the images converge in the eyepiece, you read the exact angle off the sextant. Using a little geometry, you can then arrive at the measurement of height. All this works easily on or near land, but the open sea is a different matter. There, you have no fixed point to guide you, only the clear line of the horizon. You also need the stars.

I quickly learned the most important secret of celestial navigation: the timing of the measurements. We needed a clear sighting of both a star and the horizon to determine an angle, and only two times of day, dawn and dusk, offered such conditions. Those were by far the most dramatic times on the bridge of the ship. Each day I awoke early and made my way to the bridge, sextant in hand. I asked which bright star to sight on (it had to be listed in our astronomical tables) and fixed one tube of the sextant on it. With one eye cocked on that star through the sextant, I searched for the horizon with the other eye.

At first the stars shone bright and well-defined and the horizon line was dark and hazy. But as the edge of horizon gradually sharpened against the brightening dawn, the stars faded away and rapidly became invisible. There was just one moment, and we awaited it anxiously, when the horizon stood out distinctly and the stars still shone faintly. At that critical moment I locked my sextant on the precise angle between the star and the earth.

At its surface the earth spins nearly one thousand miles an hour, changing our ship's position and angle of reference to that star constantly. For this reason, the instant I had my reading I dashed over to the chronometer and noted the time, correct to a fraction of a second. Now I could fix the position and direction of the ship, because at only one place on earth could that angle to the star be measured at that particular instant in time. I had no second chance; if I missed the first reading and returned to the sextant, the star would have vanished.

Dusk reversed the order of sighting. I stood on the bridge with the crew watching the clear horizon, as sharp and fine as a ruler's edge, and waiting for the first star to appear. On that journey we usually looked for Alpha Orion and Betelguese. Suddenly someone would shout 'There it is!' and we all swung our sextants. We focused one tube on the star and one on the horizon, flipped down the mirror that converged the images, and locked the sextants. Then, again, came the scramble to the chronometer.

Those two times of day – dusk and dawn – bracketed the passing of time on the ship. All day we could see the sea and all night observe the stars, but in order to navigate we had to bring heaven and earth together. Other sophisticated instruments on board for measuring drift, propeller velocity, and tidal forces gave us an approximate location, and these were especially useful on cloudy days. But they ran the danger of compounding the previous days' errors. For accuracy, we needed the alignment of fixed points on earth and in the heavens.

A word in the English language reminds me somewhat of my experiences with celestial navigation. It takes on several forms: orient, orientation, or the modern sport of 'orienteering'. At its most basic level it means finding the East (the Orient), and the connotation actually derives from an ancient religious practice.

In Jewish and early Christian faith, churches and synagogues had to face east, toward Jerusalem – that was the only acceptable 'orientation' for the worship of God. This practice stemmed from a belief articulated by Solomon when he prayed at the dedication of the temple, asking God to hear any call for help prayed toward the temple in Jerusalem. Later, syncretism with sun worshippers further settled the practice of facing east. Jesus discounted the notion that location mattered in worship (e.g., in His conversation with a Samaritan woman in John 4), but the tradition lived on and in some places still does.

The practice has a sort of symbolic significance that brings to my mind the principles I learned in celestial navigation. It captures the concept of planting my feet firmly on earth while sighting along a line of spiritual direction. I need a time of day to orient myself, to bring heaven and earth together. In the midst of the clamour and tumult of this material world, I must find a place of quietness to listen to the still, small voice for guidance of my life.

The Old Testament gives one striking example of spiritual orientation, as performed by a Jewish executive in the worldly government of Babylon. For Daniel, orienting toward Jerusalem meant an act of civil disobedience punishable by imprisonment in a den of lions. Regardless of the king's edict, three times a day Daniel flung open his window and turned towards Jerusalem for his prayers. Surely when he did so, the reality of Babylon – the aroma of spices and produce from the bazaar, the strange jumble of urban architecture, the alien language and traffic noise – overwhelmed his sense organs. Yet as Daniel faced Jerusalem, his body language aligned him with the God Jerusalem represented. In a foreign, polluted culture, he fell back in dependence on Jehovah God.

Orientation, aligning heaven and earth, has become for me a metaphor of my reliance on the Spirit as I live in an alien, material culture. I no longer face a city for my prayers – God does not dwell in an earthly structure – but the symbolism of prayer has changed little. To survive, I must pause to breathe in the power of the living God and consciously direct my mind to Him.

At times I find myself nearly overwhelmed by the physical realities that press in from all sides. My appointment book fills up with the names of patients who need personal attention. The hospital and government bureaucracies churn out new projects and memos and reporting procedures. I know that in a few days I will leave on an overseas trip. I have speeches to prepare, books to review, a manuscript to edit. At such moments, I am strongly tempted to shunt aside my normal time with God.

Over the years I have learned, with difficulty, that those moments amid intense earthly pressures are precisely the times when I need most to rely on the Spirit for guidance. In the morning and in the evening, I look for a time when the Spirit can bring heaven and earth together. I commit my day's clutter to Him, asking to see the details of my life in the light of His will.

Spiritually, I cannot survive the alien atmosphere of earth without live contact through the Spirit. Daniel looked out over the streets of Babylon, but his mind and soul were in Jerusalem. The astronauts walked in the cold, forbidding atmosphere of the moon only by carrying with them resources from another world that would keep them alive. I need just that kind of reliance on the Spirit of God.

A practical matter arises. What does this reliance consist of? Does the Spirit actually help with the specific pressures and choices confronting me each day? How, in fact, does God guide us?

I confess that on very few occasions have I felt clear, unmistakable guidance from the Spirit. I explain my dilemmas to Him and pour out my needs, but He does not respond by telling me what to do. And the Bible itself contains little advice on techniques of guidance. (The often cited instances of Gideon's fleece and the Macedonian call are notable because of their exceptional nature; they hardly offer a practical model for guidance.)

The Bible does, however, have much to say about maintaining a love relationship with God. He wants a conscious and willing acceptance of His presence whenever I make a decision. There is no shortcut, no magic, only the possibility of a lifetime search for intimacy with a God who sometimes seems close by and sometimes faraway. Normally, I believe, God guides in subtle ways: feeding ideas into my mind, speaking through a nagging sensation of dissatisfaction, inspiring me to choose better than I otherwise would have done, bringing to the surface hidden dangers of temptation. The Prompter supplies real help, but in ways that will not overwhelm my freedom.

If someone asked me to trace the guidance of God on my life I could do it fairly easily, I think. Looking back, the circumstances of my life do fit together with an order and design that seem purposeful. And yet, at individual points along the way, exactly the opposite seemed true.

In my childhood and teenage years I wanted to be a missionary. My parents had impressed me with a value system that ranked their own work of helping people in India as among the highest ends a person could seek.

Due partially to the influence of my father, a builder, I decided to pursue a career in building. My father had built schools, hospitals, and homes, and I knew that such skills would prove useful in India. If I could learn that trade, then surely I would find a place as a missionary builder. As I have recounted, I stubbornly resisted an uncle's generous offer to pay my way through medical school and began to study masonry, carpentry, and principles of engineering. Many of my close friends thought the whole scheme was a waste of time. They proposed to me dozens of alternative careers, but for four years I persisted.

After my full apprenticeship I spent one year at Livingstone College taking a medical course designed to help missionaries with first aid and basic treatment. There for the first time I felt a pull toward medicine (mainly because of the experience at Connaught Hospital mentioned earlier in this book). I wondered whether I had made a mistake by choosing against a career in medicine. But after finishing the course I put these thoughts behind me and went with great eagerness to call on the director of my parents' mission.

With some pride, I announced to him my willingness to serve in India. A small booklet of Scripture texts had fortified my determination. I had prayed for guidance and opened the booklet to the first text, and this is what I had found: 'I have chosen you for my kingdom and glory.' It all seemed clear to me: a second generation of Brands would carry on the work of Jesse Brand who had died in the Lord's service.

But J. B. Collin, the president of the mission, did not see matters in quite the same light. He asked numerous questions about my motives and preparation and then cordially said, 'No.' He did not dispute my direction, but rather judged me unready for the kind of work the mission required. He suggested more preparation and then a fresh application if I still felt the same. I was crushed. God's will had seemed so clear to me, and now this key person was standing in the way.

I slipped into medicine by apparent accident. I signed up for a course at the Missionary Training Colony, a Bible School that also taught how to prepare for the rigours of life in remote settings. I learned to mend boots, make my own clothes, and live off the land. There, too, I took a brief course in medicine, and the inner voice inside me got louder and louder. I felt inescapably drawn to the field of medicine. So intense was the feeling that I withdrew from the two-year missionary course and enrolled in medical school.

When I finally did sign up for medical school, the four years in construction loomed over me as a wasteful diversion. Despite the late start, I did well in school and finished my general training as a doctor.

Once again I presented myself to a mission board, now trained in two separate fields, building and medicine. Again I was turned down! This time the interference came from the Central Medical War Committee of Great Britain. They rejected my application to work in a mission hospital on the border of Nepal and instead ordered me into the bomb casualty clearing services in London. Impatiently biding my time during the forced delay, I studied for higher qualifications in the field of surgery.

Twice my good plans had been stymied, once by a wise and godly mission administrator and once by a secular committee of bureaucrats. Each time I felt shaken and confused. Had I somehow misread God's will for my life?

Now, as I look back, I can see that God's hand was directing me at every step. Eventually Dr Bob Cochrane in India convinced the same Central Medical War Committee to assign me to a new medical college in Vellore, India, and it was he who challenged me to apply the principles of orthopaedics to leprosy patients. One intense moment (the story is told in *Fearfully and Wonderfully Made*), while shaking the powerful but insensitive hand of a leprosy patient, I experienced a stirring, unforgettable call from God. Ever since, I have devoted my life to leprosy work.

Decades later, I now look back with profound gratitude on the time I spent in construction and engineering. Hardly a day goes by that I do not use some of those principles in trying to perfect a rehabilitation device, or form a better pair of shoes, or apply engineering mechanics to surgery techniques, or set up stress experiments. And I am equally grateful for the decision that forced me into surgery.

I have stood under the thatched roof of our New Life Centre in India and reflected on God's pattern in all those years. Watching the patients do carpentry in the workshop I established, I have a momentary sense of being back in my London carpentry shop; the smells of the wood shavings and rhythmic sounds of the tools come rushing back. I am among colleagues, my fellow-apprentices. But I quickly awake from my reverie and see the differences. These are all Indians with reconstructed hands and tools adapted to protect them. God has permitted me the honour of serving these patients on several levels: as a doctor treating their disease, as a surgeon remaking their hands, and as a carpentry foreman helping to fashion new lives for them.

Only the zigzag course of guidance allowed me to interact with them on all these levels. At any point – if I had gone to India earlier or had bypassed those years in construction, for example – I could easily have strayed slightly out of line and thus have proven less useful. In hindsight, I have a wonderful sense of how God planned ahead and ordered the details of my life.

The summer I sailed the coasts of Britain and France, I was responsible for guiding the boat into the treacherous harbour of St Malo, notorious for centuries as a pirates' cove. Jagged rocks hidden just beneath the surface of the water make the harbour unnavigable, except through one narrow route. To follow that route, I had to rely on two sets of leading lights to the harbour. I would fix our course by lining up the first pair, sailing southeast until the next two lights lined up. Immediately I would turn sharply starboard and keep the second set of leading lights in line. Our boat rarely headed in the ultimate direction of the harbour, but zigzagged through a pattern required to avoid unseen obstacles. I concentrated solely on the lights before me, putting my trust in the one who knew the harbour well enough to mark off that route.

Similarly, God does not ask that we figure out the reason for each change in our direction, or look on apparent obstacles with frustration. Rather, He wants us to accept the circumstances He permits in our lives and respond in obedience and trust even when they appear confusing and contradictory. Events not under my control, such as the war and the slamming of doors by the bureaucracy, served to guide me by blocking my way. These, in turn, sent me back to the Holy Spirit for help in facing a new set of circumstances requiring new evaluation and new strategies.

I take great comfort in the promise of Romans 8:

'Moreover we know that to those who love God, who are called according to his plan, everything that happens fits into a pattern for good' (v. 28, PHILLIPS). God does not promise only good things will happen; nor does the verse say all that happens is sent by God. I seek God's wisdom primarily to guide me through and around circumstances that happen to appear, moving always toward the fulfillment of His will. And I have confidence that the end result of all things will show a pattern for good. Obedience to the Spirit at every point ensures fulfillment of that promise.

I am, after all, a mere cell in Christ's Body. It is the role of the Head to direct the other members and coordinate the actions for the whole church. What He asks of me is simple loyalty, a commitment to follow the messages of His Spirit in whatever form they come, in a way that builds up the whole Body.

PAIN

19   Protection

'How much reverence can you have for a Supreme Being who finds it necessary to include tooth decay in His divine system of creation? Why in the world did He ever create pain?'

'Pain?' Lieutenant Shiesskopf's wife pounced upon the word victoriously. 'Pain is a useful symptom. Pain is a warning to us of bodily dangers.'

'And who created the dangers?' Yossarian demanded. 'Why couldn't He have used a doorbell to notify us, or one of His celestial choirs? Or a system of blue-and-red neon tubes right in the middle of each person's forehead?'

'People would certainly look silly walking around with red neon tubes in the middle of their foreheads.'

'They certainly look beautiful now writhing in agony, don't they?'

                                    Joseph Heller

In a lithography by Honoré Victorin Daumier, a distinguished gentleman in a white waistcoat is sitting on a high-backed Victorian sofa – no, not sitting, contorting. His legs are jerked up under him spectacularly and his back arches downward, nearly forming a foetal position. He is doubled up with pain. Four sets of leering little devils perch mischievously at each corner of the sofa, half of them playing tug-of-war with cables looped around the gentleman's mid-section and half gleefully brandishing a huge, jagged-tooth saw that is sundering his abdomen. His face is frozen in an expression of utter agony. Daumier added a simple title: *La colique* – the pain of colic.

Virtually everyone who views Daumier's print responds with a wince, a mirroring of the figure's anguish. We have all felt at least a twinge from a muscular spasm caused by intestinal blockage or distension. Pain is the hallmark of mortality.

We plunge into the world through the stretched and bloody tissues of a grimacing woman. 'My mother groaned, my father wept. Into the dangerous world I leapt,' wrote William Blake. Our own first reaction is a loud cry of fear, or grief, or both. Years later we exit the world through suffering, sometimes in one last paroxysm of pain. Between those two events, we live out our days with pain always lurking at the door.

Large industries exist to loosen the cables and dull the saw's blade of pain. A parade of modern mountebanks fills television talk-show slots, promising relief through a new method of foot or ear massage, or acupuncture, or a new electronic marvel sewn beneath the skin. Pain is the tainted sensation: the word itself derives from *poena*, Latin for 'punishment', hinting that the demons manning the saw are not imaginary.

Ironically, I have spent half my life among people whose faces bear the same disfigurement of punishment and torment, but for the opposite reason. Leprosy patients suffer because they feel no pain; they yearn for the demons who would alert them to impending danger.

My love/hate relationship with pain began, I suppose, in

my childhood. Wherever we went in the mountains of South India, my parents would take along a few pairs of dental forceps, for they knew that toothache was one of the most persistent and overwhelming pains. Their reputation for pulling teeth preceded them even in the most remote mountain hamlets.

Hundreds of times I interrupted my play to stand by, with wide eyes and a wildly thumping heart, as my mother or father extracted patients' teeth – without anaesthetic. I would watch my tiny mother wriggle her pointed forceps up between the gum and tooth, seeking a firm grip so the crown of the tooth would not break off when she yanked. When dealing with a very large patient, she hung on fiercely to those forceps while the patient's own thrashing motions worked the tooth loose. The patients cried out, danced around uncontrollably, and spit up blood. Yet, even after seeing those reactions, onlookers lined up for treatment. Ridding themselves of toothache was worth any cost.

Occasionally in villages on the plains we would also see the impressive *fakirs*, religious men who demonstrated their conquest over pain. Some would push a thin stiletto-type blade through their cheek, tongue, and out the other cheek, then withdraw the blade without bleeding. Others strung themselves high in the air by pulling on ropes that passed through a metal ring at the top of a pole and ended in meat-hooks stuck into the flesh of their backs. Passively, showing no signs of pain, they dangled like spiders above an admiring crowd. Still others garishly decorated themselves with scores of oranges attached to large safety pins which they jabbed into their skins. They laughed and merrily danced down the streets on stilts, jiggling the oranges in time with music.

Later, as a medical student in England I had the rare privilege of working as a house physician under Sir Thomas Lewis, one of the great pioneers in the exploration of pain. I remember those days well because Sir Thomas gained much of his knowledge of pain by using his students as guinea pigs. One gets an unforgettable perspective on pain by recording sensations while being pinched, pricked, or bound by a tourniquet. Lewis collected his findings into a book, *Pain*, that became a classic, a model of beautiful language as well as medical research.

Then, returning to India I immediately encountered the full spectrum of human misery: vast numbers of victims of poliomyelitis, osteomyelitis, joint tuberculosis, spinal tuberculosis, paraplegia, and other crippling disorders. These all came to our hospital at the Christian Medical College in Vellore.

Unaccountably, I found myself drawn to those who never came, the pitiful deformed people who lined the entrances to temples, railway stations, and most public buildings, begging for alms. They had clawed hands with missing fingers, ulcerated feet, paralysed thumbs, and every other conceivable kind of orthopaedic defect, yet no orthopedist had ever treated them or their fifteen million fellow-sufferers worldwide. Because they had leprosy, few hospitals would admit them.

Eventually, of course, I decided to spend my life among leprosy patients and concentrate on their orthopaedic problems. I have been studying pain ever since, because leprosy destroys pain nerves, making the body devastatingly vulnerable to injury. Those creatures snapping their cables like bullwhips in Daumier's lithograph – are they truly demons? Without their torments, would the gentleman attend to his colic? A lifetime among suffering people has planted such questions in my mind.

A career devoted to any sensation will inevitably distort one's perspective so that the specialist considers his or her sensation to be the richest and most wonderful. Thus a gourmet will pay thousands of dollars to visit France for the sole purpose of scraping particles of food across taste buds, or an oenophile will trade a month's salary for a bottle of vintage Bordeaux. The nuances of taste and smell have come to mean that much. Over the years, paradoxically, I have developed an appreciation for the pain system that approaches their fanaticism. To be sure, I do not seek out personal experiences of pain, but my study of its design features has overwhelmed me with awe.

The mechanics of pain resemble those of other sensations: like taste or sight or sound, pain is detected by the nerve endings of receptor cells, translated into a chemical and electrical code, and conveyed to the brain where a meaning or interpretation is assigned. One portion of my brain is receiving impulses that it recognises as the typewriter in my office while another area alerts me that a phone is ringing. Similarly, steadily firing nerve cells remind my brain that my strained back needs attention.

Pain, however, functions with such brutal efficiency that its message can preoccupy the brain and drown out all pleasurable signals. It travels along a hotline, insisting on priority. Moreover, its impact can spread out from the brain and ultimately involve the entire body. At the muscular level, my body responds to back pain by contracting or tensing. Unchecked, this response can initiate a vicious cycle in which the tension causes even more pain as it squeezes nerves.

My blood flow changes: blood pressure reacts to pain just as it reacts to anxiety and fear. I may even go pale or flush or, in the event of vascular collapse, I may faint.

Pain may upset my digestion by causing a spasm of my gut or even nausea and vomiting. My endocrine system responds to pain by secreting chemicals like adrenaline. And finally the pain may come to dominate me on the psychological level. I may complain to my colleagues and family. Perhaps I'll cancel an overseas trip to give my back extra rest. But that, too, may lead to complications: guilt from letting people down, depression about my inability to work.

Amazingly, this sensation of pain, which provokes such a powerful response in every part of my body and mind, soon fades away into oblivion. Think back to your worst experience of pain and try to remember what it felt like. You cannot. You can summon up an accurate recollection of a visual scene, like a face or a childhood home; or a sound, such as a few bars of music; or even a memory of taste or smell piquant enough to provoke salivation. But the sense of tyrannical pain has somehow vanished. You have forgotten.

Dominating, subjective, ephemeral – pain offers a target for research as elusive as the quark. What is pain? When is it really there – and where? The answers must begin with a study of individual nerve cells that first trigger pain. My old teacher in London (along with Bishop, in America, and von Frey before them) laboriously mapped out the subtleties and complexities of the nervous system devoted to pain. Having studied under Sir Thomas Lewis, I know well the real heroes who sacrificed to produce our knowledge: medical students whose potential careers depended upon their voluntary cooperation in a series of tests that might daunt the Marquis de Sade. Many professors insisted on subjecting themselves to the same tests; otherwise they would find it difficult interpreting their students' reports of pain.

Research subjects allowed blood pressure cuffs to be inflated around a metal grater that pressed into their arms, endured drippings of hot sealing wax, and dutifully performed isometric exercises while a tourniquet cut off their blood supply. Von Frey's pressure tests with boar bristles and sharp pins attached to miniature scales soon gave way to a new generation of laboratory devices: supersonic oscillators of high frequency sound waves, ultraviolet lights, super-cooled copper wires, radiant heat devices, metal rods dropped from heights onto the skin, 1000-watt bulbs intensified with mirrors. Electricity offered a creative medium for torture machines, including many repetitive spark producers and one maleficent contraption that shot voltage through the fillings of a tooth.

Today's sophisticated breed of experimental subjects have potassium sprinkled onto open blisters, balloons inserted in their stomachs, irritating chemicals applied to their nasal mucosa, and corrosive mixtures such as diluted hydrochloric acid and cowage swabbed on their skin. They submerse their hands in ice water, then hot water. They have cheeks and hands pricked simultaneously to determine which pain 'extinguishes' the other. They hear bells rung and stories read aloud and must repeat sequences of numbers in forward and reverse order, all the while being assaulted by one of the torture machines.

These exhaustive methods yield a few basic measurements. At what points does it start hurting (pain threshold)? Do you ever grow accustomed to the heat or pressure (adaptation to pain)? Where does it hurt (distribution of pain)? At what point can't you endure it any more (tolerance of pain)? Subjects may also describe each pain verbally and try to distinguish degrees of pain (as many as twenty-one have been reported).

The students come away with slight lesions, blisters, and pinpricks, and a diploma that exempts them from being victimised again. The professors come away with graphs mapping out sensitivities on every square centimetre of the body. Such experiments have proceeded unabated for a hundred years for one reason: the nervous system is incredibly complex. Each tiny swatch of the body has a different perception of pain.

I need not reproduce the charts here; everyone knows, albeit subconsciously, the principles of distribution of pain. A single speck of dust (or, worse, an eyelash) flies into your eye. You respond immediately: your eye tears, you squint it shut and dab at the eyelid with your finger to remove the speck. Such a speck can immobilise even a superbly conditioned athlete like a baseball pitcher; the pain is so great he cannot continue pitching until the speck is removed. Yet the same speck on the pitcher's arm goes wholly unnoticed. Undoubtedly, thousands of dirt particles will accumulate there in the course of the game. Why the disparity in sensitivity?

The eye has certain rigid requirements of structure. Unlike its sensitive neighbour the ear, it must lie exposed on the surface, in a straight line with light waves. An eye must be transparent for obvious reasons, which severely limits a blood supply (blood vessels would make the eye opaque, blocking vision). Any intrusion causes serious danger, since the blood-starved eye cannot easily repair itself. Therefore a well-designed pain system makes the eye extraordinarily sensitive to the slightest pressure or pain.

Every part of our bodies has a unique sensitivity to both pain and pressure, depending on function. The face, especially in the area of the lips and nose, is acutely sensitive to both. Feet, subject to a day's stomping, are better protected by tough skin and mercifully insensitive. The abdomen is moderately sensitive, the back less so. Fingertips present an unusual case: their constant use requires them to be sensitive to pressure and temperature but relatively pain-resistant. Where limbs join the trunk, protecting vital organs becomes the main concern; there, cells are four times more alert to pain than to pressure. A light tap on the foot goes unnoticed, on the groin is felt as painful, and on the eye causes anguish.

As I study pain throughout the human body I gain deep respect for the Creator's wisdom. Sometimes I could wish that the lining of the trachea were even more sensitive to irritants, causing more pain and coughing and so making lung-destroying tobacco smoke intolerable. But could humans even survive with a hypersensitive trachea in a dust storm or in the smoke of our modern polluted environment?

Or I think again of the eye. Some wearers of contact lenses might wish for less sensitivity in the eye, but the sensitivity benefits the great majority of people and their need to preserve vision. The eye has a split-second response to danger – intense pain, a blinking reflex, and an effusion of tears – that occurs numerous times each day, often below our level of consciousness.

Each part of the body responds to the appropriate danger that might interfere with it and thus affect the whole body.

Pain contributes daily to a normal person's quality of life, even in such a common activity as walking. A leprosy patient, with perfectly normal skin tissue on the soles of his feet, can take a daily five-mile walk and return with foot ulcers. A healthy person who undergoes the same stress will return without ulcers. Why? A file cabinet in my office contains a box of photographic slides that illustrate the reason.

The slides of colour-coded feet show that the way a healthy person puts feet to the ground changes radically from the first mile to the fifth mile. If at the beginning your great toe is doing most of the work, by the end of the run your lateral toes and the lateral border of your foot will take over. Later the toe and heel will come down together. When you begin a really long hike, you will start off heel-toe, heel-toe. But when you return you'll be lifting your foot and setting it down as one unit – all adjustments having been made subconsciously. The photographic evidence of these changes is quite astounding.

Muscular fatigue does not cause the shifts. Rather, pain cells in your toes, heels, arches, and lateral bones are intermittently informing your brain, 'Ease up a little. I need some rest.' You jog along oblivious, since your brain assigns these functions to a subliminal control, but every spot on your body is constantly talking to you. Even as I sit and write this, the pain cells in my hips and legs are frequently asking me to shift my weight around, and I reflexively obey.

Pain employs a tonal range of conversation. It whispers to us in the early stages of damage: subconsciously, we feel a slight discomfort and toss and turn in bed. It speaks to us as danger increases: a hand grows tender and sore after a long stint at raking leaves. And pain shouts at us when the danger becomes severe: blisters, ulcers, and tissue damage break out, forcing us to change behaviour.

A leprosy patient, having lost this incessant hum of intercellular conversation, will walk five miles without changing gait or shifting weight. The same pressure strikes the same cells with unrelenting force, and ulcers open up.

A limp graphically demonstrates in exaggerated form the body's adjustments to pain. Out of orthopaedic habit, I suppose, I have always stared impolitely at people who limp. I learn a lot from them. What they may view as an embarrassing malfunction, I view as a wonderful adaptation. A limper's body is compensating for damage to one leg by redirecting weight and pressure to the other, healthy leg. Every normal person limps occasionally. Sadly, leprosy patients do not limp. Their injured legs never get the rest needed for healing.

In an extreme form, this inability to 'hear' pain can cause permanent damage because the body's careful response to danger will break down. For example, a healthy person nearly always falls when beginning to sprain an ankle. Perhaps you step on a loose stone or curb. As your ankle begins to twist, the lateral ligaments of the ankle endure a terrific strain. Nerve cells detecting the strain categorically order the body to take all weight off the damaged leg immediately. The thigh and calf muscles will become momentarily flaccid. But if your other, undamaged leg is off the ground taking a step, you will now have no support and will lurch to the ground. (A step, says the anatomist, is a stumble caught in time.) Your body prefers falling to forcing the ankle to take weight in its twisted position. You get up feeling a fool and hoping no one was watching, but in reality you have just achieved a beautifully coordinated manoeuvre that saved you from a sprained ankle or worse.

However, I recall watching a leprosy victim sprain his ankle without falling. He stepped on a loose stone, turned his ankle *completely* over so that the sole of his foot pointed inward, and walked on without a limp. He did not even glance at the foot he had just irreparably damaged by rupturing the left lateral ligament! He lacked the protection of pain. Afterward, without the support of the ligament he had ruptured, he turned his ankle again and again until eventually, due to more complications, he had to have that leg amputated.

20 Linking

A man may perform astonishing feats and comprehend a vast amount of knowledge, and yet have no understanding of himself. But suffering directs a man to look within. If it succeeds, then there, within him, is the beginning of his learning.

Soren Kierkegaard

Compassion is the chief law of human existence.

Fyodor Dostoevsky

I admit, a professional career devoted to people with leprosy, whose main defect is an absence of pain, has biased me on the subject. And yet numbness, too, is a form of suffering. In the case of leprosy patients it can lead to a life of acute suffering.

When I reflect on pain I prefer not to think in a detached way of a hypothetical sum of the world's suffering; instead I focus on one individual with a face and body. At such moments my mind often flashes back to the refined, upper-caste features of my friend Sadagopan, whom we called Sadan. Readers of *Fearfully and Wonderfully Made* know him as the forbearing subject of my early experiments with proper footwear for leprosy patients.

When Sadan first came to Vellore, his feet had shrunk to half their normal length and his fingers were shortened and paralysed. It took us nearly two years of unflagging effort to stop the pattern of destruction in his feet. Meanwhile we began reconstructing his hands, a finger at a time, attaching the most useful tendons to the most useful digits and retraining his mind to control the new set of connections. In all, Sadan spent four years with me in rehabilitation. He personified the soft-spoken, gentle Indian spirit. Together, we wept at our failures and rejoiced at the gradual successes. I came to love Sadan as a dear friend.

At last Sadan decided he should return home to his family in Madras for a trial weekend. He had come to us with badly ulcerated hands and feet. Now his hands were more flexible, and with a specially designed rocker-type shoe he could walk without damage. 'I want to go back to where I was rejected before,' he said proudly, referring to the cafés that had turned him away and the buses that had denied him service. 'Now that I am not so deformed I want to try my way in the great city of Madras.'

Before Sadan left, we reviewed together all the dangers he might encounter. Since he had no warning system of pain, any sharp or hot object could harm him. Having learned to care for himself in our hospital and workshop, he felt confident. He boarded a train to Madras.

On Saturday night, after an exuberant reunion dinner

with his family, Sadan went to his old room where he had not slept for four years. He lay down on the woven pallet on the floor and drifted off to sleep in great peace and contentment. At last he was home, fully accepted once again.

The next morning when Sadan awoke and examined himself, as he had been trained to do at the hospital, he recoiled in horror. Part of the back of his left index finger was mangled. He knew the culprit because he had seen many such injuries on other patients. Evidence was clear: telltale drops of blood, marks in the dust, and, of course, the decimated clump of tendon and flesh that had been so carefully reconstructed some months before. A rat had visited him during the night and gnawed his finger.*

Immediately he thought, *What will Dr Brand say?* All that day he agonised. He considered coming back to Vellore early, but finally decided he must keep his promise to stay the weekend. He looked in vain for a rat trap to protect him that last night at home – the shops were closed for a festival. He concluded he must stay awake to guard against further injury.

All Sunday night Sadan sat cross-legged on his pallet, his back against the wall, studying an accounting book by the light of a kerosene lantern. About four o'clock in the morning the subject grew dull and his eyes felt heavy and he could no longer fight off sleep. The book fell forward onto his knees and his hand slid over to one side against the hot glass of the hurricane lamp.

When Sadan awoke the next morning he saw instantly that a large patch of skin had burned off the back of his right hand. He sat trembling in bed, despair growing like a tumor inside him, and stared at his two hands – one gnawed by a rat, the other melted down to the tendons. He had learned the dangers and difficulties of leprosy, in fact had taught them to others. Now he was devastated by the sight of his

---

* To prevent such tragedies, we later tried to maintain a rule at the hospital: all released patients must take a cat home to protect them from rats during the night.

two damaged hands. Again he thought, *How can I face Dr Brand, who worked so hard on these hands?*

Sadan returned to Vellore that day with both hands swathed in bandages. When he met me and I began to unroll the bandages, he wept. I must confess that I wept with him. As he poured out his misery to me, he said, 'I feel as if I've lost all my freedom.' And then, a question that has stayed with me, 'How can I be free without pain?'

Sadan represents millions of people who suffer from leprosy and other numbing diseases; taken together they offer a powerful negative lesson about the true message of pain. At its most basic level pain serves as a signal that something is wrong, like a smoke alarm that goes off with a loud noise whenever the danger of fire reaches a certain level. Sadan nearly lost his hands because he lacked such a signal.

Besides this warning aspect, pain offers a related contribution that often gets overlooked: it unifies the body. In truth, Sadan suffered because the rest of his body had lost contact with his hands. No jolt of pain informed his brain a terrible thing was happening at the extremities.

A body only possesses unity to the degree that it possesses pain. An infected toenail proves to me the toe is important; it is mine, it needs attention. Hair – yes, that matters, but we see it as a decoration. It can be bleached, shaped, ironed, and even cut off without pain. But what is indispensably mine is defined by pain.

Nothing arouses more distress in me than watching my patients in the Carville hospital 'lose touch' with their own hands and feet. When pain fades away they start viewing their own limbs as stuck-on appendages. You and I speak metaphorically of a hand or foot going 'dead' when we have slept on it in an awkward position. The leprosy patients seem to regard their hands and feet as truly dead.

The most common injury at Carville, 'kissing wound', occurs when a cigarette burns unnoticed down to the nub and brands matching scars into the skin between the two fingers. The patients think of their hands as impersonal accessories, not unlike a plastic cigarette holder. One such patient, who was gradually destroying his hands, said to me, 'You know, my hands are not really hands – they're things, just like wooden attachments. And I always have the feeling they can be replaced because they are not me.'

As rehabilitation director of the hospital, I strive to remind the patients of parts of their bodies they might 'forget about' in the absence of pain. I have spent much of my life repairing the damage that results when patients lower their guard. I would give anything to awaken in such people a sense of their bodies' unity, but overcoming this peculiar sense of detachment seems impossible without the sensation of pain. Just as pain unifies the body, its loss irreversibly destroys that unity.

In India I had one group of teenage patients nicknamed 'the naughty boys' because they tested the limits of our medical long-suffering. These rapscallions competed to appall others with their displays of painlessness. They would thrust a thorn all the way through a finger or palm, pulling it out the other side like a sewing needle. They juggled hot coals or passed their hands over a flame. In addition, they often injured themselves by doing things other boys could do without damage and then proceeded to hide the wounds from us. When quizzed about a wound on hands or feet, they grinned mischievously and said 'Oh, it must have come by itself.'

Eventually, after taxing all our skill in psychology and motivational therapy, most of the 'naughty boys' acquired a respect for their bodies and learned to transfer their ingenuity to the task of preserving their hands and feet. Throughout their rehabilitation process I felt as if I was introducing the boys to their limbs, forcing them to welcome these parts of their bodies.

Years later when I began working with laboratory animals, I learned to my dismay that they felt even more estrangement from deadened parts of their bodies. If I denervated rats or mice for an experiment, I had to keep them well fed; otherwise, the next morning I would find animals with shortened feet and legs. I am told that a wolf or coyote, losing sensation through frostbite or a trap injury, will gnaw through its leg, severing it, and limp away unperturbed. That single scene captures for me the worst curse of painlessness: the painless person, or animal, loses all normal sense of self-unity.

An amoeba, one-celled, automatically perceives any threat as a danger to the whole organism, and the whole organism responds. But organisms consisting of many cells need something more. Pain provides the crucial link that keeps a multi-celled organism informed. The head must feel the needs of the tail.

Anatomically, the method of linking is quite astonishing. In the circulatory system cells are joined by blood vessels composed of millions of intermediate cells. But in the nervous system, a single cell reaches out in unbelievable disproportion from one end of the body to the other. One thin nerve cell joining toe and spinal column spans four feet – no other body cell approaches that length.

As I turn from the network of pain in biology to its analogy in the Body of Christ, comprising all believers, again I am struck by the importance of such a communication system. Pain serves a vital role in protecting and uniting that corporate membership as it does in guarding the cells of my own body.

There are great differences between the unity attainable in a physical body of linked cells and in a Body composed of autonomous members. No tangible axons stretch from person to person in the church. Nevertheless, the Body of Christ offers a primary channel through which to share pain with others. In biology, individual cells must suffer with one another for multi-celled organisms to survive. When living tissues are wounded, they cry out and the whole hears the cry. And we in Christ's Body – loving our neighbours as our selves – are called to an even higher level of identification: 'If one part suffers, every part suffers with it,' says Paul (1 Cor. 12:26).

Deep emotional connections link human beings as

certainly as dendrites link cells in our bodies, evident even in such relative trivialities as sporting events. Watch the face of a wife sitting in the stands at Wimbledon as her husband plays in the championship tennis match. Strands of concern and affection unite them so intensely that every on-court success or failure can be read on the wife's face. She winces at every missed shot and smiles at each minor triumph. What affects him affects her.

Or, visit a Jewish household in Miami, San Francisco, or Chicago around election time in Israel. Many Jews know more about the campaign ten thousand miles away than about their local elections. An invisible web, a plexus of human connections, links them with a tiny nation of strangers far away.

Or, recall the effect on a nation when a great leader dies. I experienced the unifying effect of pain most profoundly in 1963 when I came to the United States to address the student chapel at Stanford University. As it happened, the chapel service occurred just two days after the assassination of President John Kennedy. I spoke on pain that day, for I could read nothing but pain on the faces of hundreds of students jammed into that building. I described for them scenes from around the world, where I knew clusters of people would be gathering together in prayer and mourning to share the pain of a grieving nation. I have never felt such unity of spirit in a worship service.

Something like those sympathetic connections should link us to members of Christ's Body all over the globe. When South Africa jails courageous black Christians, when a government systematically destroys the church in Cambodia, when Central American death squads murder Christians, when Muslims drive a person from town for the crime of converting, when more of my neighbours lose their jobs, a part of my Body suffers and I should sense the loss. Pain can come to our attention in whispered signals of loneliness, despair, discrimination, physical suffering, self-hatred.

'How can a man who is warm understand one who is cold?' asks Alexander Solzhenitsyn as he tried to fathom the apathy toward millions of Gulag inmates. In response, he has devoted his life to perform the work of a 'nerve cell', alerting us to pain we may have overlooked. In a Body composed of millions of cells, the comfortable ones must consciously attend to the messages of pain. We must develop a lower threshold of pain by listening, truly listening, to those who suffer. The word compassion itself comes from Latin words *cum* and *pati*, together meaning 'to suffer with'.

Today our world has shrunk, and as a Body we live in awareness of many cells: persecuted Russian believers, starving Africans, oppressed South Africans and Indochinese and Central Americans . . . the litany fills our newspapers. Do we fully attend? Do we hear their cries as unmistakably as our brains hear the complaints of a strained back or broken arm? Or do we instead turn down the volume, filtering out annoying sounds of distress?

And closer, within the confines of our own local gathering of Christ's Body – how do we respond? Tragically, the divorced, the alcoholics, the introverted, the rebellious, the unemployed often report that the church is the last body to show them compassion. Like a person who takes aspirin at the first sign of headache, we want to silence them, to 'cure' them without addressing the underlying causes.

Someone once asked John Wesley's mother, 'Which one of your eleven children do you love the most?' Her answer was as wise as the question foolish: 'I love the one who's sick until he's well, and the one who's away until he comes home.' That, I believe, is God's attitude towards our suffering planet. He feels the pain of those suffering. Do we?

God gave this succinct summary of the life of King Josiah, 'He defended the cause of the poor and needy, and so all went well.' And then this disturbing postscript: 'Is that not what it means to know me?' (Jer. 22:16).

I hear many cries for unity in the church today; a watching world sees divisiveness as our greatest failure. Calls go out exhorting one denomination to merge with another, or for many denominations to join hands in a national or world-wide campaign. Out of my experience with the nervous system in the human body I would propose another kind of unity: one based on pain.

I can read the health of a physical body by noting how well it 'listens' to pain – most of the diagnostic tools we use, after all (fever, pulse, blood cell count), measure the body's healing response. Analogously, the corporate Body's health depends on how the stronger parts attend to the weaker.

Some cries of pain in the Body come to us loudly and persistently. We cannot help but acknowledge them. Distant outposts of pain cause me more concern, the extremities of limb in His Body that we have somehow silenced. I have performed many amputations in my life, most of them because the hand or foot has gone silent and no longer reports pain. There are members of Christ's Body, too, whose pain we never sense, for we have denervated or cut whatever link would carry an awareness of them to us. They suffer, but silently, unnoticed by the rest of the Body.

I think of my Lebanese friends, for example. In Beirut, children have grown up knowing nothing but war. They carry submachine guns as nonchalantly as American children carry water pistols. They play, not in parks, but in crumbling skyscrapers gutted by bombs. Christians in Lebanon, especially the Armenians, feel utterly abandoned by the church in the West, which focuses so much attention on Israel and assumes all non-Israelis in the Middle East to be Arab and Moslem. Spokesmen for Christians in Lebanon eloquently plead for compassion or some token of understanding by their brothers and sisters in the West, but we act as though the neuronal connections have been cut, the synapses blocked. Few hear their pain and respond with Christian love.

Or I think of the homosexual population scattered throughout our churches and colleges. Some surveys show that as many as 20 percent of males in Christian colleges struggle with homosexual tendencies. The reality is so abhorrent to certain Christian leaders, though, that they simply pretend the problem does not exist. Those affected are left to flounder, cut off from the balance and diversity of the larger Body and the compassion that might help them.

Or I think of the elderly, often put away out of sight behind institutional walls that hold in all sounds of loneliness and mourning. Or of battered children who grow up troubled, unwelcomed into foster homes. Or of races who feel cut off from participation in the Body.* Or of prisoners sealed off behind huge fences. Or of foreign students who live tucked away in cheap lodging, isolated and afraid. Even those within the church judged for some minor doctrinal disagreement can feel shut off, severed.

In modern society we tend to isolate these problems by forming organisations and appointing social workers to deal with them. If we are not careful, a form of institutionalised charity will grow up that effectively isolates hurting members from close personal contact with healthy ones. In such an event, both groups atrophy: the charity recipients who are cut off from human touch and compassion and the charity donors who think of love as a kind of material transaction.

In the human body, when an area loses sensory contact with the rest of the body, even when its nourishment system remains intact, that part begins to wither and atrophy. In the vast majority of cases – 95 of 100 insensitive hands I have examined – severe injury or deformation results. The body poorly protects what it does not feel. And in the spiritual Body, also, loss of feeling inevitably leads to atrophy and inner deterioration. So much of the sorrow in the world is due to the selfishness of one living organism

---

* A terrible example of exclusion from the Body occurred in South Africa, when a young spiritual searcher named Mohandas Gandhi tried to hear the missionary C. F. Andrews. Gandhi was not allowed in the meeting because of his brown colour. Soon afterward he rejected Christianity and went on to lead 400,000,000 people as a Hindu. Concluded E. Stanley Jones, 'Racialism has many sins to bear, but perhaps its worst sin was the obscuring of Christ in an hour when one of the greatest souls born of a woman was making his decision.'

that simply does not care when another suffers. In Christ's Body we suffer because we do not suffer enough.

I must also mention one further service that members of Christ's Body perform by embracing others' suffering. I say this carefully: we can show love when God seems not to.

The great accounts of Christians who have suffered, beginning with the Book of Job and the Psalms and continuing through the writings of and about the saints, speak of a 'dark night of the soul' when God seems strangely absent. When we need Him most, He is most inaccessible. At this moment of apparent abandonment, the Body can rise to perhaps its highest calling; we become in fact Christ's Body, the enfleshment of His reality in the world.

When God seems unreal, we can demonstrate His reality to others by revealing His love and character. Some may see this as God's failure to respond to our deepest needs: 'My God, why have You forsaken me?' I see it as a calling for the rest of the Body to push through loneliness and isolation and to embody the love of God.

> Praise be to the God and Father of our Lord Jesus Christ, the Father of compassion and the God of all comfort, who comforts us in all our troubles, so that we can comfort those in any trouble with the comfort we ourselves have received from God. For just as the sufferings of Christ flow over into our lives, so also through Christ our comfort overflows. If we are distressed, it is for your comfort and salvation; if we are comforted, it is for your comfort, which produces in you patient endurance of the same suffering we suffer. And our hope for you is firm, because we know that just as you share in our sufferings, so also you share in our comfort (2 Cor. 1:3-7).

One of my favourite patients at Carville, a man named Pedro, taught me about developing greater sensitivity to pain. For fifteen years he had lived without sensation of pain on his left hand, yet somehow the hand had suffered no damage. Of all the patients we monitored, only Pedro showed no signs of scarring or loss of fingertip.

My associate went over Pedro's hand with great care and came up with a surprise. One tiny spot on the edge of his palm still had normal sensitivity so that he could feel the lightest touch of a pin, even a stiff hair. Elsewhere on the hand he could feel nothing. We also found on a thermograph that the sensitive spot was at least six degrees hotter than the rest of Pedro's hand (which supported our theory, still being formulated, that warm areas of the body resist nerve damage from leprosy).

Pedro's hand became for us an object of great curiosity, and he graciously obliged without protest as we conducted tests and observed his activities. We noticed that he approached things with the edge of his hand, much as a dog approaches an object with a searching nose. He picked up a cup of coffee only after testing its temperature with his feeling spot.

Finally Pedro tired of our endless fascination with his hand. He said, 'You know, I was born with a birthmark on my hand. The doctors said it was a hemangioma and froze it with dry ice. But they never fully got rid of it, because I can still feel it pulsing.' Somewhat embarrassed that we had not considered the option, we verified that the blood vessels in his hand were indeed abnormal. A tangle of arteries brought an extra amount of blood and short-circuited some of it straight back to the veins without sending it through all the fine capillaries. As a result, the blood flowed very swiftly through that part of his hand, keeping its temperature close to that of the heart, too warm for the leprosy bacilli to flourish.

A single warm spot, the size of a nickel, which Pedro had previously viewed as a defect, had become a wonderful advantage to him when he contracted leprosy. The one remaining patch of sensitivity protected his entire hand.

In a church that has grown large and institutional, I pray for similar small patches of sensitivity. We must look to prophets, whether in speech, sermon, or art form, who will call attention to the needy by eloquently voicing their pain.

'Since my people are crushed, I am crushed,' cried Jeremiah (8:21). And elsewhere, 'Oh my anguish, my anguish! I writhe in pain. Oh, the agony of my heart! My heart pounds within me, I cannot keep silent' (4:19).

Micha, too, wrote of his grief at Israel's condition:

Because of this I will weep and wail;
   I will go about barefoot and naked.
I will howl like a jackal and moan like an owl
   For her wound is incurable (1:8–9).

These prophets stand in great contrast to insensitive Jonah, who cared more about his comfort than about an entire city's destruction. The prophets of Israel tried to warn an entire nation of social and spiritual numbness. We need to encourage modern Jeremiahs and Micahs and to value these compassionate, pain-sensitive members as much as Pedro valued his tiny spot of sensitivity.

By shutting off pain, we risk forfeiting the wonderful privileges of being part of a Body. And a living organism is only as strong as its weakest part.

21 Adaptations

Although I still did not know that I had cancer, I hit intuitively on the correct diagnosis as regarding the tumour as an accumulation of 'swallowed tears'. What this phrase suggested to me was that all the tears I had not wept and had not wanted to weep in my lifetime had gathered in my neck and formed this tumour because they had not been able to fulfil their true function, which was to be wept. In strictly medical terms, of course, this poetic-sounding diagnosis is beside the point. But, seen in terms of the whole person it expresses the truth. All the suffering I had swallowed and dammed up could no longer be compressed inside me. The pressure became too great, and the resulting explosion destroyed the body containing all that compressed pain.

Fritz Zorn
Mars

It is a typical Louisiana summer day. Moisture hangs so heavy in the atmosphere it feels as if each breath is filling my lungs with water droplets. In the few minutes required to climb a three-storey steel fire escape outside the hospital building, I become soaked with perspiration. Fortunately, the animal research room is air-conditioned.

I glance briefly at the orderly cages lining both sides of the aisle. Rats, mice, rabbits, armadillos – not exactly species you would choose for companionship, but each animal here has contributed to the cause of leprosy research. In one large cage at the end of the aisle I can hear Clarence shuffling around. Clarence, a monkey, compensates for what the other animals lack in relational skills, and I greet him warmly.

I have developed a certain fondness for Clarence, partly because of sentimental memories of pet monkeys in India and partly because of his fun-loving disposition. We care for him well and are circumspect in our experimentation, causing as little pain as possible. He, in turn, has served us well.

After playing a bit with Clarence on a table, I take his right arm and begin unwrapping the bandages covering it. His fingers are pink and wrinkled, like a human baby's, but a shock of dark hair sprouts from the knuckles. Only the fingertips interest me. I notice a slight swelling on two of them, and the first signs of a water blister on a third. With a magnifying glass I study them more closely, looking especially for significant differences between the first two fingers and the second two. I find none.

Clarence jumps a little when I touch two of the fingers. Externally, they seem no more swollen than the others, but they are clearly more tender. When I first obtained Clarence, I surgically opened up his hand and cut the nerves of sensation to those two fingers. Ever since, he has had two normal monkey fingers and two with no feeling of pain. My research attention focuses on his partially numb hand, which I keep swathed in a protective splint so he will not injure his two painless fingers.

Experiments with Clarence – he is anaesthetised for

most of them – have revealed much about the body's responses to pain stimuli. Mainly, he has shown that insensitive fingers absorb no greater damage than normal ones when subjected to equal stresses. All four of his fingers are equally vulnerable. Thus I can prove to my leprosy patients that damage is not inevitable and that they can, with care, prevent serious damage even without pain.

Scar tissue in Clarence's painless fingers shows that his body mobilised healing processes even when the message of pain never reached his central nervous system. My scalpel long before severed the nerves that would have carried pain to Clarence's brain; thus he felt nothing. The body's healing response to pain – the swelling, extra blood supply, scar tissue – occurred *on the local level*.

In the previous chapter we looked at pain as a valuable unifier of individual cells and, analogously, of a Body. As a member of Christ's Body, I should attend to the pain of a suffering member nearby. But then what? How should I respond? The physical adaptations to pain in my own body teach me much about the appropriate responses of neighbouring cells.

To better understand the mechanisms of response to pain, I have subjected my own fingers to the mechanical devices we use on Clarence: machines that press a metal rod against fingertips with measured force and frequency. If I put my hand under the tiny mechanical hammer delivering a force of exactly one pound over one-twentieth of a square inch (twenty pounds per square inch), I find it not painful at all. It feels rather pleasant, like a vibro-massage. But if I let the machine run on for several hundred beats, my finger turns slightly red and feels uncomfortable. After 1500 beats I must pull my finger out, for I can no longer endure the pain. My finger, now sore to the touch, is distinctly warmer than its neighbouring fingers. When I return to the machine the next day I can only tolerate a couple of hundred beats before yanking my finger away. In a mysterious and complex process, my body evaluates pain not only by the mechanical forces but also by how the cells are 'feeling' when the stress begins.

My body's protective response shows visibly in inflammation, as blood surges to the affected area and the body cushions the point of stress with extra fluids. In regard to the pain system, inflammation brings on a condition called hypersensitivity. My finger that has endured hundreds of tiny hammer blows becomes hypersensitive to hammer blows, because in its inflamed condition just a few more stresses could lead to a blister or ulcer.

Similarly, a finger that has been burned becomes hypersensitive to heat, because even a little heat would harm the mildly inflamed tissues. (I have more than once put my hands in a basin only to discover, to my surprise, that my hands are sending mixed signals. My left hand tells me the water is hot; my right hand says warm. Then I remember an incident from breakfast: a drop of hot bacon grease popped out of the pan and landed in my left hand. I had not noticed it at the time, but pain nerve endings at that spot lowered their threshold and are now reporting warm water as hot.)

Who has not felt the irritation of a sore finger, from an infected hangnail perhaps, always seeming 'in the way'. It gets bumped every few minutes no matter how careful you are. That sensation has a sound physiological basis: your pain cells have suddenly become ten times more sensitive to pain. My finger becomes hypersensitive so that I won't foolishly subject it to more hot grease or hammer blows. Pain cells in effect 'turn up the volume'. In these remarkable ways, hypersensitivity builds up a shield of pain to protect unusually vulnerable parts.

All of us experience a psychological parallel to the reaction of hypersensitivity. When we are under severe strain, maybe resulting from an accumulation of small stresses – bills, work pressures, irritating habits of family members – suddenly every minor frustration hits like a blow. We have become hypersensitive, and our minds are telling us we need a respite as surely as neuronal hypersensitivity warns our bodies of a need for relief.

Following the example of cells in the human body, we members of the Body of Christ would do well to learn the place of hypersensitivity and how to respond. Cells in my fingers, although uninjured themselves, take up the cry for relief from a nearby injured cell and report it to the head. There is a place for 'intercessory pain' in the Body of Christ.

In addition, the body makes certain allowances for its hurting cells. Pain works precisely because it is loud and insistent. People in pain, physical or mental, while in a hypersensitive state may lash out against those who try to befriend them. They require from more healthy members a forgiving acceptance that sees past surface reactions to the hidden needs.

The Christian church, said one noted pastor, 'is the only outfit I know of that shoots its wounded.' He referred to a common tendency to harshly judge a person who is already in emotional or spiritual pain. In contrast, a healthy body will make far-reaching adaptations to announce the pain and make sure it is heeded. Healing agents are summoned by the area of local need, as my study of the monkey's denervated fingertips clearly confirmed.

Real love protects and defends areas of special vulnerability. We may be called on to bolster bruised egos, gently confront an insensitive person, or take upon ourselves some of the minor stresses that have accumulated. As a former missionary, I cannot overstate the life-sustaining role of people back home who invested themselves in me by praying and writing letters. These specially sensitive cells sought out my pain and nourished me in time of need. Such dedicated people make the difference between a missionary who serves twenty years and one who breaks down after a short time.

Once I had the experience of serving as medical officer at a professional boxing match. I was assigned to treat the injuries that occurred during the match. (I only accepted the assignment once – the sight of two men pounding living

cells to destruction offended all my medical sensibilities.)
One vivid scene stays with me. The trainer of one of these
heavyweight boxers ran up to his man, in the corner where I
was standing, after a particularly furious round. 'The left
eyebrow!' he yelled excitedly, pointing to his own wildly
dilated eye for emphasis. 'Pound him on the left eye!
You've landed some good ones – it's already swelling. A
couple more jabs and you'll bust it open!'

The boxer followed his instructions, bearing down re-
lentlessly on the inflamed, hypersensitive lump above his
opponent's eye. I had to sew up the remains of skin and
eyebrow after the fight. The pummeling had taken its toll.

That scene has come to my mind periodically, in very
different circumstances, such as at a dinner party at a
friend's home. Everyone is eating and conversing amiably
until the husband says something to his wife that seems
slightly charged. By itself, the comment is harmless. Yet
the wife flushes with obvious embarrassment, and the
husband appears a bit smug. Without comprehending details, I realise a blow, genteel but deadly, has landed.
Dinner proceeds with some awkwardness after the
comment.

When I intercept that kind of interchange, or hear a
remark slightly veiled in humour about housecleaning,
some past disagreement, a personal habit, sexual perform-
ance, or in-laws, I hear replayed, 'Hit him again – the left
eyebrow!' Each partner knows well the other's vulnerable
points. Intimacy increases the vulnerability of the person
who loves and makes us naked to ridicule. At such moments I wish the Body of Christ would show the consistency
of my physical body in its healing responsiveness to other
cells. Love demands it.

The human body is not so defenceless that it merely shouts
a warning, swells red with injury, and abandons the
struggle. If I had to summarise the grand design of pain in
one phrase it would be this: pain is directional. It hurts not
in order to cause discomfort, but to demand a change in

response to danger.* And hypersensitivity occurs not as part of a cruel scheme to introduce even more suffering into the body, but as a quick adaptation to force the rest of the body to devote more attention to the vulnerable part.

Once a suffering member has gained the body's attention, either by firing messages through the central nervous system or by alerting surrounding cells via enzymes, a healthy body reacts immediately. After hypersensitivity, it relies on the second level of response: distribution of stress.

I dig in my garden. Again and again I thrust the spade into the hard soil, with my hand absorbing the back-thrust on its handle. For a while the action causes no pain, but gradually the cells under the skin call out for more blood and the skin reddens (inflammation and hypersensitivity). As my hand grows more tender, without thinking about it I distribute stress by changing my grip on the spade so that a different patch of skin will take the pressure and I can continue digging.

I go through a similar process whenever I buy new shoes. Although the loafers felt comfortable during my test paces in the store, when I return home and walk a mile, a spot on my foot begins to call for help. An area of friction or pressure that I had not noticed before demands attention. If I must go on walking, my body adapts with a massive redistribution of stress out of proportion to the hypersensitive spot: I limp. The new gait, though awkward and unnatural, minimises stress on the tender area.

I was called on once to treat the star basketball player of Louisiana State University. He was leading all scorers on the LSU team and ignited each game with incredible displays of his speed and leaping ability. But he could never complete a game. Invariably, in the second half a large

---

* I believe this principle applies to all pain, not just physical. Emotional and spiritual pains are likewise directional signs. Guilt 'hurts' so that the person will repent and find forgiveness. Depression points to the need to resolve certain tensions. Marital conflict merely expresses the deeper underlying discord that must be worked out. In short, emotional and spiritual pain are, like physical pain, symptoms and not diseases. Normally, a symptom will not disappear until the disease is treated.

tender spot would develop on his forefoot that would
blister and ultimately break open and force him from the
game. Our remedy for him was simple and proved an
instantaneous cure: we carefully shaped a paste of cork dust
and rubber latex into the exact shape of his forefoot, taking
into account the stress points. By distributing the stress
over a wider area, we freed him to pivot, jump, and run all
over the court for the entire game.

Without the adaptation of stress distribution, all of our
daily activities would be fraught with danger. I know
because I have treated scores of leprosy patients who will
never walk again because a defective pain system failed to
warn the central nervous system to redistribute the stresses
being applied to just one spot on their feet. The force of
walking itself should not cause damage – feet are designed
so that the foot of an elephant, a rat, and a human all absorb
the same comfortable pressure per square inch. But unrelieved, repeated pressure on the same spot will cause
damage.

There is no escape from danger. An act of seemingly
total rest – sleeping – can destroy. The most gentle pressures can keep blood from an area and ultimately silence the
pain cells there. If the body heard a cry of pain, it would
turn a bit, distributing the stress to other cells. But with no
pain, purulent bedsores may result. I thank God for the
millions of sensors embedded in my skin that tell me when
to shift weight in my buttocks, or reposition my legs or
back, or change my step when walking.*

When I turn from my physical body to the Body of
Christ, I see the need for a similar adaptation. Just as
a healthy body wisely senses the friction and stresses on each
individual cell and adjusts its role accordingly, so a spiritual

---

* Inventors have tried to correct the problems that lead to ulcers and
bedsores on insensitive or paralysed people who do not redistribute stress.
They have designed wheelchairs and beds featuring rollers that look like
those on warehouse conveyor belts and are constantly on the move to
distribute pressure more evenly.

Body, under direction from the Head, must constantly evaluate which cells need special attention or perhaps even redeployment. Outer front-line cells will require qualities of resistance and firmness. Other, inner cells need to be protected and sequestered to lead lives of quiet contemplation.

From my own observation, the church tends to fail at this principle of redistributing stress in two crucial areas. First, when we put leaders on the front line – pastors, priests, missionaries, other public representatives – we demand too much. We exert extraordinary pressures on them to fit into our preconceptions of spirituality. When they fall short, instead of gracious acceptance and forgiveness, we respond with rejection. We give them no chance to 'limp'. I caution such leaders to surround themselves with hypersensitive friends and associates who can detect signals of damaging stress and bring about whatever changes are necessary to redistribute those pressures.

Too easily we overlook the cumulative effect of minor, inconsequential mechanical stresses. To my great surprise, my research proved that the subtle, less dramatic forces of *repetitive* stress hold greater peril for my patients than the obvious hazards of laceration or burning. Similarly, we must not overlook the cumulative effect of hundreds of everyday stresses in the lives of pastors: incessant phone calls, a fractious board, financial pressures, the burdens of counselling, loneliness, the vulnerability of public speaking, social ostracism. These represent far greater dangers than spectacular crises in the church.

The church could learn a second major lesson from the human body: certain members need protection during specific periods of their lives, especially in spiritual infancy. I have seen a consistent pattern of elevating new converts such as athletes, politicians, actors, beauty queens. Often, these enthusiastic new recruits captivate the attention of the media for a short time. After trying to project the image expected of them – an image not yet real – they abandon their faith in bitterness and disgust. When this happens, I cannot help thinking of a disease of the skin, psoriasis.

Severe psoriasis can change a person's appearance far worse than leprosy. In bad cases, red patches of scurfy, flaky skin may spread across the body. The disease has one cause: skin cells that normally take three weeks to migrate to the surface force their way up in a few days. Those callow cells arrive unprepared for the stresses of light, ultraviolet rays, temperature, and atmosphere on the surface. They die quick, ugly deaths, scarifying their miserable victims. Is there not a lesson here for the Christian world that insists on forcing newly converted celebrities toward the glare of the surface before any spiritual maturity has taken place? Distribution of stress includes the need to protect those unprepared for any stress.

Sometimes I have seen the Body of Christ react with extraordinary speed and wisdom in redistributing painful stress. In such cases, fellow members can mean the difference between collapse and survival. I think of a divorced woman I know in a small church. After her husband left her for another woman, she struggled to hold her life together. Haunted by feelings of guilt and rejection over his leaving, she also had to face four children, an empty bank account, and a house in poor repair. For that woman, the local church became the only means to health. People responded in loving and practical ways: by babysitting, painting the house, repairing the car, inviting her to special events. Her condition did not go away; today, five years later, she still 'limps' and relies on the church to help her cope. I am convinced that local church saved her from personal ruin. She is healthy today because they, like cells in a body, surrounded her with their strength and relieved the pressure that would have destroyed her.

Sometimes, even after repeated cries of alarm, individual cells still face the percussive repetition of damaging force. The affected area has one last strategy for relief, and a remarkable process springs into motion.

I push a spade into dirt two hundred times. I feel some soreness, but the garden soil must be turned, so I politely

ignore the warning signs. Finally, without my wilful cooperation, my body makes a radical architectural change on
the surface of my thumb. The top layer of epidermis
separates from the layers underneath it and mushrooms up
to form a perfect dome supported by the sudden influx of a
cushioning liquid. A blister.

My dermis, formerly mashed flat and vulnerable, now
has soothing relief from stress as the forces of my spade are
gently absorbed by this new structure. Such an adaptation
can easily go unappreciated or, worse, be viewed with
irritation. But it is a startling phenomenon, requiring the
coordination of millions of cells.

A blister is a dramatic, temporary response. It cools
the area, cushions shock, disperses stresses – in short,
gets me through the day.* Human beings have bad habits,
though: we tend to repeat, over and over, the very
stresses that bring on inflammation, hypersensitivity, and
blisters. A tennis player will work through five consecutive blisters before he convinces his body of the need
to develop alternative, more permanent adaptations.
Bones thicken and grow dense and muscles expand in
the presence of continued stress; the skin alters blister into
callus.

I can look at the feet of a runner and get a fair idea of how
far he or she runs in a week. For the serious runner, calluses
fill in crevices, build up weak spots, form-fit the borders to
running shoes, and generally add layers of protection
against the merciless forces of long-distance running. If the
stress continues long enough, a *bursa* develops in the body:
a pocket of fluid buried deep in the tissue under the
thickened piece of skin. These localised adaptations
occur so regularly among certain occupations that we have
informal medical categories for them: 'housemaid's knee',

---

* In a somewhat related process, the body responds to deeper pressures
by rushing fluid to the scene to cushion the blow. Experienced handball
players know the importance of smacking a few balls in a warm-up before
the match. This causes a condition of edema: a cushioning layer of fluid
under the skin.

'coal heaver's back', 'tailor's bunion', and my favourite, 'episcopal knee' (from the prayer rail).

Bodies adapt quickly but grudgingly, and rarely without a sense of loss. As I have mentioned, during one summer of medical school in England I joined the crew of an eighty-foot sailing schooner. At first the friction of ropes burned and chafed my hands and fingers until my fingertips were raw and bleeding. Finally, after two or three weeks, my skin added on thick layers of callus. But, to my chagrin, when I returned to school I found I had completely lost my knack for dissecting. Previously, I could feel any slight resistance of the scalpel as I cut; now I felt only gross pressure. I panicked – surely those thick pads of dead callus had forever destroyed my career as a surgeon. In time, however, when the body sensed I had no need for the extra protection, it shed the layers as gladly as an insect sheds its skin. I regained sensitivity.

Friction in human affairs can likewise cause calluses. Just to survive, a person in a stressful environment will grow extra padding to protect his own psyche from being too easily abraded. I compare my field trips out into Indian villages, where hundreds of patients lined up for treatment, to the situation at Carville where we have as many staff members as patients. The slower pace at Carville allows me time to think about problems in depth and to know each individual patient. On the Indian field trips, I had to sacrifice that personal sensitivity for the greater demands of efficient medical procedures. I could not possibly have got personally involved with each of the hundreds of patients.

Similarly, nurses, social workers, and counsellors who live among clamorous human needs must sometimes develop a protective callus. They dare not let each instance of child abuse, horrible as it is, incapacitate them. Young nurses and doctors sometimes ask my advice on how to cope with overwhelming human need without developing the hardness and cynicism they see in some of their older colleagues. They walk a thin line. Surely they cannot involve themselves with the intimate details of suffering in every patient, and yet they must not shut off personal concern. I have found it an important discipline to pray daily, asking God to identify one or two selective patients with special needs. I cannot be equally sensitive to everyone, and I must not grow insensitive to all. Rather, I depend on His Spirit to help me catch a sense of those who need more than strictly medical care.

Those of us in support roles in the Body must accept the responsibility of carefully monitoring our representatives on the front lines. We cannot expose them to infinite human sorrow. A new phrase, 'burn-out', describes a familiar pattern of self-extinguishment. These people rely on us for a balanced perspective to help convince them to pull back and rest or to shift their load to someone else. Warning signs come in the form of hypersensitivity, fatigue, or emotional trauma. Too much sensitivity or too little can immobilise either a physical body or a corporate one.

I have never seen a clearer example of poorly handled repetitive stress than that which occurred among a trio of brilliant surgeons at a major hospital in the Midwest. When I first visited there in 1952, an esteemed old man, renowned as a hand surgeon, was training two assistants to take his place. The old man had passed retirement age, and his assistants, Morris and Bates, were in their forties, already possessing impressive skills and experience. Both Morris and Bates were well-known all over the country; one edited a leading medical magazine. But the old man couldn't bear to relinquish control over any patient. He leaned over his assistants' shoulders, correcting, advising, and scolding like a parent. To Morris, a superb surgeon, he would say, 'No, don't make that incision quite so long!'

The two gritted their teeth and determined to hang on until his impending retirement. When I met with them, I could sense the venom that had been building up inside them and could see blood pressure rise as they talked about the splenetic old man.

Ten years later I went back to that hospital. Both Morris and Bates were dead. One had had a stroke and was totally paralysed, unable to speak, for several months before he died. The other died of apoplexy, a haemorrhage. Both had been in perfect health before working for the chief surgeon. The old man? He was still there, well into his seventies, training younger doctors.

No one comment from the old surgeon, taken alone, had caused the injury. Rather, the steady, repeated application of irritating force had gradually worn down healthy psyches, as surely as my repetitive stress machine had destroyed living tissue in Clarence the monkey and in my own finger. This same elderly surgeon was a model of Christian gentleness toward his wife, who had Parkinson's disease, and yet showed a blindness to the feelings of those who worked with him so closely.

I think of all the people who would have been helped had those two brilliant surgeons lived. What went wrong? Had others around them failed to notice the problem and re-spond with hypersensitivity? Should the management of the hospital have stepped in to redistribute the stresses? Should Morris and Bates have developed a layer of callus strong enough for them to confront the old man? Or sought divine resources of the cleansing power of forgiveness? Apparently, none of these responses occurred. The two simply absorbed the harmful stresses, and their bodies responded with steadily mounting blood pressure.

I have seen that pattern of destruction occur often in Christ's Body too: a captious church gossips about its minister, an employer mercilessly harasses a well-meaning employee, parents or siblings needle a clumsy child. Where is the grace that forgives and the love that accommodates to weakness? Where the power of reconciliation? All of us could take a lesson from the human body's adaptations to pain. 'Carry each other's burdens,' said Paul, 'and in this way you will fulfil the law of Christ.'

22   Chronic Pain

One wonders what will become of a society in which certain forms of suffering are avoided gratuitously, in keeping with middle-class ideals. I have in mind a society in which a marriage that is perceived as unbearable quickly and smoothly ends in divorce; after divorce no scars remain; relations between generations are dissolved as quickly as possible, without a struggle, without a trace; periods of mourning are 'sensibly' short; with haste the handicapped and sick are removed from the house and the dead from the mind. If changing marriage partners happens as readily as trading in an old car on a new one, then the experiences that one had in the unsuccessful relationships remain unproductive. From such suffering nothing is learned and nothing is to be learned.

Dorothy Soelle
Suffering

On rare occasions I have met a pain that defies understanding. Although it seems to serve no purpose, it dominates a life so that the patient can think of little else. This was the case with Rajamma. I had been in India only a year or two when she came to me for treatment. In my training in London, whenever I encountered a problem case that belonged in another speciality I promptly referred the patient to someone more experienced. In South India I had no such luxury.

Rajamma crept into my office with an expression of fear on her face. As if scouting for an enemy, she peered suspiciously around the room before lowering herself into a chair. She had many enemies: anything capable of startling her or creating a sudden noise, or even a gust of wind that might blow on her face. Her cheeks were sunken; she was thin to the point of emaciation. Burn marks of a peculiar circular pattern scarred her face; I recognised them as treatments by the traditional medicine man. She had scratched and burned the skin so often that it had taken on a tough, leathery texture like that of an animal.

Rajamma had the condition of *tic doloureux*, neuralgia of the face, in its most severe form. The pain usually attacks spasmodically, in an overwhelming shot of agony to one side of the face. It causes a sudden grimace, or it may seem to be caused by a grimace, thus the name 'tic' suggesting a twitch of the facial muscles. Sometimes the condition begins with no apparent cause and sometimes it starts from a real source of infection, such as a septic molar tooth. Even though Rajamma could not remember any tooth problems, various doctors had extracted all the teeth on one side of her face in hopes of locating and removing the source of pain.

As she told me her story, speaking slowly, she held her mouth open and moved her lips carefully to avoid sudden movements of her cheeks. Rajamma lived in a tiny earthen hut with her husband and four children. Her children never played in or near the house any more, she said. They tiptoed around and would not laugh or even tell a joke for fear of triggering one of their mother's attacks.

Chickens (which usually have the run of village houses) were kept penned so that none would fly up or startle her by cackling. Rajamma's obvious weight loss had resulted from her fear of eating. She dared not chew, so she lived on fluids, making sure they were neither too hot nor too cold.

Despite all these precautions Rajamma lived at the mercy of excruciating pain. Jolts of pain hit her many times every day and totally incapacitated her. Sometimes in desperation she or the Indian village 'doctors' would heat a metal tube in the fire and burn blisters onto her face in an attempt to quell the pain. Her mental health had deteriorated badly. Her husband tried valiantly to understand a pain with no apparent cause, but the family anxiety was clearly beginning to reach a state of critical mass, just before an explosion.

I made every effort to locate a cause, but failed. Twice I tried to deaden the trigger area which seemed to lie just in front of her right cheek bone. The first time, the sight of the needle approaching her face touched off one of her most savage attacks. My second attempt, under anesthesia, did not succeed.

Reluctantly I concluded there was only one sure way to stop this incurable pain: I must open her skull and divide the nerves supplying that part of her face. I put off this decision, because I had not been trained for neurosurgery and indeed had never even observed such a procedure. But I had little recourse. Fortunately, in the anatomy course years before I had dissected the cranial nerves and knew just where to find the Gasserian ganglion within the bony coverings of the brain.

I explained the procedure to Rajamma and her husband, emphasising two dangers. I might fail because of my inexperience. Perhaps worse, I might cut more of the nerves than should be cut. In that event, her eyeball as well as her cheek might become insensitive, which could eventuate in blindness. I painted a bleak picture of potential consequences.

Nothing I said to the couple, however, caused the slightest flicker of hesitation. The effects of her suffering were so great that even if I had told them she would definitely lose an eye in the operation, they would have readily consented.

Over the next week I studied all the books I could find and planned a strategy with our anesthesiologist Dr Gwenda Lewis. Because I wanted to communicate with the patient during surgery, we chose an anesthetic that would keep her alert enough to respond to questions. The day for surgery arrived.

We arranged Rajamma in a sitting position to minimise pressure on the veins in her head, and after the anesthetic had taken hold I began to cut. The Gasserian ganglion lies at the junction of the fifth cranial nerve, in a venous sinus surrounded by bone. Inside this cavity, veins and nerves crisscross in a skein of tangled threads, making it impossible to keep the site free of blood. I chipped away the overlying bone and entered the cavity, picking through the layers of tissue one by one. At last I could see the base of the cavity. A plexus of nerve tissue, an inch across and half an inch deep, lay glimmering under my light like a crescent moon. From under it, fine white nerve fibres fanned out, like tributaries of a river, toward the face.

One of the nerves was a motor nerve, and any damage to it would partially paralyse her jaw. I took special care to identify that one. But the other fibres all looked the same, and lay bundled so close that I could not be confident which was which. I electrically stimulated one tiny fibre and asked Rajamma what she could feel. 'You are touching my eye,' she said. Beads of sweat popped out on my forehead as I dropped that thin nerve back into place.

In most of the body, a tough sheath that tolerates a certain amount of pulling enwraps each nerve. But in the bony skull, nerves are not designed to be touched or stretched. They have no sheath, and the smallest tremor of my hand would tear a nerve irreparably.

I stared into the spreading pool of blood, pale and watery from the anaemia caused by Rajamma's malnutrition. (At that time we had no blood bank to enrich her blood before surgery.) Finally I separated two tiny white nerve fibres and lifted them away from the blood. These two fibres seemed the most likely carriers of the pain impulses that were making her life a misery. All I had to do was cut them and I would be through.

I lifted the two fibres with my probe, and an unexpected, awful sensation broke over me like a wave. I was transfixed by the significance of the tiny act I was about to perform. We surgeons are trained to maintain a certain distance from patients so that personal feelings will not impair our judgment – we are warned not to operate on our own wives or children for this reason. At that moment, I had a vision of Rajamma's family gathered around me in a circle, staring, waiting to know what I would do with her life.

As I looked at those trembling strands of soft white matter, as thin in diameter as a cotton sewing thread, I found it hard to believe they held such significance. Were these two the faulty nerves? So little is known about the physiology of nerves that I could not possibly spot a visual defect. Yet these nerves, containing hundreds of axons serving thousands of nerve endings, were tyrannising a woman's life. Nerves just like them were steadying my hands and letting me know exactly how much force to use on my instruments.

With a start I came to myself. My reverie lasted only five or ten seconds, but I have never forgotten the vision brought on by a tiny, shimmering nerve. I could not be sure which of the two carried the pain; I had to sacrifice both. So I cut them with two snips. Quickly we got the bleeding under control and closed the wound.

Back in the ward, after Rajamma awoke fully, we mapped out the area on her cheek that no longer had sensation. My knots of tension relaxed when we learned the insensitivity did not include her eye. Haltingly, Rajamma began to try the things that previously had triggered her spasms of pain. She tried a slight smile, her first intentional smile in years. Her husband beamed at her. With a quizzical look, she scratched her cheek, knowing that she would never feel anything there again.

Little by little after that, Rajamma's world fell into place. She became the gentle, sweet person she used to be. Her husband's anxiety began to lessen. Back home, chickens were welcomed into the house again. The children began to play and then to jump and skip, even when they were near their mother. In ever-widening circles, life returned to normal for that family.

In my entire career in surgery I have encountered a mere handful of patients who, like Rajamma, suffer from fierce, unyielding pain that is apparently untraceable to a physical cause. And only a few times have I been called upon to silence pain surgically by cutting a nerve. All of medicine views such a procedure as a radical one of last resort. It carries with it grave risks – the possibility of denervating the wrong areas, danger to the body parts made insensitive – and, most mysteriously, the chance that even after nerves are cut the pain may persist.

In view of the debilitating effect of Rajamma's pain on her health and family, I reluctantly concluded I had no other option but the risky surgery. The physical cause of her condition had eluded my search, and I had to go counter to all medical instinct by treating her pain itself as the problem, not as a valuable symptom. That change in perspective is the peculiar peril of chronic pain: pain is no longer a directional signal that points to something else; it is a demon that dominates and immobilises. Sufferers of chronic pain care only about how to turn it off.

Most commonly, chronic pain occurs in the back, neck, or joints, although victims of diseases such as cancer can experience such pain anywhere. Whereas painless people like my leprosy patients yearn for the warning signal of pain, chronic pain sufferers hear a blaring, ceaseless alarm. A flurry of pioneering research has focused on the problems of people plagued by chronic pain, and about five hundred pain clinics in the US now specialise in their treatment.

Yet, despite the obsessive nature of chronic pain, the preferred methods of treatment are moving away from the older surgical techniques. A new term, 'pain management', is entering the vocabulary of specialists. The director of one of America's largest chronic pain clinics has said we may need to apply a different model to chronic pain than medicine's normal surgical removal approach. Perhaps, he observes, we should view chronic pain as we view such diseases as diabetes and collagen disorders, teaching patients to live comfortably *despite* the disease.

I could fill a good-sized room with exercise machines and electronic gadgets that are sold as panaceas for chronic pain. Newspapers and magazines regularly feature other alternatives: techniques of acupuncture, foot or earlobe massage, biofeedback, self-hypnosis. And a catalogue of such exotica as transcutaneous nerve stimulators offers a more technological (and expensive) approach. Most of these techniques of pain management depend on overloading the brain circuits with diversionary stimuli and thus suppressing incoming pain signals.

(I prefer simpler methods to accomplish the same purpose. For example, I often prescribe a stiff-bristle hair brush for a person with arm or leg pain. The effect of briskly stroking the skin will excite touch and pressure sensors and often relieve pain. Or, when my chronic pains intensify I go for a barefoot walk on the rough shell-and-gravel pavements near my home.)

I cannot in this book, of course, attempt to speak directly to those people who suffer from chronic pain. Rather, I will focus on its analogies within the Body of Christ. That Body, too, has chronic pains that will not go away, and in the church we need to learn much about pain management.

In our age the spectres of poverty, famine, and violence never leave some areas of the world. Consider the impulses from the church in a region like Africa or Central America. We cannot ignore the signs of chronic suffering. They fill our mailboxes, our television screens and radio speakers with a daily recitation of gloom. Jesus acknowledged the chronic nature of this type of human suffering when He observed (in a statement that is often grossly distorted), 'The poor you will always have with you' (Mark 14:7).

Because I lived in a country where suffering is an oppressive daily reality, I know well the terrible dilemmas raised by chronic pain on a massive scale. I have stared at long rows of patients, knowing I must decline treatment for all but a handful, and knowing thousands more await attention in remote areas. Even in affluent America, pockets of human misery exist, though on a different scale.

We tend to view the worst suffering indirectly, via television documentaries, and thus pain forces a choice upon us. We can choose to extend our aid and food and wealth to help ease human misery, or we can simply numb the chronic pain by switching the channel, averting our gaze from the problems, or by dispensing token gifts without a true personal commitment.

The Bible makes clear that we in the Body have a responsibility to the sufferings of those outside the church also. Overseas relief aid administered by Christian agencies has mushroomed in recent years, indicating that we are healthfully listening to the short-term, crisis pains of the world. Christians helped spearhead emergency responses to the influx of Indochinese boat people, the drought in Africa's Sahel, and the refugee crisis in Somalia. Hundreds of millions of dollars poured in to support such efforts. We who are strong helped the weak. But in handling chronic, long-term pain, the church still seems in its infancy.

The head of one large Christian relief agency confessed, 'I must restrain myself from global ambulance-chasing. When a major disaster occurs that captures media attention, our donors respond with incredible generosity. All the agencies collect millions of dollars, and move in with a kind of overkill. When the crisis is "hot news", we have no difficulty raising support. Six months later, the desperate problems are still there, but the camera crews have gone elsewhere, and no one cares about the long-term suffering.'

Intense suffering provokes a sudden outpouring of aid, but people soon tire of hearing about depressing conditions. Instead of increasing sensitivity, as a human body does in response to injury, we decrease it. Our focus on the pain turns from 'How do I deal with the cause of the pain?' to 'How can I silence it?' No longer a motivator and stimulus for action, the pain becomes a dull, ineffective throb. It has worn us down.

The field of health services symbolises the conundrum of relief work. People eagerly donate for hospitals, drugs and medical supplies.* Yet, according to the World Health Organisation, eighty percent of all health problems derive from polluted water supplies. Parisian sewers had more impact on that city's health than a hundred hospitals. But development programmes for sanitation and hygiene simply don't have the drawing power of more flamboyant approaches to health.

Of course, chronic pain occurs much closer to home than Somalia or the Sahel. During hard economic times the United States and Europe also hear the plaintive cries of people who cannot provide for their own basic necessities. That sound, too, can become a dull throb, easier to tune out than attend to. In the early 1980s as the impact of budget cuts in social programmes began to affect individuals in the large cities, churches found themselves facing overwhelming human need. The poor began coming to the church, not a government office, for aid.

In 1982 the mayor of New York City, alarmed about the sudden increase of homeless people roaming the streets, made a radical proposal to church leaders. Thirty-six thousand people wander New York streets without shelter, he said; if each of the city's 3,500 churches and synagogues would take in ten of them, the problem of the homeless would be solved. The mayor brought to urgent attention a chronic pain that had long plagued a large city.

---

* An example: after Albert Schweitzer's death, his friends and supporters launched a campaign to build a simple, village-oriented hospital on the scale Schweitzer preferred. The fund raising hopelessly bogged down until a professional agency convinced the committee to build instead a massive, Western-style hospital with state-of-the-art technology. Only then did donors respond and funds pour in.

The churches responded defensively. One Protestant leader seemed offended that he had first read of the proposal in the newspaper. 'It is a very complex situation and the remedy will be complex,' said another. 'There are many problems of implementation.' Most asked for time to evaluate the proposal. They claimed their houses of worship were ill-equipped to shelter the homeless. Only seven congregations responded affirmatively.

Although the mayor's proposal did have a complex dimension, its simple appeal to charity stands in direct line with the message of the Old Testament prophets, Jesus, and the apostles. 'Share your bread with the hungry and bring the homeless poor into your house,' said Isaiah. And Jesus urged disciples to 'give to everyone who begs from you.' In the early church, members routinely brought vegetables, fruit, milk, and honey to distribute to widows, prisoners, and the sick.

In no way do I mean to imply that chronic pain will gradually fade away. No one who has worked in a country such as India could easily come to that conclusion. I think of a lonely woman, abandoned by her husband, left alone to raise children with insufficient resources; and of Christians under persecution in some Communist and Moslem countries; and of monumental problems of health in Third World countries. Neither governments nor the church will relieve all their suffering. More important measures are the attitude and energy with which we face these pains. Do we soon grow numb and insensitive? Do we react with a quick burst of enthusiastic support that wanes if dramatic results are not obvious?

I retain a clear memory from my childhood of the monthly charity of my Aunt Eunice. She would keep a little book from the Aged Pilgrims Friend Society and visit women from that list every month without fail. Often I would accompany her as she took money or food or clothing or Christmas packages to those elderly women. In her own quiet, unglamorous way, Aunt Eunice taught me how to turn impersonal, chronic pain into a personal experience of sharing. She insisted on visiting the women, not mailing them packages, and she kept up her simple ministrations faithfully for years.

People with chronic pain, such as quadriplegics or the parents of retarded children, describe a common pattern: friends and church members respond initially with sympathy and compassion, but over time they lose interest. Most people find an ordeal with no end in sight unsettling, and can even come to resent the person who is suffering. A similar deadening of sensitivity can occur with regard to problems of a national or global scale.

A body's health can be measured in large part by its instinctive reaction to nagging, chronic pain. Management of pain requires a delicate balance between proper sensitivity, to determine its cause and mobilise a response, and enough inner strength to keep the pain from dominating the whole person. For the Body of Christ, the balance is every bit as delicate and as imperative.

23 Pain of God

'I see everything,' he cried, 'everything that there is. Why does each thing on the earth war against each other thing? Why does each small thing in the world have to fight against the world itself? Why does a fly have to fight the whole universe? For the same reason that I had to be alone in the dreadful Council of the Days. So that each thing that obeys law may have the glory and isolation of the anarchist. . . . So that the real lie of Satan may be flung back in the face of this blasphemer, so that by tears and torture we may earn the right to say to this man, 'You lie!' No agonies can be too great to buy the right to say to this accuser, "We also have suffered." . . .'

He had turned his eyes so as to see suddenly the great face of Sunday, which wore a strange smile.

'Have you,' he cried in a dreadful voice, 'have you ever suffered?'

As he gazed, the great face grew to an awful size, grew larger than the colossal mask of Memnon, which had made him scream as a child. It grew larger and larger, filling the whole sky; then everything went black. Only in the blackness before it entirely destroyed his brain he seemed to hear a distant voice saying a commonplace text that he had heard somewhere, 'Can ye drink of the cup that I drink of?'

G. K. Chesterton
The Man Who Was Thursday

At the age of fifteen an imprisoned Jewish boy named Elie Wiesel endured unspeakable horrors at the Buna and Auschwitz concentration camps. One lives forever in his memory: an incident not of mass murder or torture but of punishment applied to a single child. The victim, maybe twelve years old, had been caught helping a Dutchman hoard arms inside the camp. He was sentenced to death.

The boy had a refined and beautiful face, so different from the gaunt, disfigured faces of most prisoners – the face, said Wiesel, of a sad angel. To execute such a child publicly before thousands of prisoners was no easy thing, even for the SS. The camp stoolies refused to assist this time, so the SS had to perform the deed themselves. They erected three gallows, one for the child and two more for other condemned prisoners.

The three victims mounted chairs and the SS placed their necks in nooses. 'Long live liberty!' cried the two adults. The child said nothing.

But from the rows of anguished spectators, a cry came up. 'Where is God? Where is He?'

The chairs were tipped over and the bodies jerked, then dangled limply from the ropes. Guards ordered all the prisoners to march past the three victims. It was a terrible sight. The two adults were dead, their tongues hanging out, already swollen and blue-tinged. But the third rope was still twitching lightly. The child, being so light, was still alive.

In all it took the boy perhaps half an hour to die. The prisoners had to file past, looking him full in the face as his life fluttered away.

'Behind me,' said Wiesel, 'I heard the same man asking, "Where is God now?"'

'And I heard a voice within me answer him: Where is He? Here He is – He is hanging here on this gallows. . . .

'That night the soup tasted of corpses.'*

That question, 'Where is God?' has haunted Wiesel and thousands of other survivors who cried out in their human

---

* Elie Wiesel, *Night* (New York: Discus/Avon Books, 1969), 75–76.

hells and heard no answer. Wiesel intended his conclusion to be understood in its most literal, atheistic meaning: God's silence proved He was on a gallows, dead, helpless, unresponsive, undependable. Others would use the same words, but with a different meaning: God had suffered alongside the young child, as He grieves and suffers with every pain of His children on earth. But if He was there, hanging on the gallows, watching the thousands – no, millions – of innocents march to the ovens, why did He not intervene? And why did they not sense God's presence? Never had He seemed more distant.

In a medical career that has spanned four decades, I have never stopped thinking of pain. I have seen its beauty and brilliant design as I have studied physiology and observed the effects of painlessness on my leprosy patients. I have seen its cruelty as I have watched patients die in agony and have listened to families traumatised by the mutilating injury of a child. In my reflections on theology, no matter where I begin, my mind circles back to this enigmatic topic of pain.

For this reason, I cannot end a section on pain and a book on the Body of Christ without raising the issue of God's concern for human suffering.

If the message of pain is directional, a call for us to link up compassionately with those who suffer, how then does the Head of the Body relate to such suffering? How does He 'feel' about those who are abused or divorced or alcoholic or unemployed or homosexual, about the needy in Africa and Central America and everywhere? The scope of this book does not permit me to address the 'why' questions of causation. But at least I must consider how God views the suffering of His creatures. Does it affect Him?

A common theme has surfaced throughout this book: that God has undergone a series of self-humiliations – in the Creation, the covenants, the failed monarchy, the Exile, the Incarnation, the Crucifixion, and finally as Head of a very human church. And, I have said, in the role of Head

He can truly – not just figuratively or analogously – feel our pain. Yet, having made that assertion, I cannot ignore certain important questions about the nature of infinite God. Perhaps they have lurked uncomfortably in your mind as you have read about God's self-limitations. Is not God changeless, eternal? Can our pain truly affect an essentially changeless God? Can He hurt? Did He in any sympathetic way share the gallows with the child in Buna? These are good questions, inescapable questions.

Such careful documents as the Anglican Communion and Westminster Confession declare that God is 'without body, parts or passions'. Can a God without passions feel our pain? Admittedly, theologians over the centuries have largely concluded that God does not feel passion or suffering. Early Christian theology, thrashed out in a Greek intellectual environment, held that such qualities as movement, change, and suffering distinguish humans from gods. God is *apothos*, or apathetic, with no disturbing emotions whatever.* Bible passages describing God as angry or grieved or rejoicing were dismissed as anthropomorphic or metaphorical.

Yet, here is a strange thing: if someone with no background in philosophy and theology simply picked up the Bible and started reading it, he or she would find a startlingly different picture. The Bible gives overwhelming emphasis to God's passionate involvement with creation. It is virtually a catalogue of His emotions in relation to humanity. From creation onward, God places Himself in the position of an anxious Father who has let His children go free.

Each key event in the Old Testament tells of God sharing the pain (or, less frequently, triumph) of His people. He

---

* Clement, for example, urged people to strive toward freedom from passion, becoming like an impassible God. Purge yourselves of courage, fear, cheerfulness, anger, envy, and love for creatures, he said. A similar prejudice against passion and emotions continued through philosophy and theology up until the Romantic movement. Spinoza called emotions 'confused ideas', and Kant urged 'duty for duty's sake'.

heard the cry of the captives in Egypt. For thirty-eight years He pitched His tent among the shifting tents in Sinai, joining Israelites in their punishment by tabernacling among them. 'In all their distress he too was distressed,' concludes the prophet Isaiah (63:9).

The prophets seem to compete in describing the depth of God's emotional attachment to His people. The books of Jeremiah and Hosea swell with the cry of a wounded God. 'Is not Ephraim my dear son, the child in whom I delight?' God asks (Jer. 31:20). 'Though I often speak against him, I still remember him. Therefore, my heart yearns for him; I have great compassion for him.' (Luther translates that penultimate phrase, 'My heart is broken.')

In Hosea God declares, 'My heart is changed within me; all my compassion is aroused' (11:8). 'Why did you forsake me?' He asks often. 'My people have forgotten me,' He laments. In Isaiah the boldest figure of speech used by any prophet compares God to a woman undergoing labour:

'For a long time I have kept silent,
   I have been quiet and held myself back.
But now, like a woman in childbirth,
   I cry out, I gasp and pant' (42:14).

Clearly, events arouse in God either joy or sorrow, pleasure or wrath. The Old Testament portrays a God who is not 'wholly other' or remote, but One involved with creation. He goes with His people into exile, into captivity, into the fiery furnace, into the grave.

A phrase like 'My heart is broken' is metaphorical, to be sure – when applied to God or to a human being. But a writer employs metaphor to point to a truth, not to its opposite. Abraham Heschel, a Jewish theologian, concludes, 'The statements about pathos are not a compromise – ways of accommodating higher meanings to the lower level of human understanding. They are rather the accommodations of words to higher meanings'.

Could it be that the church Fathers, so intent on protecting God from any deficiency of being, missed an obvious possibility: that God voluntarily put Himself in the position of being affected by creation? Love involves giving, and God, self-complete, has only Himself to give. He surely does not suffer out of some deficiency of being, as His creatures do, but from the love that overflows from His being. That is, in fact, how the Gospels define love: 'For God so loved the world *that* he gave his one and only Son.'

The pictorial Chinese language combines the two concepts of love and pain in eloquent symbolism. In the character that express the highest kind of love, symbols for love and for pain are brushed on top of each other to form a word like 'pain-love'. Thus a mother 'pain-loves' her child. She pours out her whole being on the child's behalf. In essence God showed pain-love to creation by emptying Himself and joining us in the Incarnation.

Any Christian discussion of what effect human suffering has on God must centre on the Incarnation, when God Himself lived among us. In the Gospel accounts, Jesus opposed illness and suffering without exception. At the beginning of His ministry He announced healing the sick as one of His chief goals (Luke 4:18) and used it as a proof of His messianic identity when questioned by John the Baptist (7:22). The gospels record no instances of Jesus declining to heal when asked, or of advising a sufferer, 'Be happy with your illness!' or 'Simply bear the pain of your son's death.' When His friend Lazarus died, Jesus wept. God, as revealed in Christ, takes no pleasure in the suffering of His children; rather, He is grieved.

When Jesus Himself faced suffering, He did not show the tightlipped resignation of martyrdom. In Gethsemane He accepted pain almost as a last resort. Three times He prayed, 'If it is possible, may this cup be taken from me'. And on the cross He bore pain not with silence, but with the forlorn cry of abandonment, 'My God! Why have you forsaken me?' His own deliverance from the cross was the one miracle of healing He refused to perform.

'What can I say that others have not said already . . . told many times over and drawn again and again? . . . What can these places say to you, if in your mind's eye you do not see . . . the fearful day of the death on the cross within the walls of Jerusalem?' I share those sentiments of Nikolai Gogol whenever I attempt to speak about the cross. What more could be said? Yet I cannot explore the pain of God without pausing before that most poignant moment, for it was then that God took on Himself the groaning and travailing of all creation.

What is so unique, after all, about that death in Jerusalem? Why is it called the 'day that shook the world' and 'the greatest event in history'? How did it mutate the symbol of the cross from one of execution to one of religious adoration?* The fact of Jesus' physical suffering does not account for the impact; it differed little from Stephen's or Peter's or even Socrates'. Nor could it be the unfair punishment inflicted on a person innocent of a crime; Socrates, too, was innocent, as well as Solzhenitsyn and the Jews described by Elie Wiesel. Not even the manner of execution was that momentous; *Fox's Book of Martyrs*, for instance, chronicles tortures even more horrible than crucifixion.

How can one obscure man, executed like other common men in an outpost of the empire and virtually ignored by contemporary secular historians, claim to occupy the centre of history and affect what goes on before and after him? Scoffers call it 'the scandal of particularity,' and the question looms before our faith. The answer, of course, is nonsense but for the acceptance of one belief – that the man executed was God Himself in the incognito of history. The cross expresses the suffering of God Himself. He

---

* Charles Williams writes, 'When St Paul preached in Athens, the world was thronged with crosses, rooted outside cities, bearing all of them the bodies of slowly dying men. When Augustine preached in Carthage, the world was also thronged with crosses, but now in the very centre of cities, often in processions and above altars, decorated and jewelled, and bearing all of them the image of the identity of dying Man.' Even the Colosseum, the imposing site for so many bloody spectacles, was ultimately crowned with a Christian cross and the single word 'Benedictus'.

joined humanity by stepping into the historical plane and letting us see Him in shame and nakedness and pain.

At this point, the doctrine of the Trinity becomes so mystifying that other religions shrink away. Did Almighty God simply allow His Son to suffer for us, or did He suffer in Christ on our behalf? Moslems believe that God, unable to go through with the execution of His prophet Jesus, substituted another victim at the last moment. One Jewish Rabbinic argument against Christ's Sonship goes like this: 'If God could not bear to see Abraham's son slain, surely he would not let his own Son die.' Could the thrust of the gospel be missed more widely? In Christian belief, God gave up His own son precisely because He could not, in love, bear to see those such as Isaac suffer. '*He who did not spare his own Son*, but gave him up for us all – how will he not also, along with him, graciously give us all things?' (Rom. 8:31–32).

And still today we miss the point. American television personality Phil Donahue, explaining why he became disillusioned with Christianity, asks, 'How could an all-knowing, all-loving God allow His Son to be murdered on a cross in order to redeem my sins? If God the Father is so "all-loving", why didn't He come down and go to Calvary?' The answer, of course, is that in some incomprehensible way it *was* God Himself who came to earth and died. 'God was in Christ reconciling the world to Himself' (2 Cor. 5:19 NASB).

When I contemplate the pain of God in the suffering of Christ on Calvary, invariably I turn back to the passage by Isaiah, that most eloquent of prophets. He captures the pain of God in the description of the Suffering Servant in Isaiah 53, a passage the New Testament authors apply to Christ. *

---

* Jewish interpreters often apply the symbol of the Suffering Servant to themselves as a race. Could this be the reason, asks Japanese theologian Kazoh Kitamori, that Judaism has attracted so few converts in the world? No race has suffered more than the Jews. But human pain, no matter how great, is meaningless and barren unless it can become a symbol of God's pain sharing in it – unless God really is on the gallows with the boy at Buna.

He was despised, the lowest of men:
  a man of pains, familiar with disease,
One from whom men avert their gaze –
  despised, and we reckoned him as nothing.

But it was our diseases that he bore,
  our pains that he carried,
While we counted him as one stricken,
  touched by God with affliction.

He was wounded for our rebellions,
  crushed for our transgressions;
The chastisement that reconciled us fell upon him,
  and we were healed by his bruises.

All of us strayed like sheep,
  each man turned to his own way;
And Yahweh brought the transgressions of all of us
  to meet upon him.

Oppressed he was, and afflicted,
  but he did not open his mouth;
He was led like a sheep to slaughter;
  and as a ewe is speechless before her shearers,
  he did not open his mouth.

By a perverted judgment he was taken away;
  and who was concerned with his case?
For he was cut off from the land of life;
  for our rebellions he was struck dead.

He was given a tomb with the wicked,
  with the evildoers his sepulchre,
Although he had done no violence,
  and there was no deceit in his mouth.

  (ANCHOR BIBLE)

The Incarnation made possible one further aspect of the
pain of God, one that has direct bearing on our analogy of
the human body. I think of my futile attempts to develop an
artificial pain system. All my patients intellectually understood pain, acknowledged its value as a warning signal, and

abhorred the injuries and wounds on their painless hands and feet. Yet until they 'felt' pain for themselves, inside their own brains, they had not suffered.

It seems inappropriate to think of a 'developing aware-ness' within God, but something like a progression did occur as implied in the mysterious phrase in Hebrews 2:10, 'made perfect through suffering'. Imagining pain is one thing – God as designer had surely understood its physio-logical values and limitations. Grieving in response to pain, feeling with His people, suffering with humanity – all these, too, link God and man. Still, something was missing.

Until God took on the soft tissue of flesh along with its pain cells just as accurate and subject to abuse as ours, He had not truly experienced pain. By sending His Son to earth, God learned to feel pain in the same way we feel pain. Our prayers and cries of suffering take on greater meaning because we now know them to be understood by Him. Instinctively, we want a God who not only knows about pain, but shares in it and is affected by our own. By looking at Jesus, we realise we have such a God. He took onto Himself the limitations of time and space and family and pain and sorrow.

Christ has now ascended, and in the new role of Head He receives messages of pain reporting in from all over His Body. My brain does not feel pain inflicted on its own cells – protected in a skull of bone, it needs no such warn-ing cells. Yet it desperately feels the pain of other cells in the body. In that sense, Jesus has now placed Himself at the receiving end of our pain, with actual consciousness of the pain we endure.*

---

* It would have been far easier and more pleasant for God simply to abolish pain rather than to share it. Pain exists not as a proof of God's lack of concern, but because it has a place in creation significant enough that it cannot be removed without great loss. I, of course, see the effects of that loss every day in my leprosy patients. For this reason, if I held in my hand the ability to eliminate human pain, I would not exercise the right. Pain's value is too great. Rather, I lend my energies to doing all I can to help when that pain turns into suffering.

Christ did not, however, stop at identification and shared experience. I have focused on the cross, but in the resurrection that followed He transformed the nature of pain. He overthrew the powers of this world by first allowing sin to do its worst, then transmuting that act into His best. The most meaningless of all acts, His own innocent death, became the most meaningful.

The apostle Paul explored this change in a hymn at the end of Romans 8. No one can condemn us, he says, because of Christ Jesus who died and was raised to life and now is present with the Father. Now, nothing can separate us from the love of Christ, not the pains of trouble or hardship or persecution or famine or nakedness or danger or sword. No, he concludes, we are all more than conquerors through Him who loved us. And then this summing-up: 'For I am convinced that neither death nor life, neither angels nor demons, neither the present nor the future [time], nor any powers, neither height nor depth [space], nor anything else in all creation, will be able to separate us from the love of God that is in Christ Jesus our Lord.'

This, then, is the conclusion of pain. God takes the Great Pain of His own Son's death and uses it to blot up into Himself all the minor pains of our own confinement on earth. Meaningless pain is absorbed.

Jesus Himself had told His followers to 'take up a cross' and follow Him and to 'drink of the cup' that He drinks. Paul went even further, alluding to 'the fellowship of his sufferings' and to a process of filling up what is lacking in Christ's afflictions (Col. 1:24; Phil. 3:10). He seldom missed a chance to refer to such terms as crucifixion with Christ, union with His death, sharing in His sufferings. In one passage he said explicitly, 'We always carry around in our body the death of Jesus, so that the life of Jesus may also be revealed in our body' (2 Cor. 4:10). All these fragments of mystery speak to me of the miracle that has taken place. God absorbs our own pain so that what we endure becomes a part of what He suffered and will become a part of what is resurrected in triumph and transformed into good. Following a similar train of thought, the apostle Peter concludes buoyantly, 'Even angels long to look into these things' (1 Peter 1:12).

In two profoundly suggestive passages, Christ identifies with suffering people so completely that He fills their place and bears their pain. Matthew 25:35–40 shows Him accepting ministry to the hungry, the thirsty, the sick, the naked, the vagrants, the prisoners, as though it were done unto Him. In Acts 9:4, during Saul's blinding epiphany en route to Damascus, Jesus asks, 'Saul, why do you persecute *me*?' The whips and stones directed against persecuted Christians had fallen on Jesus Himself. In these cases, at least, it seems inappropriate to ask, 'Why does God allow their suffering?' 'Why does God allow Himself to suffer?' would be closer. His identification with our pain is that complete.

Elie Wiesel was right: in a way, God did hang on the gallows with the lightly twitching body of the young boy. He hangs on our private gallows in our own private pains. He has been here in person, serving a sentence for a crime He did not commit; He is here still, receiving every sensation and making it His own.

The portion of human anatomy I have specialised in is that marvellous creation the hand. To my mind, nothing in all of nature rivals the hand's combination of strength and agility, tolerance and sensitivity. Our most wonderful activities – art, music, writing, healing, touching – are performed by hands. It is natural, then, that when I think of the Incarnation and the pain of God, I visualise the hands of Jesus Christ.

I can hardly conceive of God taking on the form of an infant, but He once had the tiny, jerky hands of a new-born, with miniature fingernails and wrinkles around the knuckles and soft skin that had never known abrasion or roughness. 'The hands that had made the sun and stars,' says Chesterton, 'were too small to reach the huge heads of the cattle.' And too small to change His own clothes or put food in His mouth. God, too, experienced infant helplessness.

Since I have worked as a carpenter, I can easily imagine the hands of the young Jesus as He learned the trade in His father's shop. His skin must have developed calluses and rough spots and tender spots. He felt pain gratefully, I am sure. (Carpentry is a precarious profession for my leprosy patients who lack the warning of pain that allows them to use tools with sharp edges and rough handles.)

And then there were the hands of Christ the physician. The Bible tells us strength flowed out of them when He healed people. He chose not to perform miracles *en masse*, but rather one by one, touching each person He healed. He touched eyes that had long since dried out, and suddenly they admitted light and colour. He touched a woman with a haemorrhage, knowing that by Jewish law she would make Him unclean. He touched people with leprosy – people no one else would touch in those days. As He did so, people could feel something of the Divine spirit coming through. In small and personal ways, His hands were setting right what had been disrupted in His beloved creation.

The most important scene in Jesus' life also involved His hands. Then, those hands that had done so much good were taken, one at a time, and pierced through with a thick spike. My mind balks at visualising it.

I have spent my life cutting into hands, delicately, with scalpel blades that slice through one layer of tissue at a time, to expose the marvellous complex of nerves and blood vessels and tiny bones and tendons and muscles inside. I have been on treasure hunts inside opened hands, searching for healthy tendons to reattach in order to free up fingers that have been useless for twenty years. I know what crucifixion must do to a human hand.

Executioners of that day drove their spikes through the wrist, right through the carpal tunnel that houses finger-controlling tendons and the median nerve. It is impossible to force a spike there without crippling the hand into a claw shape. Jesus had no anesthetic. He allowed those hands to be marred and crippled and destroyed.

Later, His weight hung from them, tearing more tissue, releasing more blood. There could be no more helpless image than that of a God hanging paralysed from a tree. 'Heal yourself!' the crowd jeered. He had saved others – why not Himself? The disciples, who had hoped He was the Messiah, cowered in the darkness or drifted away. Surely they had been mistaken – this figure could not be God.

Finally, in one last paroxysm of humanness, Jesus said simply, 'Father, into your hands I commit my spirit.' The humiliation of the Incarnation ended. The sentence was served.

But that is not the last glimpse we have of Jesus' hands in the biblical record. He appears again, in a closed room, where Thomas is still doubting the unlikely story he thinks his friends have concocted. People do not rise from the dead, he scoffs. It must have been a ghost, or an illusion. At that moment, Jesus holds up those unmistakable hands His disciples had seen perform miracles. The scars give proof that they belong to Him, the One who had died on the cross. The body has changed – it can pass through walls and locked doors to join them. But the scars remain. Jesus invites Thomas to come and trace them with his own fingers.

Thomas responds simply, 'My Lord and my God!' It is the first recorded time that one of Jesus' disciples calls Him God directly. Significantly, the assertion comes in response to Jesus' wounds.

Why did Christ keep His scars? He could have had a perfect body, or no body, when He returned to splendour in heaven. Instead He carried with Him remembrances of His visit to earth. For a reminder of His time here, He chose scars. That is why I say God hears and understands our pain, and even absorbs it into Himself – because He kept those scars as a lasting image of wounded humanity. He has been here; He has borne the sentence. The pain of man has become the pain of God.